Praise for *Wha*

MW01200268

"Tormented by grief and his own death, Kristina . addiction and self-destruction until she sets out on a journey to unravel the mystery of his uncanny foresight. Her relentless search for truth ultimately leads to her own healing and profound spiritual awakening. *What My Brother Knew* is a beautifully written, spellbinding memoir."

—Judy Reeves, author of *When Your Heart Says Go*

"A devastatingly tragic yet fierce memoir filled with gripping visuals of love, loss and death which open into an infinite portal beyond rational meaning and definition to preconscious, intuitive, and inter subjective realms of meaning and a reality where we no longer look *at* things but *through* them. Amelong vividly reveals a shockingly tender and gorgeous glimpse of the truth of reality and the eternity of Love."

—Kristina Kincaid, author of *A Return to Eros*

"It is said that 'The two most important days in your life are the day you are born and the day you find out why.' Kristina Amelong reminds us that those days can be separated by a gulf of hurt, despair, and longing. The death of her younger brother at an early age, in an accident he had predicted, sent Amelong on a harrowing journey through this uncharted territory. Ultimately, she was brave enough and wise enough to turn the chaos of grief and uncertainty into a journey of self-examination—and a compelling memoir. For those who are searching, Kristina Amelong reveals that it is possible to 'find out why' and, in so doing, to achieve renewal and, yes, joy."

—John Nichols, author of *The Fight for the Soul of the Democratic Party*

"Amelong writes from the heart and has a gift for arresting imagery...A sincere and valiant attempt to understand the unfathomable."

— Kirkus Reviews

What My Brother Knew

A Memoir

Kristina Amelong

SHE WRITES PRESS

Published 2025
Printed in the United States of America
Print ISBN: 978-1-64742-908-9
E-ISBN: 978-1-64742-909-6
Library of Congress Control Number: 2025900944

For information, address:
She Writes Press
1569 Solano Ave #546
Berkeley, CA 94707

Interior Design by

She Writes Press is a division of SparkPoint Studio, LLC.

For Jay, and all the great lovers of life.

Author's Note

Some names, locations, and identifying characteristics have been changed to protect the privacy of those depicted. Also, please excuse my identification of a daddy longlegs as a spider, I'm now aware that it is not but didn't know when I was seventeen.

Death. The certain prospect of death could sweeten every life with a precious and fragrant drop of levity—and now you strange apothecary souls have turned it into an ill-tasting drop of poison that makes the whole of life repulsive.
—Friedrich Nietzsche

. . . from so simple a beginning endless forms most beautiful and most wonderful have been, and are being, evolved.
—Charles Darwin

Part I

—1—

The feeling of immortality, it seems to me, has its origin in a
peculiar feeling of extension in time and space . . .
—Carl Jung

On May 27, 1981, I skipped my last class. I don't remember why. I was a junior in high school and didn't need much of a reason. My mom was at work. I went down to my basement bedroom, which was empty except for the haze of marijuana smoke—I must have just missed my thirteen-year-old brother Jay. We often skipped school together, but he had made other plans that day.

I don't remember much. I probably watched some stupid soap opera, and I must have had a snack, because I was washing dishes when the call came. Even stoned out of my mind, I knew better than to leave dishes in the sink.

I squeezed the soap bottle and watched as the hot water poured from the faucet, creating a foamy storm. Bubbles rose over the sink, and for a moment, I pretended to float with them. It was fun—I would ride a bubble until it popped, imagining myself disappearing with each bubble.

Then I caught a glimmer of light from the front yard. I brushed my hair from my face and pulled myself away from the sink to investigate. A City of Madison police car had pulled into our driveway.

Stepping outside, I noticed some handlebars and a rotating bike wheel protruding from the vehicle's open trunk.

It seemed to take me five minutes to travel the ten feet from the front steps to the end of the driveway. The sidewalk was hot beneath my bare feet. The officer had been writing something on a clipboard in his car, which he set down when he noticed me. I could hear his every move—the clinking of his keys in the ignition, the shuffling of his feet, the creaking hinges as he pushed open the door. He started talking to me as he walked around to the trunk, his words falling on the driveway just short of my ears. As he walked toward me holding the silver BMX bike, one sentence sliced through: "There's been an accident." Then he set my brother's twisted bicycle on the lawn, got back in his car, and drove off.

I stood rooted to my spot. My mouth tasted of metal. A roaring grew in my ears, dulling the sounds of our sleepy, mostly white and working-class neighborhood. My eyes lost focus, as if I were seeing and hearing the world around me from inside an aquarium. Some part of my brain attempted to construct an equation of possible events that would lead to the current situation.

I decided it was a misunderstanding and returned to my chores. Back in the kitchen, the bubbles had dissipated and the air seemed odd. I picked up a glass, scrubbed it with the sponge, and plunged it back into the water, my whole body floating, as if I were swirling in the murky dishwater.

Bringgggg, bringgggg, bringgggg.

The phone's ring wrenched me back. I swam through the swampy kitchen to answer it. "Hello?"

"Kris, it's Jan Anderson." Our neighbor's raspy voice registered in my brain. "I am picking you up in five minutes. Your brother's at the University Hospital."

I clutched the green phone receiver to my face, listening to the sharp dial tone, then pulled the receiver away from my head and stared at it, examining each hole in the earpiece. What did she say? I stared at the numbers on the circular dial plate. I set the receiver on the metal hook. Still, I couldn't move.

Jay's voice echoed in my head. When did he last tell me? A few days ago, before school? *I will die young. It's not going to be much longer.*

I looked at the clock, faintly surprised to see it was only three o'clock in the afternoon. I watched the second hand, feeling a widening gap between myself and time. I counted the seconds, as if I could count out the rest of my life. *One thousand one, one thousand two.* My eyes closed and I was playing hide-and-seek. I heard the other kids scurry off to hide. I was it. *One thousand seven.* I remembered finding Jay hiding in the lilacs in the neighbor's yard, tucked in the center of the old blooming tree. *One thousand ten.*

A horn blasted out front. The cat rubbed against my leg and I looked down. I couldn't make sense of this creature, of my leg, of anything. Another series of honks started my legs moving, out the kitchen and to the front door, where I managed to put on my shoes. Outside, I walked past the bike, bent in half on the lawn. What would we want a broken bike for?

Perhaps it was the smell of cigarette smoke enveloping me, or the way the sunshine fell on my Calvin Klein jeans, or possibly it was the NPR host on the car radio, discussing the recent assassination attempt on Ronald Reagan, but for a moment, as we drove away from the one-story ranch I'd lived in since I was three years old, my eyes filled with tears.

"Buckle up, Kris," Jan said.

I pulled the belt over my waist and clicked it in place just as Prince, my gray cat, sauntered across the road, causing Jan to swerve ever so slightly. Our neighborhood was full of animals running the streets.

Jan drove quickly and calmly, her white knuckles and utter silence the only indication that anything was awry. We slipped through a stop sign at Forster and Troy, passed the PDQ gas station where a woman in a Green Bay Packers T-shirt put gas in her car, and made a right turn on Sherman.

I stared out the window at my small world, the north side of Madison. We passed the McDonald's where I'd worked for a year, the Noah's Ark Pet Center where we got Prince, the Hartmeyer Ice Arena where Jay's hockey team had home games. As Jan patted my knee, I thought back to the bike in our yard, lying not far from the unplanted yellow rose bush. *Why did Jay buy Mom a birthday present six weeks early?* stuck like a song in my head.

We arrived at the University of Wisconsin hospital. I remember walking into the silent waiting room where Mom sat next to Jay's dad, Dick. Both were hunched over, shaking with sobs. Neither looked up when I sat down. I didn't know what to do. I hadn't seen my stepdad since he left five years ago. I stared ahead at the white clock, following the motion of the second hand. My mom shifted in her seat. Her expression was vacant, eyes puffy, face wet with tears. The pain in her face made me feel as if nothing would ever be okay again. I looked back at the ticking clock.

What happened next remains fuzzy—a blur of sterile hospital rooms, blinding fluorescent lights, and blood. Someone comforted me, and it was not my mother. I think it must have been the nurse who led me to see my brother. I can see her now, an image that must be a combination of memory and imagination.

She enters the room, wearing a stark, white uniform. She looks around. She is beautiful. She smiles at me gently. "Do you want to go and see your brother? You're his sister, right?"

I don't know what awaits me, but I'm desperate to get out of this room with my two sobbing parents who hate each other. I nod.

I watch the nurse's face soften, her lungs fill. Then I follow the pull of her gravity as she turns around and leaves the room. I follow her around a corner and down a long corridor, then into the first door on the right. I focus on the way her long, curly, brown hair falls in waves against the back of her white dress. She stops abruptly and turns to face me.

We are standing in a large white room. In the center is a stainless steel table with a body, facing up. I want to keep looking at the beautiful nurse's hair, yet the body I do not yet recognize demands something of me. I can see that the left leg is turned left and upside down. Bile rises in my throat. Every muscle in my body screams, *Stay back!* But I can't. I take a few steps forward, looking closely at him. His head is larger than it should be. It looks like a broken-open watermelon. A few more steps and I can see blood still dripping out from his left ear and both of his eyes, like tears. His hair is matted with dried blood, but a small patch is still dishwater blond.

"What the fuck did you do this for?" I ask his lifeless body.

"I don't think he did it on purpose," the nurse says, putting her hand on my shoulder.

I pull away. She does not know Jay's story.

—2—

Memories saturate my heart and the story of you
spills from my eyes.
—Grace Andren

The day Jay died, I became one-dimensional. So did the chairs and the couch where, like paper dolls, my mom and I took turns lying down. We were a paper doll family, and our tabs were missing. Motion had drained out of us. We lay flat against a flat world. We had no interest in food. We no longer had space within us to hold a stomach, let alone intestines, or a liver.

Family from the country and friends from the neighborhood passed through all evening that first night, bringing food, scrubbing dishes, sitting with us. No one knew what to do. We sat and stared past each other, finding walls or framed photographs—a snow-covered forest, a gaggle of smiling children, a new baby boy who wouldn't live to finish puberty.

My cousins Mary Jo and Marty sat with me in the basement while the adults milled around upstairs. Mom hollered down, "Will you two take her somewhere? She needs to get out of the house."

Mary Jo and Marty looked at each other from across the room. Somehow, they alone were vertical in this flat world. They stuck up like cacti in a desert—distinct, prickly, sucking up all available life force.

"Let's go to the drive-in," Marty offered.

My cousins herded me to the car and we drove to the theater. They insisted I sit in the passenger's seat so I would have the best view. I sat there while Mary Jo fiddled with the speaker, trying to get it to rest on the window next to me. "What movie is this again?" I asked, not really caring.

"*Friday the 13th*," Marty answered, as the screen grew black and the outline of a scene in the woods began to appear. So began my love affair with the genre of horror movies.

I stared, fixated, as a gruesome tale unfolded in two dimensions. A man was sliced open with a machete. A spear skewered the two lovers. A woman was stabbed to death. I began to think that maybe death was just for show.

I felt my breath begin to inhabit my body. It gave shape to my lips, full lips against a paper-thin face, like two slugs mating on hard cement. I began to tremble, imperceptibly at first, but soon I was sobbing. A strange, flat girl with slugs for lips, sobbing in the front seat.

"Shh, it's okay, Kris," Mary Jo whispered.

I cried louder.

"Come on, cut it out." Marty looked nervously around. Heads were starting to turn. "Kris, everyone can hear you."

After a few minutes of trying to cajole me into silence, they gave up. Marty started the car and maneuvered out of the drive-in. As we left the gravelly parking lot, I grew eager to get home, to find Jay smoking pot in the basement, wondering why we hadn't taken him with us.

Later that night, I lay flat and thin under a sheet on the couch. The rest of the house had disappeared. I lay still, barely breathing. I watched myself, felt myself, heard myself. Did the couch creak or was that my skin? I couldn't stay here but had nowhere to go. It seemed that even if a new self could emerge and reclaim motion, no new location existed.

I was not aware of falling asleep, but I awoke with the sunrise. I went to the kitchen and got an apple from the refrigerator. I turned the faucet on, holding the pinkish-red apple in my hand under the falling water. I felt my hand becoming cold, the water changing me. I focused on the red of the fruit. The telephone rang. I bit into the apple, walking past the phone and into the living room. It was way too early for calls. I drifted to the front window and watched as the white *Wisconsin State Journal* van threw two stacks of newspapers onto our front lawn.

Jay's paper route. Any minute now he'd bound out the door. I stood, frozen, waiting for Jay to appear. I'd stepped back into the day before, when Jay stuffed the newspapers into his dirty canvas bag.

I wanted to stay outside the arrow of time, in a world where Jay would deliver papers as he did every day. So I stood, immobile, as a skirmish broke out inside me, each side fighting for ownership of reality.

All at once, I had to see the paper. I crossed to the front door, stopping in my tracks when I noticed my mom in her light nightgown, sitting in her chair in the living room, smoke spiraling from her cigarette. I hadn't even heard her get up.

We stared at each other. What was there to say? Good morning?

Instead, I heaved open the door and crossed the lawn. Perhaps the newspaper would have answers for me. The front page had a couple of headlines, one about nuclear power, one about abortion laws. There was a large photo I couldn't really make out. I pulled the strings binding the stack until they snapped, snatching the top newspaper and stuffing it under my arm. My mind raced as I traipsed inside.

I flopped down on the couch and flipped the paper over. Below the fold, a headline grabbed my attention:

DRIVER BLACKS OUT; BOY, 13, KILLED

Blacks out? He reported feeling nauseous after eating lunch. Does that make a person black out? How could Jay have known?

I continued reading, lifting the paper closer to my face to bring the last few sentences into the light.

"Oh!" my mom shrieked from the chair directly across from me.

I looked up to see her staring in horror at the newspaper, tears streaming down her face.

"What is that photo?" she wailed.

I turned the paper around. A small body lay crumpled in the grass, bare arms and T-shirt and jeans smeared with dark marks—asphalt and blood, presumably. A paramedic bent over the boy, blocking his head from view, seemingly giving him mouth-to-mouth. His legs were twisted like a pretzel, his arms hung limp and bent on the grass. *I'll be watching people bring me back to life, but they won't be able to.*

"Take that newspaper out of here!" my mom screamed.

Her voice pounded in my ears, and I reacted instinctively. Clutching the paper, I strode into the kitchen, grabbing the box of Cap'n Crunch cereal from atop the fridge. Then I bolted out the back door, letting it slam behind me. As I rounded the house on my way to the street, I set the paper back on the pile of papers on the lawn. Without breaking stride, I headed to the marsh. My body hurt all over.

I waited to cross the street as a car puttered by, to me a death threat. When I reached Warner Park, I found a spot to sit in the grass near the reeds. I jammed my hand into the cereal box and filled my fist with sticky, sweet squares. As I was about to cram the entire handful into my mouth, I noticed that a daddy longlegs had crawled onto my leg. I moved my hand with the cereal next to her and she crawled up onto my palm. I lifted my hand. She was the color of dead grass with two small darker squares across her back. I counted her legs—one, two, three, four, five, six, seven. She seemed to have lost one. With a twinge of guilt, I remembered how Jay and I used to pull the legs off those insects.

"I won't hurt you," I whispered.

She seemed to use her front two legs as both antennae and arms—feeling the space around her, reaching out to touch the cereal. I noticed what appeared to be two huge teeth on the front of her body gnawing at the cereal. As I watched her rhythmically working away, I began to feel the tightness in my chest loosen, my breathing slow. I pretended I was in the spider's body, felt the vibration of nibbling and crunching.

I held my breath as I inched my left hand to pick up another piece of cereal for myself, keeping my right hand as still as possible. I needed her to stay. I popped the piece in my mouth and exhaled, staring at the tiny creature. She existed. I existed. We were in the right place together. But what about the rest? I looked around. What about my brother? What about my mother? When I returned my focus to the daddy longlegs, she was gone.

As I took another bite, I stared at the ground, noticing that the grass around me was glistening with blood. I jumped up, scattering Cap'n Crunch. When I looked again, the blood was gone, but my brother was still dead. I walked home.

I checked the mail on my way in the door to find an envelope addressed to me and Mom. It bore no stamp—someone must have dropped it directly at our house. I didn't recognize the name on the return address.

"Mom?" I said as I entered the house.

She didn't respond, but she sat right where I left her, smoking in her chair. She was no longer crying, but her eyes were red and stared vacantly at the wall.

"Who are Mr. and Mrs. Russell Hall?" I asked.

Again, no reply. I decided to open the envelope anyway, revealing a store-bought card with flowers on the front and the words *Our deepest condolences* in a swooping cursive. Our first sympathy card.

I tried again. "Mom, this card is addressed to us. Want to read it together?"

Lost in a trance, she said, "Okay."

I sat down next to her and opened the card, and a check fell into my lap. I read out loud:

We were shocked and saddened, as was everyone, to learn of Jay's tragic death. We always looked forward to having him collect for the newspaper because he was such fun to visit with (and tease a little). We will miss him, and our heartfelt sympathy is with you and your family.

We had written Jay a check for $6.60 on April 7th, which took us through April 18. At that time we asked him to discontinue the paper for a month after the 18th, as we would be on vacation, and to start it again on May 17. I enclose a check for the week of May 23 and thru May 27.

Lorna and Russell Hall

My mom sobbed silently. I put the mail on my lap and sat like a spider.

—3—

For this moment, this one moment, we are together.
I press you to me.
Come, pain, feed on me.
Bury your fangs in my flesh.
Tear me asunder.
—Virginia Woolf

"Your mother was a wreck," Char said, her voice rough, just as I remembered it. It was 2015 and I had called one of my mom's oldest friends to see what she remembered about the days after Jay died. I wanted to revisit that time from my mom's perspective, and she would never discuss it with me. I gripped the phone with one hand and scribbled notes with the other.

"Fran and I were waiting when you two got back from the hospital. It was as if her brain had up and left the building. She just stared into space."

I had no memory of this, but I pictured my mom standing there, frozen on the stoop.

"Fran made soup, I think," Char mused.

Campbell's split pea soup with saltine crackers. My mother's go-to for every ailment. It was the only thing she ate when she was sick or sad or did not know what to do with herself. I could almost smell it, the rich, creamy aroma wafting from the kitchen.

As Char told the story, I imagined every detail, even constructed a dialogue in my mom's head. Fran walked off to prepare the soup and perhaps my mom wondered if the kitchen was clean, wanted to check but was paralyzed. She should wash the dishes, and she hadn't mopped yet this week. Had she mopped last week? Yes, last week Jay had come in with muddy shoes and she'd had to mop. No sense mopping today, it was supposed to rain later and Jay had a baseball game and—

"Carol?" Char's voice jerked my mom back to the present. "Why don't you sit down?"

Instead, she bolted out the front door. She opened her purse and fumbled for her pack of Virginia Slims and her purple BIC lighter, gasping for air as she lit the cigarette. She would often close her eyes when she inhaled, letting the nicotine wash over her. Then perhaps she opened her eyes as she exhaled, gasping as she looked across the lawn. She coughed and dropped the cigarette. She ran back into the house and collapsed into her orange chair, sobbing.

I was amazed at the details Char could remember, and she was an animated narrator, her voice full of emotion. "We were so startled, we rushed over to her, asking, 'What happened?!' 'What's wrong?' But she just cried and cried."

Tears welled in my eyes.

"It was a while before we figured out what it was all about. Her eyes were all bloodshot when she lifted her head and said, 'Jay's bike. Please get rid of Jay's bike.'" It had still been lying on the lawn.

"Your brother was always on that bike," Char said. "Always in a hurry to go to the park or his friends' houses. But you know, I had girls and he wasn't too interested in girls yet."

I smiled, holding the phone to my ear and waiting to see if she had anything else to add.

"He was a beautiful boy, so charming, dishwater-blond hair. Almost golden in the sun."

"Yeah," I said. There was a pause, so I risked the question I most wanted to ask. "Did my mom ever talk to you about Jay, ah, telling us he was going to die?"

"Oh, yeah, she was torn up about that. Actually, one time we were sitting in the kitchen, she was having her coffee. And then Jay came in and started talking about lying on the ground and then being up above his body, watching. Your mom listened a little and then said, 'I don't want to hear any more.'"

I tried to picture Char and my mom at the kitchen table, something I must have seen many times, but the memory was faint. After Jay died, my mother seemed to lose all her friendships, one by one, and I never saw Char again. My heart ached for my mom.

"It's been so traumatic for her," I said. "I mean it's one thing to have your child die, and it's a whole other thing to have been told about it, in advance. Why do you think Jay told her?"

"I think they just had an open relationship. He could tell her anything." Her usually boisterous voice had grown softer.

I was quiet for a moment, trying to imagine I could tell my mom anything. A lump lodged in my throat. "You talk about my mom as very open. But since Jay died, she will never, ever talk about his death. We've never grieved together. I've tried to bring it up a thousand times, and it never goes anywhere."

"And I don't think it ever will," Char said. "It's something she keeps locked to herself. I think she *should* talk about it, but I don't think she's going to."

"Why not?"

"It's too painful. She can't handle it. There's some people who can't talk about that stuff. She's never discussed it with me either."

"Never?"

"Actually, I do remember after he passed she said maybe it would have been a good idea if she had locked him up to keep him safe. And I said, 'Oh, Carol, he was a thirteen-year-old boy! You wouldn't have been able to keep him safe forever.' But that said, if one of my children had started telling me something like that, I'd probably try to lock them up. And she did try. How could she have kept him from skipping school? It seems fated."

Fated. Meant to happen. That's how I'd always felt too. My poor mother.

"Well, I should probably start cooking dinner," Char began. It seemed our conversation had reached a natural end, but I didn't want to let go of this connection.

"Okay," I sighed. "I really appreciate you taking the time to talk. Before you go, is there anything else you remember about, about my mom? You know, the kind of mother she was or the food she liked to cook?"

"Oh, I remember one damn thing. Oh my gosh—it was cow's tongue!" She erupted in laughter. I could almost see her then, doubled over at my mom's kitchen table. "That just blew my mind. I mean I just couldn't handle it." We both cracked up, and amid the laughter I smelled my mom's cooking. "But yeah, she was a very good mom. She was very open. And she was good about listening."

My heart swelled. Char could remember a time I had forgotten. She was bringing my mother back to me. "I love that memory," I said. "You know, so much of my memory of my mom is after Jay died. It's so good to remember this other side of her."

"Yeah, she really went down a hole, poor thing."

"She was haunted by Jay's death. Did she ever tell you about the footprints and the picture frames?"

"I can't say as I recall anything about that."

"Well, for weeks after, he lingered in our house." I told Char the story of how Mom found his muddy footprints on the kitchen floor and doormat, down the basement stairs. How his dog Terra, who was generally quiet and well behaved, would start barking ferociously for no reason. How once my mom heard the back door slam shut and rushed to see who was there. All she found was more muddy footprints.

"The day after Jay's funeral," I continued, "the pictures began to fall off the walls." First it was the picture of Grandma and Grandpa Winslow, next Jay's hockey photo, then one of the three of us all posed in Victorian garb.

"Spooky," Char said.

"Right? And the next morning, a heart had been perfectly traced in the velour chair—you remember the beige one?"

"I remember that chair."

"It was like someone had drawn it with a finger. My mom says she didn't do it, and I know it wasn't me."

"Wow. It's like he was haunting her."

"Exactly."

Another story crossed my mind. One day, my mom was home alone, napping with Terra, when she awoke to the sound of barking. She followed the sound down the hallway and found Terra outside the closed door to Jay's room.

The day before, my mother had tidied the room and made up Jay's single bed, tightly tucking the navy-blue threadbare bedspread into the mattress and plumping the pillow in its clean pillowcase. Afterward, she had closed the door, trying to block out the emptiness that seemed to scream at her. Now, with the dog barking at the door, my mom thought she could hear a noise coming from inside. Curious, she opened the door and stepped in. It was brightly lit with afternoon sunlight. Terra bounded in after her. The minute they entered, all the racket stopped. Silence. My mom searched for the source of the noise, while Terra sniffed at the bottom of the bed. Then my mom gasped. The bedspread was disheveled, unmade, as if the bed had been jumped on. The pillow seemed smooshed and cocked at an angle.

Not knowing what to do, she took herself and Terra to bed,

smoked half a cigarette and put it out in the glass ashtray on her oak nightstand. She adjusted her pillows, pulled the covers up to her chin, and closed her eyes. The house was silent except for a lone cardinal's warning cry outside her window.

She drifted into a fitful sleep, waking with a start to remember she had left something in the oven. Annoyed, she sat up, smoked the second half of her cigarette, dragged herself out of bed, and ventured into the silent house. In the kitchen, she looked for the muddy footprints and found only sparkling-clean kitchen floor tiles. When she opened the oven door, she found Jay's head roasting. He had an apple in his mouth. When she reached in and removed it, he said, "Close the door. I'm not done yet."

She awoke with a jolt of horror.

"That's terrifying," Char said, when I'd finished the story.

"I know! My mom told me that nightmare came back over and over. So I guess that's the one time she talked to me about Jay. Maybe she was able to talk about him only in the context of dreams. She said it felt like Jay didn't want to let go."

"Or maybe she couldn't let him go," Char said.

One way or another, Jay's death haunted her until the day she died.

—4—

He who kisses joy as it flies by will live in eternity's sunrise.
—William Blake

On a Wednesday afternoon in late April 2013, I sat on the grass at a park on Lake Mendota, the sky a dome of blue holding streaks of clouds. White-capped waves pounded the lake's shore and a man and woman prepared their sailboat, its sail flapping loudly against the mast. I was waiting for Sheri, Jay's childhood sweetheart. A couple of weeks earlier, I had run into Marybeth, whom I'd gone to high school with.

"Yes, I remember Jay!" she'd said. "My sister's best friend, Sheri, was Jay's girlfriend at the time. I bet we could find her telephone number."

I had completely forgotten that Jay had a girlfriend, but as soon as Marybeth said Sheri's name, she appeared in my mind: tomboyish; white-blond hair falling in perfectly straight, silky sheets; chubby, pink, freckled cheeks; a big, sparkly-eyed grin.

Now at the park, I called up my memory of Sheri. A chocolate Lab ran by, stopping a few feet away to shake, spraying me with water and the smell of dead carp. I scanned the cars and trucks passing the parking lot for anyone who might look like Sheri. Then I realized that Sheri would no longer be the thirteen-year-old girl I remembered. I tried, but failed, to create a forty-five-year-old version of the girl.

A huge, green City of Madison work truck circling the park for a second time pulled into a parking space. I squinted to see if the driver was Sheri, but a guy in baggy work clothes and a neon vest stepped out, leaving the engine running. He started walking toward me, and I saw he was smiling, so I smiled back. It wasn't until she was about ten feet away that the thirteen-year-old Sheri Kuhl emerged.

"Sheri?" I asked, waves of familiarity and grief washing through me.

"Hi, Kris," she said.

We hugged and sat down on the grass and she explained that she had only a twenty-minute lunch break—she worked for the city repairing potholes in the roads, and I could see she had left her truck running. The pressure was on, but before I could decide which question to begin with, she jumped right in.

"I think about Jay every day, especially when I'm on the north side," she began. "When I drive by Sanitarium Hill, I 'member going over to your house and stuff like that, when we would cut classes."

I nodded.

"And, um . . . Kurt Smith, Kevin Orrick, Jay, and I—they had their BMX bikes and I just had a ten-speed, but Kevin didn't have anything and Kevin always carried, like, a *ton* of books. So we're going down Sanitarium Hill and he's on the back of my bike, I'm giving him a ride."

"Wow," I said, as she paused to catch her breath.

"And we're going and he's pushing me, pushing me, forward and forward 'cause it's so bumpy. I could barely stay on the seat! Then the next thing you know, I'm flying over the handlebars, Kevin's right behind me, we're flopping down the hill, the bike is going, his books are going everywhere!"

"Yikes!" I said, giddy with Sheri's infectious excitement.

"Yeah. And them two buttheads sat at the bottom of the hill and laughed their butts off."

I figured out she was referring to Jay and Kurt.

"Nobody came up to see if we were okay." She was laughing hard now. "I don't know if the people in the office building saw us, because I was too embarrassed to look. I mean, it's an office place. Can you imagine someone looking out their windows saying, 'LOOK AT THESE IDIOTS!' What the hell, you know?"

Sheri and I doubled over, grabbing each other's arms. Then, quite abruptly, we were silent, staring out at the lake. I had so much love for Sheri and her story and that ragtag group of kids. I'd been waiting for this moment for over thirty years, and I basked in the warmth of new memories of Jay.

Sheri began again. "I mean, it was, it was just little things like that. Just some little things you kinda think about and always remember." Her voice was soft, and she looked at her hands as she launched into a stream of stories.

"Did you know Danny McCarthy committed suicide after Jay died?" she asked.

I shook my head.

"That really hurt. I wanted to kill myself many times, and I tried once by overdosing on pills from the medicine cabinet."

I grabbed Sheri's hand, feeling her rough, calloused fingers against my own.

"My mom put me into treatment and I lost a lot of friends. I didn't use drugs for the rest of high school."

She continued on to tell me that if she had had kids, she would have named one of them Jay, that Jay was the best thing that had ever happened to her. She started sobbing, and I pulled her into my arms. I wished we could sit here on this grass, in this wind, under this sky for eternity. There was so much I wanted to ask her, to share with her. I felt as if my heart was breaking anew, but we were repairing cracks my brother left behind. For a moment we were evolving together, and the impact rippled across the lake and rustled through the trees. Then it was over.

Sheri pulled away and wiped her eyes. "I really loved that boy." She stood and I joined her.

"Me too." I smiled sadly. "Thank you for sharing this with me."

She nodded, then turned and walked back to her truck. Since that day, we've never spoken, though I do see her around from time to time, on the job, filling holes in Madison's streets. I drive by and wave, and sometimes she waves back, the faintest sparkle still in her eyes.

—5—

Ignoring your death is like dying a slow death.
—Oprah Winfrey

I clutched my Starbucks oat milk venti latte, sipping anxiously as I drove toward Warner Park. The dogs panted loudly in the back seat, eagerly awaiting their afternoon walk. I hated the dog-food smell of Holiday's warm breath, so I cracked a window and pushed her head toward it, shivering as the icy blast of January air hit me. It was 2018 and I was on my way to meet Stevie Anderson, one of Jay's best friends growing up.

The last time I encountered Stevie, over two years ago in 2015, he was high on heroin and lying on the sidewalk outside a friend's house. I hadn't been terribly surprised to find him in that condition. A couple of years earlier I'd heard he had been in jail for a drug-related offense, possibly involving guns. I had given up hope of hearing from him and was surprised when he messaged me at the end of 2017.

I had been in Los Angeles attending a Miracle-Minded New Year's Eve weekend with Marianne Williamson. Deeply moved by the workshop, I'd gone back to my hotel room and prayed to any powers that may exist: "I am all yours. I want you to take my whole life. I beg you."

The next morning, I'd awoken to a miracle. As I looked through

Facebook Messenger, I found a message from Stevie: *Hey, Kris, you probably hate me, but I was thinking about you.*

The universe had heard me! I responded immediately, my heartbeat pulsing in my fingers as they tapped across my phone screen. I had prayed, I had begged, and life had given me Jay's best friend.

Stevie and I had exchanged a few more messages before I made it back to Wisconsin, and through our correspondence I'd come to learn that he was homeless, used the library to get warm and go on Facebook, and slept nights under a bridge. I shivered to think of sweet, beautiful Stevie, the boy from my youth, sleeping outdoors in the Wisconsin winter. How far off the rails had his life gone?

We had planned to meet upon my return, but as the day had approached, doubt seeped in. I brought up my concerns with Marta, the woman who cleans the offices of my business, Optimal Health Network.

"Are you sure this is a good idea?" I asked, watching Marta wipe the counter and rinse the cloth in the sink. "I need answers. But what if he's not safe? Maybe I should just cancel."

Marta put down the dishrag and placed both hands on my shoulders, her blue eyes wide. "Kristi, look at me."

I gazed at her big smile, her round, pleasant, Polish face.

"I believe in you." She patted my cheek tenderly.

I tucked Marta's love into my heart and loaded the dogs into the car. Pulling out of the driveway, I paid attention to the sensations in my body: the fierceness of my love for Stevie, the allure of digging deeper into Jay's story, and the mystery of embodied prayer. I had felt brave.

Now, however, in the twenty minutes since leaving my house, some of my courage had slipped away, out the window into the biting winter wind. I noticed three crows crossing the blue sky. I took a deep, calming breath.

The dogs and I arrived at the Warner Park Lagoon and ice skater's warming shelter, the same rainbow-painted structure where, years ago, Jay and I had warmed up near the fire with friends, instant hot chocolate and hockey sticks strewn everywhere. I drove to a remote end of the parking lot, away from the bustling community center, and parked near a stand of pine trees.

Outside, when I grabbed the back-door handle, Holiday forced the door wide open and jumped out, spinning around in attack position. She'd always done this in moments of transition, her way of claiming control in a moment when she had little.

As the usual target of Holiday's bullying, Toby didn't move from his spot in the back seat while Sheeta, unconcerned, pushed past him and joined Holiday on the ground. Holly and Toby were locked in a standoff, one snarling, the other whimpering as they stared at each other, then at me, then back at each other.

"Come on, Toby," I encouraged. "I'll make sure she doesn't attack you." A moment later, as I held Holiday by her collar, Toby scrambled out, and the dogs chased each other across the snow-covered field and into the woods. Through the trees, the afternoon sun hung low over the lagoon.

I trudged through the snow after the rest of my pack, emboldened by their energy and bundled under my purple wool hat and scarf, my feet cozy inside blue rubber boots with toe warmers. In the woods, I saw Toby and Sheeta chasing a squirrel while Holiday hung back. She was always afraid of any potential pack separation.

I arrived at the picnic table on the edge of the lagoon where Stevie told me to meet him. He wasn't there yet. I started to wonder if he'd even show, and I couldn't tell which outcome I preferred. The dogs and I could still have a nice walk. I ran to the frozen lagoon, calling them to follow. Technically, this park required all dogs to be leashed, but I'd found a loophole: leashes weren't required on frozen water anywhere in the city. As I reached the shore, I took a deep breath and stepped down, enjoying the familiar exhilaration of not knowing for certain whether the ice would hold my weight. I heard faint cracks and a gurgle, but it seemed solid. I ran, then slid across the ice, the dogs running behind me. A man's voice drew my attention back to the shore, and I whirled around.

"Why are you coming from the ice?" Stevie said, his first words to me since the day of Jay's funeral. They echoed in my head: *Why are you coming from the ice?* I stepped back in time.

"Stevie!" I called, sliding toward where he stood on the shore. "I came from the parking lot. You told me you were going to be at that picnic table, remember?" I pointed to the lone table. Sticking to a plan was something Stevie could not do. I was lucky to have found him.

As I got closer, his face came into focus and I could tell he was drunk.

"Oh, my God. Hey, Kris!" He started laughing. "Oh, my God, it's really you."

I joined in his laughter. "It's really me! And it's really you!"

"How you doing, Kris?" he asked, his words slurring as he continued without waiting for my response. "God, you are looking good."

I opened my arms, overtaken with love for this disheveled, drunken remnant of my youth. We looked at each other for a moment before he opened his arms to me, and I fell into his bright-red Wisconsin Badgers jacket, his boyish innocence.

The years had not been kind. His wrinkled skin was a pale, grayish color and he stooped slightly.

"How old are you, Stevie?" I asked. "Fifty?"

"Same as you, Kris." Stevie raised his arms to the sky, a gigantic smile on his face. "Your birthday is March 18, and mine is March 15."

"Of course!" He was three years younger than me but I didn't bother pointing this out. I was just impressed he remembered this detail of our matching birthdays after almost forty years.

"I'll always remember, Kris. You are the only girl I've ever loved."

I didn't know what to say to that, so I introduced Stevie to my dogs. "This is Sheeta, Toby, and Holiday Napkins."

"Holiday Napkins? That is hilarious," Stevie said.

"A collaboration between myself and my four children."

"You have four children?" Stevie came to an abrupt stop, turning to face me. "Kris," he grabbed my arm. "I've always wanted four children. This means we *have* to get married!"

I started to laugh.

"I mean it!" he insisted.

"Okay," I giggled. "Let's do it! Let's get married right here, with the dogs, on the ice, where we played as children."

"Okay, I can totally get behind that." Stevie reached into his jacket, pulled out a fifth of vodka, and took a swig.

I'd been expecting Stevie to bring up marriage. He'd already asked me about it a few times during our Facebook correspondence. I looked into his eyes and felt his impossible longing. It was a feeling I had known myself.

When he finished with the vodka, I grabbed his hand, running in a circle, sliding on the ice. "Do you think the ice is thick enough?" I asked, remembering I'd seen open water near the shore.

"Fucking no, but who gives a shit."

We both laughed.

"Sorry, Kris, sorry about the swearing, it's just the way I've always been."

"I love swearing!" I said. "I miss it, it's fun. Keep swearing, Stevie."

Inside a miracle, we slipped and slid arm in arm along the surface of the ice, taking turns wobbling and saving each other. Some color had returned to his cheeks and his eyes had come alive.

When we rounded the corner of the lagoon, Stevie pointed to a spot on the ice. "I almost drowned right here."

"Really?"

"Jay and I were swimming. We were both really high. I'd been swimming here so many times, but that day, I don't know what happened to me. I just plummeted to the bottom, you know that muck at the bottom? I was just sinking down, drowning."

"What happened?"

"Jay. He came down, pulled me up, brought me to the shore and literally gave me mouth-to-mouth. Oh, my God, I thought I was gonna die, you know?"

A red-tailed hawk flew overhead, casting a shadow across the ice.

"I'm glad you didn't die."

"Me too." A shudder coursed through Stevie's body as he stared down at the frozen marsh water beneath his feet. "Thank God for Jay," he said, more to the ice than to me.

I stayed quiet, still holding his arm.

After a moment, Stevie looked up at me, eyes wide. "Now that I'm telling you this, Kris, I just remembered something."

"What?"

"When Jay and I were walking home, he stopped and made me face him. And he said, 'That would have been okay, if you died. I've seen my death. I saw it one time, when I was on acid. I'm going to die young, and it's okay.'"

I stared at Stevie, shocked by his willingness to tumble into the unknown together. In his eyes, behind the wrinkles and the alcoholism, was the fourteen-year-old boy I once knew. I wanted to hear more, to tell him my story of Jay's visions, but Stevie said, "This is getting too heavy. Would you be willing to buy me a meal? I haven't eaten since yesterday."

"Absolutely." I didn't want to push him.

We walked in silence to my car.

"Where do you want to go?" I asked as we all piled in.

"There's a little Mexican restaurant in that strip mall, you know, where the Milk Depot used to be? It's only a couple blocks away."

I started the engine as Stevie continued rambling. "Remember it, Kris? The Milk Depot? Where Jay should have gone and then he wouldn't be dead?"

I looked over to see he was crying.

"Sorry, Kris," he sniffed, wiping tears away with the sleeve of his jacket. "I'm sorry."

"Oh, honey." I put my hand on his. "Tears are good."

Stevie took another swig from his vodka, and by the time we arrived at the restaurant, he'd tucked his grief away. We ordered and sat down at a table by the window, barely waiting five minutes for our food: three lengua tacos and a Coke each, plus a beer for Stevie. We attacked our plates, stuffing messy bites of tender cow's tongue into our mouths.

"You know," Stevie said, "sitting here with you—eating tacos and drinking Coke—is a dream. It's a dream, Kris."

I beamed at him. I felt it too, the beauty of this moment amid the tragedy of our impossible story.

A younger man in a baggy coat walked into the small Mexican grocery and restaurant, took his sunglasses off, and sat at the next table.

"Hey, Duke," Stevie yelled, cracking open his beer.

Duke smiled.

"Duke, this is my friend, Kris. I was telling you about her. She is the sister of my best friend, remember?"

"Yeah, wasn't that years ago?"

"Yes, it was. See, Kris? I wasn't lying to you. I've been into you ever since we were little."

I sipped my Coke, feeling thirty years younger. I hadn't had soda in years. I savored the food and the experience, knowing it would end soon. Before long, I heard the dogs barking in the car. "I've got to go now, Stevie."

"No."

"Yes. Am I leaving you here or taking you somewhere else?" Stevie had nowhere else to go, but I asked anyway.

"No, Kris, you can't leave," Stevie said.

"Gotta go, dogs are barking." I picked up my red plastic tray and brought it to the garbage.

I walked past the owner of the shop, sweeping, back to where Stevie sat slumped in his seat. Stevie's friend stood up to leave as well, and Stevie perked up. "Duke, man, you know how much I love her. Won't you tell her to marry me?"

"Bye, Stevie." I kissed the top of his head before pushing the glass door open and jumping into the car.

Driving home, I reflected on the strong historical entanglement between us, allowing myself to feel Stevie's pain. I reminded myself that uncertainty is best held loosely, so I focused on the experience of syncing with another person who loved Jay. Tears blurred the lights of cars in front of me.

One week later, I picked Stevie up at his sister Karen's house, only a few blocks from the site of Jay's death. We were going to visit the tree.

Stevie sat in the passenger seat beside me. Having him there reminded me of when he and I rode home together after laying Jay's casket in the earth.

He turned to me abruptly and said with drunken sincerity, "I'm in love with you, Kris," slurring his words as he unzipped his dirty red jacket and pulled out his vodka. "If you don't feel about me that way, it's okay. I don't care."

I turned left onto Goodland Drive. Some part of me was in love with some part of him, though not in the way he wanted.

"What I am trying to tell you about, Kris, is the moment I found out I was in love with you."

I pulled up to the curb alongside the maple tree with the healed-over scar. The gnarled gash wasn't visible in the dark, but the tree itself had a presence, looming tall and black in the yard beside us, barren of leaves. I wanted to focus on what we'd come here to do, but I turned the engine off and directed my attention to Stevie.

"You remember your bedroom in the basement?" He unscrewed the cap of his vodka.

"I remember."

"We were in your room," Stevie continued. "And we were dancing like there was no fucking tomorrow. Queen was playing—'Crazy Little Thing Called Love.'"

I nodded enthusiastically and sang the chorus.

Stevie watched me sing as he raised the glass bottle to his lips, tilted his head, and tossed back a shot, swallowing hard. "You were dancing on your bed, you remember?" He screwed the cap back on and wiped his mouth with his sleeve.

"I remember the song. I don't remember dancing."

"Yeah, we did," Stevie insisted. "I jumped up on the bed to dance with you, and then—" he shook his head. "It's embarrassing to talk about. I am fifty-one years old, but it's still embarrassing."

"What?"

"I skipped the record, and you hauled off and hit me like a son of a bitch." Stevie looked over at me, grinning wryly. "I'll never forget it."

I was in awe of Stevie. Drunk and decrepit, he still remembered the details of our young lives, like a magic trick.

"I hit you?" As an adult, I'd often felt the desire to hit someone.

"Yup," Stevie said, without anger. "You hit me, and ever since that moment, I've been in love with you, Kris."

I could see the love in his bloodshot eyes, and my initial shock gave way to an opening in my body, gratitude for a healing I'd never thought I would be allowed.

"Did I hit you a lot?"

"I mean . . ." Stevie shrugged. "You were a protector. You protected all of us. I swear to God." Stevie drank again from the half-empty bottle. "You were the big sister!"

I considered this. I was three years older than Jay and his friends, and up until I turned sixteen or seventeen, I'd spent a lot of time hanging out with them, being the boss, the protector. But I couldn't protect Jay.

"You stood up to our enemies," Stevie added when I didn't respond.

I swallowed the knot in my throat and tried to keep the conversation going. "Who were our enemies?"

"The Websters!"

I flashed back to the Webster family, children in ratty, stained clothes living in a yellow house that smelled of stale alcohol. They'd lived three doors down on Novick Drive and moved out after a couple of years. "Right," I said. "Beanie Webster. I remember her. I remember punching her."

Stevie cracked up, and I joined him.

I wondered now if our regular beatings had anything to do with their leaving. I doubted it, but even now I could feel in my body how willing we were to throw fists.

"Hey," Stevie said. "Do you remember when I threw Tootsie Rolls at your picture window because you were kissing Bob Rosenmeyer?"

"No way!" I laughed.

"No, I'm serious. I don't think a day has ever gone by without thinking about you, Kris."

The heartbreak in his voice was too much. I opened my door, which triggered a loud dinging sound—the key still in the ignition—echoing into the silent night air. I quickly removed the key, returning us to quiet reverence. I'd visited this place before, but always alone. Now, for the first time in thirty-five years, I was with someone who knew Jay.

Before I could step out of the car, Stevie grabbed my arm and pulled me toward him. "Where are you going?"

I turned to look into his clear blue eyes. "I want to touch the tree."

Stevie surprised me with what he said next. "I lived in that tree."

I shut the car door, turning back to this quiet shell of a man beside me.

"After Jay died, I climbed up that tree every day."

I looked through Stevie's fourteen-year-old eyes at the reddish buds swelling into hand-size leaves.

"No one bothered me either. No one came around here after Jay died."

It wasn't the first time I'd heard this. "Why?" I knew what he'd say but I had to hear it.

"Blood," Stevie said quietly. "There was a lot of blood on the road."

I resisted the urge to look at the pavement, knowing I would see nothing in the dark so many years later. Instead I looked at the tree. "You climbed up there every day?"

"Sure did. With my jackknife. Lived in that tree, carving."

I felt the jackknife in my hand.

"What did you carve?"

Stevie hesitated, then said softly, "I miss you, Jay, inside my heart."

A weight lifted off my own heart. I was not the only one who visited this place. My whole body resonated with his process of grieving. I only wished we could have grieved Jay together.

—6—

*Write what disturbs you, what you fear, what you have not
been willing to speak about. Be willing to be split open.*
—Natalie Goldberg

A few years earlier, twenty thousand feet above the Mississippi
River on the way home from a silent writing retreat, I began
writing a poem. An elderly man in the seat next to me had been
sound asleep and snoring, but he rearranged himself, crossing and
uncrossing his knees.

"What are you writing?" The tang of stale pipe smoke entered my
awareness.

I lifted my blue pen to my lips. "It's a poem about what I see out
this window."

"Want to read it to me?"

I fought with my desire to say no, then surrendered, composing
myself before beginning. "Shiny river, I gaze—"

"Can I get y'all anything to drink?" A stewardess with ruby-red
lipstick and a crooked smile broke in.

The man took a plastic cup of Pepsi and pretzels. I asked for a can
of seltzer with two slices of lemon.

"Begin again." He shifted his body to lean in a little closer, sipping
from the cup of Pepsi.

"Shiny river, I gaze; a we from above. The wind blows across your snaky body, changing your surface shapes. Do you and the wind speak in code? Are those lines atop your surface a song, or maybe something about the wind's love?"

"That's lovely," he said, lighting me up inside. "Who's the we?"

"Well . . ." I paused, setting my notebook down. "I'm writing about . . . about . . . my soul and I . . ." I finished quickly. "Like Walt Whitman in *Song of Myself.*" I hoped the reference would cover my lack of confidence, but when he chuckled, I shrank, squeezing my two lemon slices into my seltzer water.

"It's lovely," he repeated.

I sipped my drink. "I'm returning from a Natalie Goldberg writing retreat."

"Is she a writing teacher?"

"It's a writing practice, a meditation. She gives a prompt—a color or a line from a book. You put pen to paper. No stopping. No looking back. No deleting. Twenty minutes, depending."

"That's interesting," he said, opening his pretzels with his teeth. "Got anything from the workshop to share?"

Again, resistance arose, but I paged through my notebook to find my writing about the day Jay died.

As I began, he stopped chewing and sat silently. I read three full pages.

When I finished, he said, "You should write a book about that."

My heart skipped a beat. "I want to. But I don't remember much about my brother. It's only when I am given a prompt and the timer starts to tick that he arises."

"Can you give me a piece of paper?" he asked.

I tore out a blank page as he pulled out a ballpoint pen from his shirt pocket.

"Who can help you remember?"

"Well, my mom. But she won't talk to me about it. And I've tried.

I even locked her in a bathroom in California." I peered out the window, seeing a small lake, and watched the wind change its surface. Then I turned back to him. "No, it was Italy. I was trying to get her to talk."

"You locked your mother in a bathroom in Italy?" The warmth in his voice caught me by surprise.

"Well, yes. I was in my twenties. I had just stopped using drugs. They'd encouraged me to tell my life story, but there was so much I didn't know." I pulled a lemon slice out of my drink, extracted the fleshy segments with my teeth, and set the rind on my napkin. "At the time, I felt she just needed encouragement to tell me all the details." I laughed. "She came to visit me in Europe for winter break. I was there for a year of college. It was crazy. I was newly clean and sober, and I had started having flashbacks of my brother and of trauma from when I was a baby . . . I wanted answers and she was our mother. Jay was close to her. She was the first person he told that he was going to die."

"He knew he was going to die?" He drank from his Pepsi.

"Something about a green car, he'd say. And he knew he would be young. He had some kind of vision and it came true."

"I'm a retired English professor," he said with a smile, "and this story would make a phenomenal book."

I shivered. Wrapped in the silence of Natalie's writing retreat, I had found myself writing about Jay's death, but all I could find were pea-size flashes of light from a meteor shower, the falling stars of a childhood consciousness. Not for the first time, I'd begun to fantasize about taking a college writing course. Now my writing course had come to me. In silence, the professor and I watched the stewardess shuffle backward along the aisle, pulling the metal service cart.

"Want my last pretzel?" he asked as he handed the flight attendant his plastic cup.

"No, thanks. I don't eat gluten." I listened to him chew his remaining pretzel.

He swallowed. "Who else knew your brother?"

My mind went blank. I'd been processing my brother's death for over twenty-nine years. How could this question be a shock? *Who else knew your brother?* My first response was, *no one,* or only my mother. I looked out the window again. Clouds. A setting sun. A feeling of universal connection arose.

"My stepfather," I blurted out.

"Excellent! What's his name?"

"Dick. Dick Amelong."

As I watched him write I realized I had not thought about my stepfather in years.

"How do you spell the last name?" he asked.

I spelled it slowly.

He paused. "Okay. Dick. Your stepfather. Do you ever talk to him?"

"No, he's dead. Died in his sleep. Alcoholism."

"Well, that won't work then, will it?"

"No, I haven't learned the trick of talking to dead people." I laughed.

"Who else?"

How was it that, after all these years, the only people I'd ever talked to about Jay were people who'd never met him? When Jay died, everyone close to him had seemed to die as well. What had happened to the fabric of my community?

Then a name popped into my head. "Kurt Smith."

"Who is Kurt?"

"He is the boy who was with Jay the day he died."

"Do you ever talk to him?"

"No. I don't even know how I'd find him."

"Maybe you should call your book *Seeking Kurt*," he said as he wrote those words on the piece of paper I gave him.

"Hmm, *Seeking Kurt*," I pondered aloud, as the flight attendant announced we were about to land in Chicago.

* * *

I decided that my cousin Marty was the safest person to ask about Jay. We'd been very close as children.

Besides, I didn't have a way to find Kurt Smith.

Shortly after returning from the Natalie Goldberg retreat, I private-messaged Marty on Facebook: *"Hey Marty! I am writing a memoir about Jay. Can we meet over coffee?"*

I hadn't seen Marty for years. He and I are the same age. When we were children, he had a way of creating a world for us out of haylofts and cow manure. Unlike my other relatives, he worked in Madison, a fact I'd discovered a few years ago. At the time, my ninth-grade son was football-bound. He and I had met with Marty at a diner over a summer lunch to quiz Marty, a high school football coach, about what to expect. He'd been very helpful. Now, at Cafe Zoma, an artsy hangout on Madison's east side, I hoped he'd be helpful in my search.

"I was playing baseball. My team had an away game," Marty began, jumping right to the day Jay died.

Looking into Marty's eyes, I saw my brother.

"My parents—or was it just my mom?" Marty mused as he sipped his coffee. "Yes, my mom. She came up to me at the game. She walked onto the field. I'll never forget . . ." Marty seemed to lose himself. "I'm standing there, and all of a sudden, my mom is there. *Moms do not walk onto the field in the middle of a game*, I'm thinking. She doesn't even come to my baseball games, for crying out loud. We're farmers. She needs to be milking. But she's there. So I think, *Well, this is nice.* Then all of a sudden she comes up, asking if she can talk to me. I think I blurted out, 'What's going on?'"

Marty and I both looked up as the front door of the cafe opened and a family with two toddlers walked in. Our eyes met again, and Marty continued. "Then she said it: 'Jay was killed in an accident.'"

His words brought me back to that night. We were silent, both of us fighting off tears.

"Even though you guys lived in Madison, you both were a part of our lives, both of ya. You'd come down in the summers. Both of ya," he repeated. "Jay and I just always got along. I think it was because both of us were into sports. Jay was a very good hockey player. I was a wrestler. We talked a lot, even though he was four years younger than me."

I picked up my almond milk latte.

"I was down there almost every day for the first few days," Marty said.

"In Madison?" I asked.

"Yeah."

"For what?"

"To see you." He cocked his head.

"Really?"

"Hey, we were there the day of . . . I can remember coming down and that was tough. You were struggling, and I was too. It was hard to accept. As a child, I thought I knew how the world worked. In my world things were simple: You wake up. You work on the farm. You try to escape by getting into sports. You get away for a while and then you go back. That's just the way it is."

I nodded, hoping he'd continue, hanging on to his every word.

"I remember your mom. She was a mess."

I had no memory of my mom that night. "What was that like?"

"She was shaking. She could barely talk. I remember when we walked in . . . that was tough. That, for me, was the hardest day of my life. You didn't know what to say. You didn't know what you were feeling. It was just very intense."

—7—

Only love gives us the taste of eternity.
—Jewish proverb

One morning, in 2016, I was meditating in my bedroom, floating down a vine-covered river in my mind, when my phone shook me into awareness. My friend Mike was calling me. He and his husband, Genio, were visiting from Colorado.

I swiped the phone to answer. "Hello, Mike."

"Class reunion," Mike said. "1985. East High School."

I've known Mike for over twenty years (we dated in the late eighties and now talk on the phone often) and he's always had this habit of blurting out whatever is on his mind, as if others would obviously be just as interested in his need for chocolate, his exercise status, or when he naps. I usually ignore him, but this time I took the bait.

"What?" I asked.

"Class reunion. 1985. East High School. Looks like it's happening this weekend."

I pulled the lingering vines of meditation from my mind and sat up in bed. *1985, East High School.*

"How do you know about this? Where is it?"

"Right across the street from you, at the East Side Club. I'm out front reading the sign. Some guy's up on a ladder, changing the letters out right now."

I jumped out of bed. "Are you serious? Tonight?" I lived kitty-corner to the East Side Club, but its sign never drew my attention. If not for Mike, I may never have noticed this important information.

"Yeah, why?"

"That's my brother's class!" I ran downstairs in my pajamas. I looked out the front window and saw Mike standing there with his phone to his ear. Across the street a guy was taking down his ladder in front of the sign.

"Oh, my God, I've got to go!" I began to hang up. "Bye, M—"

"Wait!"

"What?" A slight irritation had crept into my voice. I wanted to make plans for the night.

"Should I leave Genio the car and bike to Picnic Point to go running? Or should I drop him off at the gym and drive to Picnic Point?"

I sighed, only half listening as I scrolled through my email inbox. "Which do you want to do?"

"Not sure."

"Take Genio, and then go run."

"Okay, thanks."

"Bye, Mike!" I hung up and ran back upstairs to get dressed.

I couldn't believe my luck. Perhaps this would be the night I would find Kurt! My stomach squirmed at the thought of talking to people I hadn't seen in over thirty years.

The whole day was a blur of anxious anticipation. By the time the sun was setting over the lake across the street, my nerves buzzed. I lay my Rummy 500 hand down on the table—189 points. I'd won for the second time in a row and Genio and my fourteen-year-old daughter Rayna hung their heads. Mike had met up with another friend for dinner.

I looked down at the dogs wrestling on the hair-coated carpet next to the table and realized I was avoiding the reunion.

"Anybody wanna play another game?"

Genio and Rayna shook their heads.

"Okay, fine. Anybody wanna go with me to Jay's class reunion? I'm terrified!"

I put on a dress, and Genio changed his clothes to match my outfit. I trembled as we crossed the street. *You're okay.* I said to myself. *We're okay. We need to find Kurt.* We entered the square brick building and walked down the steps to a small bar where music blared and disco lights skimmed across a mostly empty dance floor. Groups of two or three people huddled together around the room.

I grabbed Genio's hand, pulling him closer so he could hear me. "Let's look at the class list." I led him to the wall, and ran my pointer finger along the letters *K – U – R – T.*

Genio, a native Spanish speaker, followed me with his own finger, *K – U – R – T.* "Who is Kurt?" he asked.

"That's who we're looking for," I said. "I think he's the key to unlock the mystery of Jay's story. I'll explain later." I pulled him into the sparse room. "Let's see if we can find anyone with this name tag." We walked around, smiling shyly and peeking at the name tags.

Middle-aged men and women stood in clumps of three and four, clutching plastic cups and leaning on walls and tables as if the empty center of the dance floor were a black hole that they might fall into. Some stared into their drinks or up at the DJ. The few eyes I managed to catch looked away quickly. Each new cluster of people we approached brought the same spike of anxiety followed by the disappointment of more names I didn't recognize. Halfway around the room I paused.

"No Kurt?" Genio asked.

I shook my head. "Should we leave? What if he comes later?"

Genio shrugged. His face looked pained. Poor guy. What was I putting him through?

I scanned the room again to see if any new faces had entered. This was hopeless. I pressed my cool fingers to my hot forehead.

"Are you okay?" Genio asked.

I should have been asking him that. I put myself in his shoes, a Spanish-speaking, Brown, gay man in a sea of Midwestern whiteness. I wanted to protect him, but I was at the edge of my emotional capacity. I wished he would perk up so I wouldn't have to worry about him, then felt guilty for having that thought. I smiled and squeezed his hand. "Let's go ask those women."

We walked up to a small card table where two women sat behind a bucket labeled *Milton McPike Scholarship Fund*.

"Hello," I yelled over the music. "Do you know a Kurt Smith?"

They exchanged a look and nodded.

"Do you know if he is here?"

"I don't know," said the taller woman. Her hair was curly and thin. She put a hand on my arm, leaning closer to my ear. "Let's go ask Shannon. He's the DJ. He can announce it."

I followed her across the dance floor, where two women were bobbing to the music, beckoning for others to join them. As we passed, they stopped moving and stared at me. I didn't recognize them, but I paused. Their lips formed the words, "Are you?" And, again, "Are you?"

"Am I who?" I asked.

"Are you Jay Amelong's sister?" they yelled, huddling closer.

I nodded.

They whispered something to each other and then enclosed me in a full-blown hug. "I'm so sorry," they said. Suddenly, the music stopped, and I heard a voice over the PA system. "Is there a Kurt Smith here? There is a lady up here looking for Kurt Smith."

I smiled at the two women and squirmed away, Genio bobbing in my wake. I needed to talk to the DJ, who was already starting up the next song. He was a big guy with silky dark skin and a warm smile. Did she say his name was Shannon? I walked up and tapped him on the shoulder. He turned, eyebrows raised. I stood on my toes to speak into his ear. "Can you tell them I also want to talk to anyone who might know how to find Kurt Smith?" He smiled and nodded, then turned to talk to another woman.

The music stopped again and Shannon announced, "If anyone knows how to make contact with Kurt Smith, please come up front, there is a lady here who wants to talk to him."

I wanted to grab the mike from Shannon's hand and make him stop talking about the "lady." I approached him again and he bent his ear toward my mouth. "Did you know Jay Amelong?" I asked, as Katy Perry sang in the background.

Shannon's body seemed to be hit by a force equal to gravity. He swayed for a moment, then pulled me into his arms and held me.

"I'm so sorry. *That* day. I'm so sorry. How did *that* happen? Jay was the best BMX bike rider in the entire neighborhood. He designed the BMX bike course back up against . . . what was that place? Mendota Mental Health Institute?"

I nodded.

"He got air. Everyone wanted to be him, to have his bike, to ride like him. It was impossible that he was killed. And we never went on that street again, even though I lived right around the corner and had to go by there every day. I went four blocks out of my way, every day, to school and back."

"Why?"

He swayed forward and back again. "Are you ready for this?"

"Yes."

He smiled sadly, studying my face, then shook his head. "No, I don't think so." But he continued anyway. "The blood. The blood of your brother. On the road. Nobody went down Goodland Drive ever again."

—8—

You'll drift apart, it's true, but you'll be out in the open, part
of everything alive again.
—Philip Pullman

Jay died on a Wednesday. His funeral was on Friday at the Ryan Funeral Home, not far from our house. I can remember all these facts but have only snatches of actual, visual memories. It was an open-casket ceremony and the line to see his body stretched out the door of the small, brightly lit chapel. I remember waiting in that line for ages, but I have no memory of seeing Jay. I know they played "Stairway to Heaven" during the service, because Jay had requested it, and to this day, the song still makes me think of him. I know we all drove to Neptune Cemetery after the ceremony, but I don't remember the burial. I can recall only the rivers of tears, flowing from my eyes and the eyes of those around me.

My whole extended family from Richland Center came, including my Aunt Alice, who I spoke with one Christmas about the event.

"You know I've always felt so bad about how I treated your poor mother that day," she said to me, her kind face taking on a mournful expression, wrinkled brow furrowed.

"Why?"

"Well, I remember I was in a tizzy thinking about that sweet boy dying without having a proper baptism. No one in the family could confirm whether he'd been christened, and I was desperate to know. It was silly, really, what was there to do at that point? But I think I was frustrated with your mother for moving away from our roots. Of course, my feelings were misplaced but—" she paused and her face fell. "Anyway, I cornered your mother on her way to the bathroom. I said, 'Carol, did you give that boy a proper baptism or not?' And you know your mother, she's so stubborn, she wouldn't answer, no matter how much I pestered her. That's just awful, don't you think? It wasn't the time or the place. She had lost her son, for God's sake!"

I grimaced and chuckled in sympathy.

"Ah well, we all make mistakes."

"It's true!" I touched her hand. "We were all hurting that day."

She shook her head. "You know, I never did find out the answer . . . was Jay baptized?"

I smiled at her shameless persistence.

"I mean, it's not relevant anymore is it? I just—I worry about his soul."

My father was there—my real dad, Steve, whom I hadn't seen since I was a baby. I asked him about it one day, when we were adults and had begun to repair our relationship. I wasn't yet ready to start calling him "Dad," but I appreciated the increased contact. He had started coming over every week to wash my dishes, my least favorite chore. That day, Steve had asked me to teach him to write, and I suggested we try writing toward the same scene, as an exercise.

"Really?" he said, raising his bushy eyebrows. "I'd love that." His nose twitched, a familiar tick of his, and he took off his Navy Vet trucker's hat.

I smiled at him, gazing into the depths of his watery, blue eyes, feeling this "we" space of creativity and imagination.

"Jay's funeral, when I was seventeen. Let's work on that."

He nodded and opened his notebook, pen poised over the paper.

"What do you remember from the funeral?" I asked.

"Your mother. That cast on her foot." He gazed out the window. "I walked up to you and we hugged for a long time. That made me happy." I watched him write, *Lost, everyone was lost.*

My father and I sat in my sunny living room and wrote in silence for ten minutes, until the timer went off.

"How was that for you?" I asked.

"It's one of those moments in my life I will never forget. The moment, the precise moment, will never go away." Steve's eyes grew hazy as he began to read. "I am at my office, Town and Country Ford Tractor. I am reading the newspaper. I have my cup of coffee in my hand. And out of nowhere—there is your brother on the front page. He's dead. I see your mother's name. I can't believe it. I just can't believe it. The kid's only thirteen. I go home, I tell my wife, Cheryl. We go to the funeral together, at the Ryan Funeral Home on Sherman Avenue."

I nodded.

"The first thing I see is your mom. She turns around and looks at me. She hobbles over to me and opens her arms. I am a little surprised she remembers me. She has a cast on her leg. I give her a hug. Then I see you. I don't even recognize you, but I know it is you. You are wearing a long blue dress. Your mom introduces us: 'Kris, this is your dad.' You hug me, and don't let go for a long time. You are crying."

My dad looked up at me, then back down at his writing. Through his words, the memory came back, all bright colors and sharp images, like a cartoon. I saw a seventeen-year-old girl, tall, lost in a crowded funeral home, floating untethered, not even knowing she needed an anchor. Then an anchor appeared in the form of a long-lost father with sad eyes and alcohol on his breath. He held her. She felt more held than she had ever known.

A tear slipped out of my eye. "Thanks for sharing that."

"What did you write?"

"Um." I blushed. I didn't expect him to ask to hear my writing. "Well, I couldn't remember much . . . but here's what I have." I cleared my throat and shifted in my chair.

"For the first time in my life, crying was allowed. I cried more than I ever had before, while all around me, Jay's friends and classmates—a sea of thirteen-year-olds—sobbed in each other's arms.

"The love everyone had for Jay was palpable, and it made me feel loved by extension. As sad as it was, when I look back now on what I can remember, I see it as a slice of heaven, a moment free from the numbness and isolation that would plague me for the next seven years. The most tragic event of my childhood was also one of the most beautiful."

"Wow." My dad reached for my hand and squeezed it.

Recently I uncovered a box that held the newspaper clipping with the announcement and several sympathy cards. One is handmade with a rose drawn in pencil on the front. Inside, penciled in incredibly neat cursive, is a quote: *"Life is like a rose . . . full of thorns and dying buds."* A personal message follows, written in the same tidy handwriting:

> *I know no amount of cards, sympathy, or flowers will end your grief. It didn't end mine either when my 16 mo. old brother died. I was only 3 and I still remember. The only thing that comforted me was a good cry and lots of love. I can't shed your tears for you, but I can love and care. So, I do. I am NOT just saying this. I MEAN IT! I am praying that the good Lord God in Heaven will keep you in his hands, protect you and comfort and love you. I know you don't know me, nor I you, yet I LOVE and CARE for you. I don't know anything else to say, except, my family is praying for you.*
>
> *Love in Christ, Dawn Wilson, 18*

I don't remember ever meeting Dawn Wilson, but when I read her card it was like being back in that funeral hall, awash in love and loss, beauty and tragedy. Even now, knowing that Dawn was out there, praying for me and loving me, brings me healing.

—9—

Conscious evolution inspires in us a mysterious and humble awareness. We are created by this awesome process of evolution, and are now being transformed by it.
—Barbara Marx Hubbard

We buried Jay; we went home. My mother and I returned to our beds, to the couch. Family came and went. I suppose they couldn't bear to see the suffering in our faces. I went to school—I was given no other choice. I don't remember much of it. I finished junior year, and three weeks after that, my friend Cathy and I took a train out to California to visit her cousin. Cathy's brother had died a few years back, and she wanted to help me get my mind off Jay.

We traveled across the Midwestern plains, through the Rocky Mountains, and around the high desert, eventually arriving at Disneyland, "where dreams come true," or so I was told. We spent the weekend riding roller coasters, jostling among the crowds, eating turkey legs, and watching acrobats and magicians accomplish impossible feats. I tried to forget about my brother.

On Saturday afternoon, Cathy and I stumbled into a public bathroom in Frontierland, giggling and squealing, our hands covered with sticky pink cotton candy. Approaching the sinks, we inspected ourselves in the mirror. Cathy reached for her faucet first.

At the rush of running water, I thought I heard a phone ringing somewhere in the distance. Instead of my own face in the mirror, I saw Jay's hair matted with dried blood, his bloody tears still weeping. I tried to swallow it down like cotton candy but it stuck in my mouth, sickly sweet. I thought I might vomit, but I started sobbing instead.

"Stop that," Cathy snapped.

"I'm sorry," I blubbered. "It's just—Jay has only been dead a month."

Cathy grabbed some paper towels to dry her hands, then a few more that she thrust into mine. "It's time to put it behind you. I know what it's like—my brother shot himself in the head, remember? The best thing to do is forget." Under her breath, she added, "Two years now."

I used the towels to wipe my tears, sniffling and blowing my nose loudly before splashing water on my face. I couldn't stop my breath from catching in my throat, but I refused to let another tear leave my eyes.

We left the bathroom and boarded the Jungle Cruise for a wet ride down the tropical rivers of Disneyland. As my eyes dried, I vowed to rid my body of Jay, to toss him into the water, to leave behind all traces of the brother I once had.

Home. The endless expanse of summer stretched in front of me, and I did whatever I had to do to avoid being alone with my mother. When I wasn't working at McDonald's, I hung out at the Warner Beach parking lot with my girlfriends. We would sit in the car waiting for the "older guys" to talk to us. They were in their midtwenties and drove roomy American-made cars that they parked there all day while they got high. The cloud of marijuana was so thick over the parking lot you could barely see the lake below.

We didn't have to wait long to be approached. We were young and sexy—jailbait, the guys called us, teasing and flirting, staring at our low-cut tank tops and high-cut shorts. On Thursday, Friday, and Saturday nights, we'd add alcohol—Budweiser, Kahlua and Cream when we could get it, straight vodka as a last resort. We'd drink all night, and sometimes I'd show up drunk for work the next morning. Most of those nights I blacked out.

I met Joe on a Friday night. I had bet a group of guys I could out-drink them, from the keg of beer they had nestled in a pool of ice—this was our ticket to free booze. I guzzled beer until I couldn't guzzle any longer, but I won. Joe wasn't the loudest or even the cutest guy there, but he had a quiet confidence. And we couldn't keep our eyes off each other.

At some point I followed him down to the lake. He laid me down on the beach. It was hot, our legs in the water, the waves gently lapping against us, his tongue lapping against my clitoris. His desire edged out any vestige of my grief. The whole world disappeared and there was only me and Joe. Then there was only Joe, his fingers, his mouth.

I faded into blackout, coming to in Joe's car as we pulled into my driveway. The next thing I remember is lying in my basement bedroom while Joe fucked me, banging my head against the cement wall. It didn't hurt too much. What hurt was waking up the next morning to discover that I'd lost my virginity and barely remembered the experience.

Sitting up in bed, head pounding, I looked at the naked man sprawled in bed beside me. He opened his eyes and said, "Nice cans," smirking and gesturing at the collection of green and gold beer cans lining the wall opposite us. My stepdad had collected them but had left them behind.

I wasn't sure what to say, and I really had to pee, so I made my way upstairs. Mom was sitting in her orange paisley chair, shrouded in a cloud of cigarette smoke, reading a mystery novel. I tiptoed past, somehow thinking if I was quiet enough, she wouldn't notice me.

"Whose car is in the driveway?" she said, stopping me in my tracks. I looked back to see her head still buried in her book.

"Don't worry," I said immediately, as if I had prepared the response. "It won't happen again." And that was the end of it, the only conversation my mother and I ever had about my sex life.

But it wasn't the end of me and Joe. He became my first boyfriend, and we were together for the next five years. Years of doing whatever I could to forget Jay.

Part II

—10—

I want to go when I want to go. It is tasteless to prolong life artificially. I have done my share; it is time to go.

—Albert Einstein

One Mother's Day in 2015, my mom and I attended *Listen to Your Mother* at the Historic Barrymore Theater, an old, eccentric venue on Madison's east side where the ceiling is sprinkled with tiny lights designed to look like the night sky. This was the second year in a row my mother had agreed to come along to this show, which featured local participants reading aloud pieces of heartfelt prose they'd written about mothers and mothering. We sat on creaky theater seats upholstered in dingy blue fabric, in the back row near the aisle. "So I can easily get to the bathroom," Mom said, hunting in her white crocheted purse for a menthol lozenge for the sore throat that would never go away, though she'd quit smoking years ago. Across the crowd of heads, on the worn, well-lit wooden stage, at least ten women and one man sat in an assortment of old, mismatched armchairs.

The first woman who stepped to the podium was easily the oldest on the stage, her silver hair shining bright under the stage lighting, her papery skin washed white. "My son James was only eighteen when he got the letter." Her voice was thin and increasingly quavery. "He promised he'd be home as soon as his two years was up. But somehow I knew he would not return." She paused to pull a crumpled tissue from the pocket of her floral dress, and as she wiped her nose I glanced behind her at the faces of those yet to read. Some watched the woman's back, stricken with secondhand grief. Others stared blankly into the audience. "He was so young. Nothing could have prepared me for that."

I noticed a soft sniffling and turned to see my mother weeping. Was this the first time I'd seen her cry since Jay died? Surely not, though I couldn't remember any other. She didn't acknowledge me, just stared straight ahead as she dabbed her eyes. But I sensed that she could feel me there, witnessing her tears. I wanted to hold her hand, but I was afraid to touch her and break the connection.

I looked back to the stage and realized the man had started reading. He wore a gray suit with a navy-blue tie, his round, bald head pale and shiny with sweat. "She sure was a fighter." He smiled. "Life dealt my mother a tough hand, and she took it all in her stride, even when she was diagnosed with cancer."

The entire audience seemed to hold their breath, and I noticed I had stopped breathing too.

"She stayed strong, right up until the end, never once broke down. She kept her cards close to her chest. I didn't know how to be close to my mother, and then she was gone."

I chanced another glance at my mom. Her eyes were dry and focused on the stage.

Two more people read, a young woman with long black braids who read about the ever-present fear that came from raising a Black son, and the founder of the event, a charismatic woman a bit younger than me with a bright, loud laugh.

Then came a small woman who seemed to be in her early forties. She approached the podium gingerly, as if navigating a field of land mines. She proceeded to read a piece about choosing to have an abortion. "I was only nineteen. One minute my whole life seemed to stretch in front of me, the next all was black. I felt doomed to a singular fate of mother-hood, something I did not yet know if I wanted." She was thin to the point of fragility, with a long, narrow face. The sound system could barely pick up her soft voice, and I leaned in to catch every word. "My mom drove me to the appointment, but she wouldn't come in. She was ashamed of me. I sat alone in the waiting room. I lay on a hard metal table, legs spread wide open, knees bent toward the sky, feet in stirrups."

Her words dropped me back to 1983. I pictured myself, eighteen and scared, also alone in an abortion clinic.

Shortly after I'd moved in with Joe, we had sex in the back seat of his blue '72 Chevy Nova. He loved that car. He hadn't even bothered to take off my pants. I was on the pill, but I had intentionally not taken it that month. In hindsight, I believe I was trying to ground myself even as I spun further out of control. Unable to grieve Jay's death, I was playing with my own life—with life itself.

I have always been able to feel a new life when it enters my body. Three weeks later, a nurse at the UW Hospital confirmed what I already knew. I went home and took bong hit after bong hit, watching the giant red tiger oscars in my fifty-five-gallon fish tank swim endless circles in their glass-walled home.

The next day, still stoned, I met up with my dad for drinks and pool at the Nau-Ti-Gal, a bar along the Yahara River near the bridge where Jay and I had fished for bullheads when we were kids.

I can still remember sinking the black eight ball in the side pocket, beating my dad for the first time in thirty-three games. As he began racking up a new game, I said, "I'm pregnant, Dad."

"That's great, kid!" he said.

"I'm going to have an abortion."

He frowned, bushy eyebrows furrowed. "That's not a good idea, Kris."

"It's my decision," I said. Then I whacked the cue ball for the break, dropping a single ball into the corner pocket.

I ran five balls, then missed. I chalked up my stick while my dad took a drag off his cigarette, took a swig of beer, and leaned over the table, dropping all his balls exactly where he called them, including a fabulous bank shot of the eight ball in the side pocket.

Pleased, he straightened and said, "Think of it this way: we could have aborted you."

I thought about that now as I sat next to my mother and applauded, watching the tiny woman sit down. My mother had been nineteen when I was born. I doubted whether abortion had been an option for her, but would my mother have made the same choice I had made? I had never considered a scenario in which my mother was not shackled to an angry young sailor and where I didn't exist.

My thoughts were interrupted by loud applause, and I looked up to see everyone on the stage take a bow. All around us attendees rose from their seats, so I stood up and helped my mom to her feet. I pulled her arm into mine, and we made our way out, the spilled popcorn crunching beneath our feet, the crowd flowing toward the glass doors. Since she'd become unstable, we'd been able to break the no-touch rule, one of the few blessings of my mother's aging. I grabbed a door before it shut and pushed it open for her.

"Want to wait here while I get the car?" I asked as we moved onto the sidewalk.

"It's pretty nice out," she rasped. "A walk would do me good."

I squeezed her arm, grateful for the continued closeness. I welcomed the May afternoon sun into my body. We were silent, walking south, arms linked, bodies close. Mom pointed out a sprinkling of tulips. I watched the red and yellow petals wave in the wind against a Normandy brick building.

As we continued walking, my mind returned to that question. In the wake of my mother's tears, I felt more connected to her than ever before, and that gave me courage.

"Mom?"

"Yes?"

"If you could have, would you have aborted me?"

She was silent as we took the next few steps.

"Yes."

Her single word bloomed in my body, true. I considered my mother: the youngest of five daughters in a farming family that longed for sons. I pictured her at eighteen, her resentment growing as I grew inside her.

"I completely understand," I said.

We crossed the street in silence, arms still linked.

"Mom?" I said again.

She grunted.

"Thank you for not aborting me."

"You're welcome."

After helping my mom into the car, I gazed at the clouds passing above us. I was alive, from the beginning of time, through my mother's body.

As a teenager, I got to choose my life over that of a baby. As a teenager, my mother had carried me against her will. I do not think this was a coincidence.

As I drove away, I reached for my mom's hand and she reached back.

—11—

Grief turns out to be a place none of us know until we reach it.
—Joan Didion

I was twenty-two on the summer day in 1986 when I pulled my green Rambler into the driveway of my mother's house, yanked the screwdriver out of the makeshift latch I'd attached outside the driver's door to hold it shut, and ran into the house to make popcorn. I was back living with my mom, having broken up with Joe. My mom and dad had recently gotten back together, so more often than not, he was around when I got home, as was the case today. "Hey, Steve!" I called as I burst through the kitchen door.

He sat at the kitchen table reading the Sports page. Through the kitchen window behind him, I could see black-capped chickadees flitting around the sunflower-seed-laden bird feeder on the back patio.

"Hey!" He shuffled his paper aside to reveal his crooked smile. It was nice having a father figure again. Almost overnight I'd gained a whole new family—new dad and new brothers and even a sister.

"What are you reading?" I asked.

"Summer Olympics. It's in Los Angeles this year."

"That's cool."

"What's not cool..." he began, unconsciously and characteristically twitching his nose, "... is that the athletes use drugs to enhance their performance."

"No way!" I matched his outrage.

"Yep. Started in Ancient Greece with Olympians eating lizard meat."

"Want some popcorn?" I asked.

"Absolutely," he said, diving back into his paper.

I turned on the stove burner and watched the sun setting into a grove of aspen trees. Bending down to pull the stainless steel pot and its glass lid out of the oven, I remembered the question that had haunted me all week. I set the pot onto the flames, scooped out a heaping tablespoon of Crisco, and dropped it in the bottom of the pan. I looked at my dad, absorbed in his reading. My words seemed lodged somewhere behind my collar bone. Outside, the sun had disappeared, and with it, the birds. As I replaced the pot lid, I saw that my dad was lighting up a joint. The tension in my throat cleared as the lighter flashed. I walked over to the table and waited for him to pass me the joint, which he did without so much as a glance.

"Steve?"

"Yeah?" he croaked from the corner of his sealed lips.

"I think you might be an alcoholic."

He coughed hard and his eyes began to water. I sucked on the joint, watching as he regained composure.

"Well, Sherlock," he said, his nose twitching rapidly, "how'd you figure that out?" He motioned for me to hand back the joint.

"I'm doing volunteer training at Briarpatch."

"What's Briarpatch?" He touched the joint to his lips for another long inhale.

"It's a teen and family crisis center. They specialize in drug and alcohol abuse."

At that moment, the popcorn began to pop wildly. I turned away from my father's raised eyebrows to shake the pot, knowing he'd take his time exhaling the hit. I turned off the burner as the pops died down, removing the lid and walking to the refrigerator for the butter. Before my first week at Briarpatch, I had never even known that alcohol was something that could be abused; I just thought it was a part of life, a tool that all grown-ups used to have fun and survive the pain. For my whole life, alcoholism had been a part of the wallpaper, but Briarpatch was ripping that down. For the first time, I was invited to consider that perhaps living one's life constantly under the influence was not healthy or desirable. My dad drank more than anyone I knew (besides myself), so I was eager to share my new information.

As I drizzled butter over the popcorn, I heard his gentle exhale and turned to see him shrouded in a cloud of smoke.

"A crisis center?" Steve repeated. "What are you doing that for? Don't we have enough of our own problems?" At that, we both burst into laughter.

I shook the bowl to stir the butter around, then plopped it on the table, sitting down and reaching for the joint. My dad had gone back to his paper, shoveling popcorn into his mouth as he read. Inhaling deeply, I looked out the window again at the darkening sky. My father knew he was an alcoholic. He didn't deny it. Though my training was leading me to believe alcoholism was a problem, my dad didn't seem to care. I looked at his lined face, and a deep sadness welled up inside me. I felt like a small child who needed a grown-up's help, but no grown-up could be found. I took another deep hit of the joint, passed it back to my dad, and stood, calling over my shoulder, "I'm going out, don't forget there's leftover lasagna in the fridge for dinner!"

As had become my new routine, I was heading downtown with Tracy, my new friend from my job as a rental agent for University of Wisconsin students. Tracy and I went drinking every night, egging each other on to get more and more fucked up, competing to see who could get the most guys. I, too, was an alcoholic. And my addiction didn't stop with booze. I had marijuana, cocaine, and loads of casual sex.

Shortly after breaking up with Joe, I started having sex with as many people as I could. I needed it—the skin-to-skin contact, the orgasms, the temporary erasure of my grief and self-hatred, the complete surrender to another person. I wanted to be used up. To be fucked open into something greater than myself.

That summer, I saved up enough money to enroll in classes at the UW. I had a dream of being an English teacher. The night before the first day of classes, Tracy and I went out and hit a few bars downtown for the nineteenth night in a row. I had bet her that I could fuck a different guy every night for a month, and I was winning—but on the morning after, I wanted to throw up.

Squeezing past a row of college students' knees in the lecture hall for my first class, I accidentally knocked the metal base of the chair. *Fuck it!* I almost screamed out loud, cringing as I imagined the other students sneering. I landed in my seat like a meteor striking Earth. The familiar words, *I hate my life!* rang in my head.

I opened my green, college-lined notebook and raised my eyes to the harsh fluorescent lights showering me like a hot, painful rainstorm. I reached down, yanked off one of my Birkenstocks, and rubbed my toes. After a night of White Russians and line after line of cocaine followed by sex with a faceless stranger, every cell in my body vibrated with self-hatred. I wanted to disappear.

Professor Dave Dixon strolled onto the stage, smiled, and rustled his papers before speaking. "Welcome to Psychology of Personality, which will be a hot-and-heavy summer version of the semester-long course I usually teach, condensed into three weeks. Well," he chuckled, "hopefully it won't get too hot in here. Last year the AC broke and we were all sweltering for a week." His brown eyes twinkled as a few students laughed nervously. "I tell ya, summers in Canada are never as sweltering as they are down here."

More laughter.

"So," his voice had changed to a businesslike tone, still charismatic but more serious. "You've heard of type A personality, right? The list-makers, planners, rigid ones."

I looked around. A few people were nodding, so I nodded along.

"And type B is the opposite, the more artistic, easygoing, relaxed type. We'll discuss more about those personalities, and others, with a major focus on type T personality." He paused for emphasis.

I noticed the girl two rows in front of me furiously scribbling notes, and I hastily opened my notebook.

"The United States is a type T nation," he continued. "*T* is for *thrill*." I wrote down his words. "As many as thirty percent of Americans are thrill-seekers, those who pursue risk for its own sake."

I tried to continue taking notes, but as another wave of nausea rose in my throat, I laid my head down on my notebook. The rising and falling of Dixon's voice faded, and I sank into a familiar puddle of misery: *This is pointless. What was I thinking, trying to go to college? I'm never gonna pass this class. I wish I was dead, like Jay*—no. I needed to stop that line of thinking. I turned my head to the right, where the sight and feel of my long hair touching my naked arm gifted me a few moments of relief. Hoping my classmates wouldn't notice my strange behavior, I turned my head to the left and again melted into pleasure.

Dixon's voice broke my spell. "Type T personality. They drink more. They experiment more with drugs. They experiment more with everything." Fiercely, I returned to taking notes, digging my black-ink Bic into the college-ruled paper.

My pen seemed to take on a life of its own, flying across the page in several voices.

Blackout sex with a different guy every night . . .

Perhaps prayer could work better?

You don't even believe in God!

Maybe I could be one of the great experimenters of life?

You are at least a miracle. After all, you should be dead.

I set down my pen, wondering where these distinct voices were coming from. I looked around the room and saw that the other students were packing up their notebooks.

At that moment, Professor Dixon's voice seemed to rise from the lecture platform. "If anyone wants to pick up an extra credit this summer," he said, "see me for independent work-study."

The other students filed out of the hall like the day escaping the night—but not me. Hungry for anything that would speed me toward my degree, I wanted extra credit. I walked down to the front and told the professor I would like to do independent research, my vision settling on his full beard flecked with gray hairs.

"Can you come to my office tomorrow at noon?"

I nodded and threw my backpack over my bare shoulder, heading down the aisle to the door and then off to the Student Union for my daily mocha chip ice cream cone.

In a tree-lined neighborhood with large old houses, Dave sat at the desk in his home office, talking loudly on the phone. Loose papers, psychology journals, and open notebooks were strewn in piles on every surface of the room, including the floor.

"It's a breakthrough," he was saying to an interviewer from *People* magazine, "understanding the risk-taking personality, how these people seek novelty, excitement, and thrills. Imagine if society channels these people's creativity into sports. This could be a highly positive cultural trait, if we just knew what we could do with it, as a nation."

I wished Dave would say something about young, drunk women who will fuck anything in the hopes of surviving another day. I sat up in the bunk bed across the room from his desk, a foul taste in my mouth. Our afternoon sex had been quick, as usual. After six months, I was already bored. I had hoped to let my body sink into the pleasure of sex with this prominent man, but every time he kissed me, I cringed as if my skin were being consumed by scabies (he did not seem to notice). And yet, I kept going back, addicted to the desire I felt from this powerful man. He was a leader in a world that had few paths of entry for a working-class, alcoholic woman, and he wanted *me*.

As I scanned the room for my underwear, Dave laughed hard at something the interviewer said. When I looked over at him, he winked at me, and I flinched. Suddenly I was desperate to shower off his smell. I grabbed my undies from the floor and pulled them on, then covered my breasts with the jumbled pile of clothes as I walked to the bathroom.

"I need to run an errand," he called to me before I shut the door. "I left the tests that need to be graded on my desk."

"'Kay!" I hollered back, breathing a sigh of relief. I hurried to scrub off, wanting to take advantage of having the house to myself for the first time ever. There was one room I had never been in, which Dave said was his bedroom before he started sleeping on the bunk bed in his office. I had always been curious why we slept on the bottom bunk.

After I'd dressed and found some food, I padded over to the closed door. I put my hand on the knob and could almost feel the pressure of whatever waited on the other side, like something or someone was pushing to get out. I hesitated, heart pounding in my ears. I thought I heard a faint rushing sound coming from the other side of the door, but when I pressed my ear against the dark wood, I heard nothing but my own breath, short and trembling. I could not understand the dread in my stomach. There was an unspoken rule that the bedroom was off-limits, and that made it irresistible. I swallowed hard, twisting the doorknob and wrenching it open in one swift motion.

It took a moment for my eyes to adjust to the darkness; heavy curtains blocked out the sun. As I stepped into the room, dark forms began to take shape—a dresser, a vanity, a bookshelf, the bed. Every object seemed to be a shade of gray, until I realized it was all carpeted with a thick layer of dust, from the books on the shelf to the sheets on the unmade bed. I took another step inside, stirring up a storm of dust motes, and covered my mouth with my hand. The stale air was heavy with a suffocating must.

Dave had told me his beloved wife had died young. I noticed the dust-covered makeup and jewelry strewn about the vanity and shivered, feeling as if I had entered a tomb. On the bedside table, I noticed a glass Coca-Cola bottle. My stomach lurched, but I couldn't resist a closer look. A rubber band held a plastic bag over the half-full, twelve-ounce glass bottle. I picked up the bottle and examined the green and white mold colony floating on the brown soda. It was as if I were meeting Dave's dead wife. Was this bottle the last thing her lips had touched?

I set it down and ran from the room, hastily gathering my things and scrawling a note to Dave on his desk. Then I slammed the front door shut and stumbled down the steps to the sidewalk, my breath coming in shuddering gasps. I never wanted to see Dave again.

I couldn't get the image of that room out of my mind, and I worried Dave's life was a window into my future, a life destined to be haunted by death. I went right back to my nightly drunken hookups, and one frigid night has always stayed with me. The memory begins downtown, in the middle of State Street, in the middle of the night. I am yelling at a man I don't recognize. I can taste vodka and bile, and everything is blurry. Aside from the time spent sitting with my friends at our usual bar while we began our fourth pitcher, I don't remember any events leading up to this moment.

"Why the hell are we out here?" I hear myself screaming. "Where is my coat, asshole?" *Did I fuck this guy?*

"You can't stay the night!" he yells back, tugging up his jeans.

With a jolt of recognition, I see this man on top of me, in a strange apartment. We were making out and he was humping my leg. I don't remember taking my clothes off, but I do remember when he came in his pants. The rest is a blur. What are we doing outside?

"You have to leave." He sniffs and turns toward the door of the nearest walkup.

"Why?" I realize I'm shivering, but my blood is boiling. Who is this man to ditch me on such a cold night? "How am I going to get home?"

"I can't sleep with you!"

"Why the hell not? You seemed to want to a few minutes ago."

He stares at me, eyes bloodshot and dull with inebriation.

Something about this situation has made pinpricks of terror rise up my spine. I react with anger. "What the fuck is wrong with you?"

"I have HIV," he blurts, and I stop short. Then he turns and starts running up State Street.

I stand numbly, gaping after his figure careening away from me as it grows smaller and disappears into the distance. I can't move. The image of a stranger with HIV ejaculating on my leg plays in my mind on repeat. *I have to get home.*

I don't know how I found the strength to make the three-mile walk to the apartment my mom and I now shared, and without a coat. I still marvel that I didn't get hypothermia or give up halfway and fall asleep forever next to the flock of geese in Tenney Park. A large, vacant part of me wanted to. With each step I grew less intoxicated and more suicidal. Music still blared from behind closed windows of the fraternities along Langdon Street, and I tried to let the beats fill the tight, empty space in my chest. The wind blowing through the swings at James Madison Park made high-pitched squeaks. As I worked my way along Johnson Street, the streetlights glared at me like searchlights, hunting me, exposing my recklessness. Looking back now, I realize that a single thought kept me alive: I was my mother's only living child. I wasn't allowed to die, from HIV or hypothermia or any other tragedy that could come from my partying. I needed to commit to my survival. I let myself into the empty house and walked straight to my bedroom. *I need to stop drinking*, I thought as I fell into bed and passed out.

The next day, I slept until noon. Luckily, my mom was out of town. When I woke up, the whole night came rushing back to me. *What the fuck is wrong with you, Kris? You could have gotten AIDS. Think of what your mother would do if you died.* My thoughts grew like a monster, spreading out of my head and through the house, threatening to devour me. I spent the rest of the day inhaling bong hits, eating Ben and Jerry's White Russian coffee ice cream with Kahlua coffee liqueur, and masturbating. Anything to stay numb, to keep the monsters at bay. Around 9:00 p.m. I flushed my bag of marijuana down the toilet and cried myself to sleep.

—12—

Two swimmers wrestled on the spar
Until the morning sun,
When one turned smiling to the land.
O God, the other one!
The stray ships passing spied a face
Upon the waters borne,
With eyes in death still begging raised,
And hands beseeching thrown.
—Emily Dickinson

In 1987 I got myself into a drug and alcohol treatment program. I started by attending outpatient counseling at the Meriter Hospital Newstart clinic, but when I arrived stoned for my second appointment, my counselor Shelley suggested putting me into a month of inpatient treatment. Her brown eyes were kind and sharp, eyes that could spot a lie a mile away but wouldn't shame you for it. "I'm going to help you make the right decisions for a while," she said, and I felt what it would be like to be mothered, to have someone guiding me, laying out my options. At last, I wasn't the only person in charge of my life. But I wasn't prepared for what would come next.

The physical misery and discomfort of detoxing were nothing compared with the shame and self-hatred that arose when I was no longer numbed by a constant stream of substances. Repressed thoughts and memories flooded my mind, things I had hoped to never think about again. For the first time, I became aware that I had been holding myself responsible for Jay's death. I'd been the one who got him into smoking weed and I believed he was hit on his bike because he was high. This caused my shame to spiral further, and the only thing that kept me in control was the structure of my daily life, the twice-daily Narcotics Anonymous and Alcoholics Anonymous meetings. Still, I could never fully open up about the degree to which I blamed myself. Memories of Jay haunted me.

One in particular kept coming back. He and I were ten and fourteen, perhaps. My mom had told me to go walk Jay home from his swimming lessons one evening.

"Mom, no."

"Yes."

"Ugh, I hate you. You always make me do stuff when I have other plans."

"I have to work," Mom said, "and I don't want him walking home alone. He's grounded from last night."

Jay and the Anderson boys had been caught kicking a flaming tennis ball soaked in gasoline around the backyard while three-year-old Jennifer Krause sat in the middle of everything, watching and cheering them on. It was bad but I couldn't help smirking.

"Wipe that smile off your face and get going. Now."

My smirk changed to a scowl. "I hate your stupid job," I mumbled, letting the back door slam as I stomped outside.

I walked to Warner Park, still seething. I wanted new shoes. All my friends had Nikes but we couldn't afford them. It was all Dick's fault for leaving us. *I hate my life, I hate my life,* became a rhythm that propelled me forward to the beach. Then I saw Jay splashing out of the water. I smiled and waved, feeling the dark cloud above me start to clear. But Jay didn't smile back.

"You suck," he said sullenly, ignoring the towel I held in my out-stretched hand.

"Why?"

"For putting a . . . a pad on my bike." His face flushed.

I burst into laughter.

"It's not funny!" Jay fumed. "I rode around like that for three days until Kurt said, 'Why you riding around with a girl's blood pad on your bike?'"

I continued cackling.

He sat down on the ground with his arms crossed. "You told me it was to protect me if I fell," he said softly. "And I believed you, Kris."

I stopped giggling. It was true, last week I had put a pad on his bike, right after he had slipped off his pedals and knocked his balls so hard that he was on the ground in pain for five minutes.

"I'm sorry." I crouched next to him. "I really did think it might make your next fall easier. That last one was rough."

"True." He considered for a minute, then said, "Want to swim?"

I nodded, dropping his towel and standing to strip down to my suit. I sensed something deep within my body, a rearrangement, a vision of Jay and me living as brother and sister through ripe old age.

"Let's see who can do the most figure eights," I suggested. "You go first."

We waded out into the lake, diving into the water and splashing like dolphins. Once the water had reached our thighs, we stopped. I planted my legs in a wide stance, facing Jay, swaying in the waves. The sounds of the other kids at the beach and the traffic on the road faded away as Jay dove under. He swooped around my legs in figure eights and I counted: one . . . two—I almost lost my balance—three . . . four—*Wow, how many times can he do this?* When he got to fifteen I started to worry. My record was twenty-two. I couldn't let him beat me. I loved the attention I got from being the best.

At last, Jay broke the surface at a particularly strong crest of a wave, bobbing past me, disappearing into the next curving crest.

"Wow!" I yelled. "Did I count twenty figure eights? That's scary shit."

"Twenty-one," he said, wearing a triumphant expression.

"No way!"

He sprayed lake water at my face, mouth puckered in revenge for humiliating him. "Don't ever do mean stuff to me again, promise?"

"Promise."

After I successfully defended my title as figure-eight champion, we splashed out of the water, dripping and hungry for dinner. We shared Jay's towel before heading home amid long shadows cast by our neighborhood oak trees. As we walked, I pictured the look on Jay's face when he said, "I believed you, Kris." It was wrong to set him up for humiliation. In that moment, I resolved to always have Jay's back, to protect him no matter what. I repeated the vow in my head: *I promise, Jay, I promise.*

In the program, I became friends with people quite different from me. I learned that addicts and alcoholics can be hippies, mechanics, lawyers, doctors, mothers, and grandfathers. I'd sit in a circle with all these other hurting, healing people. When my turn came, I would say, "Hi, my name is Kris. I'm an alcoholic and drug addict," and then share my story and update them on my journey. I did not share my darkest revelations, but being with others in a similar position, combined with the framework of the twelve-step program, was enough—for now—to keep me sober. I even tried to turn my life over to a higher power, whatever that meant, and experienced some comfort in trusting in and praying to a god that might be there.

After thirty days in rehab, I moved into a halfway house on Ingersoll Street. I quickly fell into a rhythm of daily twelve-step meetings, continuing to practice connecting to people without being drunk or high—a new experience for me as an adult. I was no longer all alone with the words that rang in my head like church bells—"unwanted," "dead," "fucking anyone who would have me." It turned out there were other people with similar voices in their heads.

Following the advice of my recovery counselors to avoid sexual or romantic relationships in my first year of sobriety, I became celibate. Then one day after an AA meeting I heard a woman's voice behind me as I stood refilling my Styrofoam coffee cup from the silver percolator on the snack table. "Congrats on six months."

Turning to see who the voice belonged to, I dripped scalding coffee on my fingers. Gasping and mopping up the mess with some napkins from the table, I looked up to see Elizabeth, smiling grimly. I had noticed her before with some interest; her stocky, strong build and short haircut suggested that she might be a lesbian, and I was curious about lesbians. We had never spoken but had exchanged smiles in the past.

"Sorry about that." Elizabeth gestured to the coffee pot. "But seriously, six months is a big deal." Her voice was low and slightly rough.

"Thanks," I stammered, rising to stand in front of her. "I'm trying to figure out how to celebrate it, now that going out for drinks is out of the question." I gave her a wry smile and she grinned back.

"You should do something relaxing and rejuvenating, focus on yourself." She helped herself to some stale cookies from the tray as I loaded my coffee with cream and sugar. "For my one-year anniversary I got myself a massage."

"Hmm," I said. "I don't think I could afford a massage." I took a sip of my burnt, milky-sweet coffee. "I was thinking of maybe going out to dinner with some friends."

"That sounds nice!" She seemed a bit older than me, her pale face lined with faint wrinkles and gritty confidence.

I looked down at my coffee, conscious that I had been staring at her.

"You doing anything right now?" Elizabeth asked.

"Not really. Seems like it's snowing pretty hard so I was gonna take the bus home."

"Would you wanna hang out for a bit? I'm house-sitting for some people on Lake Monona and they have a big fancy house. They even have a sauna if you want to try it, that would be relaxing."

"A sauna?" I said. I had a vague image in my head of rich old people wearing nothing but towels, sitting in a hot room with a fire in it.

"Yeah!" Elizabeth nodded. "You get really hot and sweat out all your toxins, and it's good for your muscles as well. What do you think?"

I hesitated for a moment, not totally trusting the feeling of excitement in my stomach, then said, "Sure!" I had been wanting to make more friends in AA.

We took the bus from our meeting site to the edge of a nice neighborhood. The houses were huge, with expansive, snow-covered lawns. By the time we reached Elizabeth's temporary home, we had covered our addiction and recovery stories in detail, as well as sharing some information about our childhoods. Our conversation had flowed easily and felt electrically charged, but the sun had gone down, and when we stomped off our boots and clambered in the front door, we were both shivering from the cold.

Elizabeth cranked up the thermostat and went into the kitchen to put on the kettle. "What kind of tea do you want?" she hollered.

"I'll have whatever you're having." I took off my coat and boots and followed her to the kitchen.

"You want any cream? Sugar?"

"Yes, please."

She smiled at me as she bustled around the kitchen, and a feeling of warmth grew in my stomach despite my frozen fingers and toes.

When we had finished our tea, Elizabeth asked if I wanted to try the sauna. "I usually go in it naked," she said, shyly. "We can take turns, it's not that big."

I blushed. "Okay." I was confused by my embarrassment. Was it just the idea of being naked around another person?

Elizabeth went down to the basement to turn on the sauna, then came back up and filled two glasses of water. I watched her in silence as she disappeared down the hall, returning with a couple of plush, white towels.

"Follow me," she said.

Downstairs was a tiny wooden box with a glass door.

"So you can hang your clothes there and here's your water," she said, setting the glasses on a table. "I think it's probably warm enough by now. Just come on up when you're done and I'll take my turn." She started to walk back up the stairs.

I peered in the box. "I don't mind sharing," I said softly, forcing myself to meet her eyes.

She turned back to me and sighed, smiling and shaking her head slightly. "What the hell." She pulled off her sweater and T-shirt in one quick motion. I started to unbutton my jeans, realizing that this was the first time I had been naked around another person while sober. My stomach squirmed but I continued undressing, then wrapped the towel around myself as well as I could and squeezed into the sauna.

I soon found myself wedged between Elizabeth and the wall, our arms pressed against each other's, skin already moist with sweat. She smiled at me and the look in her eyes took me back to my nights of partying and chasing men—it was an expression I always sought out, a certain glint that would indicate which men I could get. It made me feel desirable, sexy—the most important person in the room. The rush brought on by Elizabeth's desire was stronger than if I had flooded my bloodstream with my old favorite chemicals.

Making out in the sauna, hot and slick with sweat, soon led to fucking in the bedroom.

Sober sex with a woman was unlike anything I had experienced before. It was more intimate. We talked about our lives. We gazed into each other's eyes. She wanted to know me, to hear my entire story, to pay me deep and lasting attention. She seemed to want the very best for me, listening to me and asking what I wanted. As we kissed and cuddled, I started to taste a more whole version of myself.

I called her the next day, hoping for a repeat.

"I can't see you again," she said, her voice wobbly.

"What do you mean?"

"It was a mistake. You haven't made it to a year yet, you're not supposed to be dating people in the program. I fucked up. I'm sorry." She was crying now. "I've been on the phone with my sponsor all morning and she helped me see how bad this could be, for both of us."

"No!"

"Kris, I really like you, but we can't do this. Please don't make it any harder than it has to be."

There was nothing I could say to change her mind.

I spent the rest of the day in bed. I had found salvation from my loneliness and isolation, only to have it whisked away. Dark thoughts swirled back into my head, and it was all I could do to crawl out of bed and make it to the Thursday AA meeting. Some small part of me was hoping to see Elizabeth there, but she didn't show. I sat near the back, quiet and alone, barely listening to the words of those who were sharing. In my head I was already formulating my plan for after the meeting. I would swing by the liquor store on my way home and get a six-pack—just one—and drown my sorrows in that, then get back on the wagon. My sponsor would be so pissed. I imagined what Shelley might say, the disappointment that would register in her eyes. That made me pause.

" . . . and I've just realized that the comfort I'm seeking won't come to me from another person, not even my boyfriend." The voice of the woman sharing cut into my thoughts. "I have to sit with the painful stuff I've been avoiding, to learn how to be my own foundation. I need to be okay on my own before I can learn how to be with someone."

She was right. I had already decided not to mask my grief with alcohol, and I couldn't use sex or intimacy either. I needed to sit with my pain. I raised my hand to share next.

—13—

I believe a leaf of grass is no less than the
journey-work of the stars.
—Walt Whitman

After one year sober, my life looked quite different. The daily support-group meetings gave me space to be listened to and share my inner life, a complete turnaround from my raised-poor, Protestant upbringing. Through Briarpatch and AA, I had made a wider circle of friends than I'd had since childhood, people who genuinely seemed to like me and supported my sobriety. Through working the steps, my relationship with my mom had improved, though I had to stop spending time with my dad due to his constant drinking. I had re-enrolled at the University of Wisconsin, where I discovered how to be in an intimate relationship with Shakespeare, sentence structure, and Pink Floyd. I lived on lattes and gyros. I had started to believe that I could *want* to be alive.

Everything seemed possible. I discovered a world outside of partying and temporary pleasures, and I wanted to see it all. I decided I was stable enough to study abroad in Europe. It didn't matter that very few kids I grew up with even attended college. When the time came, my friends made plans to drive with me and my mom to a hotel in Chicago, then drop me at the airport in the morning.

Shortly after we arrived at the hotel, as we got ready to go down to the swimming pool, I discovered that I had left my passport at home. Like a knight in shining armor, my mom swung into action, telling us to stay and have a fun night—she was going to drive the three hours home, sleep in her bed for a couple hours, and drive back to the hotel in time to pick me up and bring me to the airport for my 6:00 a.m. flight.

The next morning, my friends and I piled into her car, rubbing sleep from our eyes. Mom looked alert, if a bit haggard, the pleasure of a job well done evident in her posture.

At the gate, my friends hugged and kissed me farewell, giddy and effusive despite the early hour. My mom and I shared a stiff embrace, then she patted my arm and said, "Be safe." Looking back, I imagine she felt torn between the pride of her daughter leaving to study and see the world and the terror of possible dangers that might await me. She made herself useful until she was no longer needed, then turned away so she wouldn't have to watch me board the plane.

In my window seat, I took out my journal and began an entry. I wanted to document all of my travels. As I wrote the date, September 3, 1988, my stomach dropped. Jay's birthday. Jay's . . . I did the math . . . twenty-first birthday. In my mind he was still thirteen. I grabbed a bag of M&M's from my backpack and started shoveling them into my mouth, staring out the window, wishing the plane would start moving. I wasn't yet ready to see synchronicities as the powerful messages they are.

From New York, I took two more planes and then two trains and finally arrived in Den Haag, Holland, where I was meeting my friend Tommy Bender. Tommy and I had met volunteering at Briarpatch, and when he heard I was traveling to Europe, he proposed we meet up. "I'll be in Holland this summer visiting my sister. You can crash at her house and then we can backpack around Europe together before you have to start school!" I liked Tommy. He was kind and mild-mannered, a short, queer, middle-class Jewish man who was different from anyone I had grown up around. It was a relief to have a traveling partner for this big adventure.

After arriving at his sister's house, I vomited for a couple of days in the guestroom—some combination of nerves, lack of sleep, jet lag, and heaps of candy, cookies, and Diet Coke. I felt bad for Tommy, because this meant pushing our travel plans back, but he reassured me that he was more than happy to spend time with his family and catch up on reading. He sat in the living room and checked in on me from time to time, bringing water, tea, and anything else I needed.

Once I recovered, Tommy and I took a train to Amsterdam. A few minutes into our train ride, I started to feel nauseous again. Something about the rumble of the tracks below, the roar of the world rushing by outside, the sway of our car as it passed through towns and countryside made it seem as if the walls were closing in on me. The air felt thin and I thought my lungs might have collapsed.

I leaned my head against the window, closed my eyes, and forced myself to take slow, even breaths: *In through your nose, out through your mouth.*

We finally made it to Amsterdam, where I staggered into an AA meeting, leaving Tommy outside with his backpack full of books. Over the course of the meeting, my stomach settled and my breathing returned to normal. It was a mixed group of Dutch and American people, and I let the blend of familiar and foreign voices soothe me. When it was my turn to share, I kept it brief, not wanting to upset my stomach again. I introduced myself, then said, "Thanks so much for inviting me into your meeting, I really appreciate it. And if anyone has room for me and my friend to crash tonight, let me know after the meeting!"

The meeting closed. I sat in my seat for a moment as others rose and shuffled around, mingling or heading toward the door. It didn't seem as if anyone were going to offer us a home for the night. In a minute I'd have to stand up, walk outside, and find Tommy so we could go off in search of the nearest youth hostel before it got dark. I hoped it wouldn't be too far away. I didn't think I could handle a long walk or another train ride. What was it with me and trains anyway? An image of a baby with brown curls appeared in my mind but was interrupted by a soft touch on my shoulder.

I flinched, opening my eyes—I hadn't realized they'd been closed. The hand belonged to a short-haired woman, eyes merry and full lips twitching at the corners. Her baggy T-shirt said *Lavender Menace*, with the female symbol below it.

"You gonna sleep here then?" she asked. Her voice was teasing, almost as if she were offering a challenge.

I giggled, suddenly shy. "Sorry, I still have jet lag."

"Oof, jet lag's a bitch." She shook her dark curls. "I remember when I first got here it was a week before my sleep was back to normal."

"Where are you from?"

"New York—well, I grew up in Jersey. You said you're from the Midwest?"

I nodded. "Madison, Wisconsin."

She smirked and my stomach squirmed. Why was she looking at me that way? I couldn't decide whether I liked it.

"You can crash at my flat if you want." She stood up abruptly. "It's not far from here. You mentioned you're traveling with a friend?"

"Oh, thank you! Yeah, he should be right outside."

She raised her eyebrows. "He's not your boyfriend, is he?"

"No, why?"

She smirked again. "Just curious." Then she turned and headed out the door.

Her name was Leah, and her flat was small and grungy. We picked up a pizza on the way back, and as we sat around her living room eating, she told us about all the places in Amsterdam we had to see before we left. She sat next to me on the couch, and every now and then she'd lean her shoulder against mine or rest her hand on my knee. I didn't mind. She was the kind of person who could make you feel important anytime she looked at you. Poor Tommy buried himself in a book at some point in the night, seeing that we only had eyes for each other. We made out on the couch for a bit before Leah dragged me into her room where she taught me to fist-fuck her.

The sex was rough, hot, desperate. For the first time in days I didn't feel sad or anxious or nauseous. I just felt good. We fucked all night, passing out in each other's arms as the sky became light and the birds started chirping.

The next day, I awoke after noon. Leah had gone to work, leaving a note that we could stay another night if we wanted, that she hoped we would. I sat down next to Tommy on the couch where he sat, writing in a notebook. He didn't look up.

"You mad at me?" I asked.

"No." He kept writing.

"Well, are you upset about something?"

"Nope." He still didn't look up.

"Okay." I stared at him, growing annoyed. "What would you think about staying here a couple more nights instead of going to Paris?"

He stopped writing, closed the notebook and sighed. "That's fine." He stood and walked over to his dark green army surplus backpack. "I'm gonna go out for the day." He grabbed a different book from the bag and headed to the door. "No need to wait up for me, I'll see you in the morning."

I felt bad for changing the plans on Tommy. But the guilt didn't last. I had to fuck Leah again. That night, Leah took me out, to a party or a show—I can't remember. The whole night is blacked out in my memory, except for our train ride home. The fluorescent lights in the subway car seemed to pound my head, and nausea crept back in. Hunkering down in the seat, I mumbled something to Leah about motion sickness and cradled my head in my hands. The regular clicking and bumping of the train along the tracks dropped me into a trance.

Tk-tk-tk-tk-tk-tk-tk-tk-tk.

My stomach squirmed with hunger, nausea, terror?

Tk-tk-tk-tk-tk-tk-tk-tk-tk.

The heat of Leah's body beside me brought the memory of her mouth on mine, my fist inside of her.

Tk-tk-tk-tk-tk-tk-tk-tk-tk.

I am a baby in my mother's arms.

Tk-tk-tk-tk-tk-tk-tk-tk-tk.

I am in Leah's bed; she brings me to orgasm.

Tk-tk-tk-tk-tk-tk-tk-tk-tk.

I see Dad push Mom to the floor through the bars of my crib.

Tk-tk-tk-tk-tk—

The train sounds disappeared, and I opened my eyes to figure out why. Leah was staring at me in horror, moving her mouth soundlessly. That's when I realized I was screaming.

Shaking uncontrollably, I began sobbing. "What's happening to me?"

"Kris." Leah's voice got through at last. "KRIS!"

I had stopped screaming, but I continued to sob and shake, my arms clutched around my body in terror. What had I just seen? Was that a flashback?

Leah rubbed my arm and tried to calm me as the train thundered toward our stop. The tentative foundation I had carefully constructed in my year of recovery had begun to crumble and my hopes of a stable life along with it.

My breakdown seemed to cast a pall over the rest of my time in Amsterdam. I just wanted to get out of there. When Tommy and I departed after another night, Leah embraced me tightly. "I'll come check on you in London," she whispered, kissing me. I could sense the hunger in her tongue, but I felt nothing in response. The desperation had left me feeling scraped clean, hollow.

We left the picturesque stony canals blanketed in gently wafting autumn leaves and headed to Yugoslavia. Since I couldn't bear to ride another train, we took up hitchhiking, passing through Germany and Italy on the way. We saw truly spectacular sights, but some part of me had been missing ever since the flashbacks in Amsterdam. Tommy and I parted ways at the airport and I flew to London. We didn't keep in touch after that trip, and I've always regretted my treatment of him.

As I pushed through the gray, bustling streets on the way to my host family in Ealing, flashes of the incident on the train kept leaking out of my subconscious, and I fought to ignore them. I thought only of making it to the start of classes and my daily AA meetings. I needed to survive.

I soon began classes at Ealing College of Higher Education. I studied film, photography, and William Blake's poetry, clinging to and memorizing his words. In a ceramics class taught by a tea-leaves-reading Iraqi, my hands, skin, and soul embraced clay, and I sculpted earth into lumpy mugs, bowls, and vases.

Back in Madison there had been no passenger trains, but here in London I was always riding a train or subway somewhere; I couldn't avoid them. My body was trying to tell me something. I kept having flashbacks of being a baby in my mother's arms, and it felt as if we were running from something. I remembered so little of my childhood, of life before we moved in with Dick, before Jay was born. Why had we left my father?

On top of the flashbacks, I dreamed of Jay almost every night. I couldn't focus on my classes because I saw his face everywhere. It

made no sense that I was alive and he was dead. I cried all the time—
at home, in class, and at the regular twelve-step meetings I attended.
Sometimes in those meetings I sobbed hysterically and couldn't stop.
People began to look at me with frightened or pitying expressions. I
had become too much.

One day, as I was slicing bread for breakfast—Nutella on toast, a
new favorite—I cut my finger. Blood spurted from my hand, and it
was all I could do to stop from passing out. I grabbed a dish towel
and sat on the floor with my hand above my head, panting heavily. A
memory swam into my mind.

*Mom, Dad, Jay, and I are camping up north for Jay's eighth birth-
day. Jay saws a log and throws it on the fire with glee. Dad throws his
beer bottle into the fire where it clinks and cracks. My mom cuts yellow
cheese, the shiny knife glinting in the firelight, making a rhythmic tapping on the cutting board. I grind my teeth, turning a marshmallow
speared with an elm shoot over the fire.*

"Carol, get me another beer," Dad says. He is already drunk.

*She sets down her knife, walks around the picnic table, and rum-
mages in the red cooler. She pops the cap off with a church key and
hands the beer to Dad.*

*Jay tosses another log on the woodpile and says, "Ma? Can you
make me a pudgy pie?"*

*She picks up a pie iron, butters a slice of Wonder Bread, and
places it butter-side down on the cast iron. Then she lays cheese
slices in a double layer and folds a piece of ham atop the cheese. As
Jay places the toothed edge of his saw against the last two feet of the
tree trunk he is working on, Mom butters the second slice of Wonder
Bread, places it onto the sandwich, hooks the pie irons together, and
walks toward the fire, narrowly missing Dad's head as she maneu-
vers the long handles.*

When Jay screams, I look up to see him throw his saw, which whizzes along the picnic table and crashes into the side of our silver pull-up camper with a loud CLANG! *Blood drips from Jay's left pointer finger.*

"Jay!" Mom gasps.

"What the fuck is wrong with you?" Dad yells. "Can't you all just leave me in peace?" He stands up and walks off into the dark, his curses echoing into the woods.

My mom runs into the camper and brings out the first aid kit.

I look away, focusing on my marshmallow, licking the sticky residue from my fingers.

With a jolt, my eyes snapped open. I inspected my finger—my left pointer finger, same as Jay's. It was a deep cut, one that would surely scar, but the blood had stopped, so I grabbed a Band-Aid, then finished preparing my breakfast. I savored the creamy, sweet chocolate in my mouth, trying to get Jay's face out of my mind. *I need to get out of the house!*

Seeking a subject for my Black-and-White Photography class, I decided to go to Bunhill Fields Burial Grounds and find William Blake's grave. As I waited for the red double-decker bus, I heard his words in my head: *A little black thing among the snow, / Crying "weep! weep!" in notes of woe!* I was the black thing, clothed in death and crying in woe. If Blake had written about me, he must have something to say to me. I wanted to be near his bones.

The tombstone was small and unassuming, surrounded by cobblestones. I took a deep breath and raised my camera.

Nearby Lie the Remains of the Poet-Painter William Blake

I looked around at the cemetery, at the rows of old, rough gravestones covered in bright green moss. I set my camera down and took a can of Diet Mountain Dew from my bag.

I wanted to hear the dead.

I sat down with my back against the tombstone and closed my eyes. The cobblestone was cold beneath my fingers.

"William," I said to the chilly air. "I don't want to live like this. I can't do it."

I paused and strained my ears. The silence was deafening.

Perhaps a question from his own poetry . . .

"What immortal hand or eye, / Could frame thy fearful symmetry?"

I listened.

Again, nothing.

All the strength seemed to drain from my body, and I slumped over, head cradled in my arm. I longed to join Blake in the ground, to join my brother in death. The wind rustled through the bare trees. I began to weep. A light rain covered my glasses, soaking the ground below me, above the dead.

"William," I whispered to the ground. "I want my life." As I lay on his grave, I remembered that someone I'd met at an AA meeting had suggested I go to a Survivors of Incest Anonymous meeting. I heard these words through my bones: *You are alive. You can live.*

I stayed with William until the sun set. Then I walked through the dark to McDonald's to soothe myself with french fries.

The following week, I stepped off a bus in south London, my body burning with terror. I walked toward a tiny, ancient church and stared up at it for several minutes, frozen in place. The wooden church doors loomed over me. I hauled them open and found my way to a room where four scruffy English men of varying ages and one young Jewish American woman sat around a table, shrouded in cigarette smoke. When it was my turn to share, all the thoughts I'd been having tumbled out. For the first time, I could verbalize the terrifying combination of sex, violence, and babyhood that were coming up in my flashbacks. I felt safe to cry, held by the warm faces and kind eyes of the people in the group.

The woman, Nina, bounced right up to me after the meeting

adjourned, pulling me enthusiastically into a hug and talking a mile a minute. "I'm so glad there was another woman here! They seem like great guys, but it's just not the same, you know? I was so happy when I saw you walk in the door. This is my first time coming too. How did you find out about the meeting?"

She had a very pretty face and dark curly hair. She was much shorter than me, but somehow her bright, squinty eyes seemed to be level with mine—perhaps it was her warm confidence. She reminded me of my recovery counselor, Shelley, and I felt immediately close to her, cared for. We chatted for a bit, both reveling in the familiar sounds of each other's accents. The current of excitement running between us made me wish we could stay in that church and talk for hours. Unfortunately, we had to give up the room to another group, so she invited me to visit her flat sometime, writing down her phone number and address with step-by-step directions on a slip of paper. Then she embraced me, kissed me lightly on the cheek, and rushed off to catch her train.

Days later, I took Nina up on her offer to visit her flat in Hammersmith, near Charing Cross Hospital, above the winding Thames.

It was one of those days when the sun is shining and somehow that makes things worse. I left my flat feeling as if I couldn't face my life. Still, I didn't want to die. The prospect of a new friend gave me a shred of hope.

I took the Tube to Hammersmith and began to follow Nina's written directions. After twenty minutes, I was lost in a neighborhood I'd never seen before. Darkness was falling. Last week I'd had to flee a man who flashed me in a dark alley. I pulled my jacket closed and picked up my pace.

Eventually I came to a train station. I pulled out my pound sterling coins and bought a Diet Mountain Dew and a custard pie. Hands trembling, I cracked open the soda. As I gulped it down, I noticed a red phone box across the train platform. I rummaged about in my notebook, looking for Nina's phone number. I couldn't find it. I was crossing over into panic when I came to the page. It took all my focus to make my fingers press the right buttons.

"Hello?"

"Nina?"

"Kristina! It's you. Where are you, honey?"

I burst into tears. "I'm sorry," I stammered. "Excuse me, I don't mean to cry, but . . . I'm lost."

"Oh honey," Nina said. "Why don't you take a minute?"

"What?" I asked, confusion momentarily stopping my tears.

"Oh, never mind. Where are you now?"

"Hammersmith Station?" My voice sounded high-pitched, childlike.

Speaking calmly and softly, Nina gave me clear directions to her flat. As I walked up the steps of her row house, tears burned my eyes. She greeted me at her door with a smile the size of the country, opening her arms in a big hug.

"Why don't you take a minute?" she said again, leading me to sit on the couch in her living room. "Go ahead and cry, honey. You deserve the chance."

I broke down in loud sobs that shook my whole body. Nina just sat there, unconcerned, rubbing my shoulder and murmuring soft encouragement.

"That's right, sweetheart, let it out."

Why wasn't she repulsed or frightened by this audacious show of emotion? "Sorry," I blubbered. "I d-don't . . . know what's . . . wrong with me."

"There's nothing wrong with you, Kris. Crying is a very normal, human thing to do. This is so good; you're doing just right." Nina looked straight into my eyes as she said this, and I saw no fear, no discomfort. There was only love, and that made me cry harder.

After a few minutes, Nina handed me some tissues.

"What are you feeling right now?" she asked.

"Um," I sniffled. "I feel . . . afraid . . . of everything."

Nina nodded.

"I just . . . want to die!" I began wailing again.

"Keep telling me, honey." Nina clasped my hand and I held on tight.

I had never cried this much in my life. I started to wonder if I would ever be able to stop. My breath came in short, heavy gasps and I looked at Nina in panic.

"You're okay, Kris, I'm with you. Just breathe."

I stared into her brown eyes and gripped her hand until the tight feeling in my chest went away.

"What's happening to me? Why can't I stop crying?"

"You'll stop when you're ready. I'm not worried about you. And I won't leave you alone with these big feelings."

At some point during my weeping, Nina's husband, Crispin, came in, bringing hot tea and biscuits. Another wave of embarrassment hit, and I tried furiously to wipe my tears away, to go back to normal. I barely even knew these people!

"Don't worry about it, Kris." Crispin smiled. "We've both been where you are. Just let it out."

"Okay," I whimpered. Jay popped into my mind, the feeling of his hand in mine as we walked home from the park. A fresh burst of tears followed, and there was something relieving about being allowed to cry about my brother, like scratching an itch I'd had for years but couldn't reach.

"What are you thinking about?" Nina asked when I paused after a particularly heavy sob.

"I miss my brother!"

She squeezed my hand, and though my face must have been a snotty, blotchy mess, the flood of tears seemed to sweep away some shame in their current.

I was blowing my nose and starting to look around the living room when I noticed a piece of art on the wall. "That's a beautiful painting."

"Thanks!" Nina said. She started telling me about it, and as I listened, a sense of ease gradually settled upon me, like a down comforter. I noticed that I no longer felt embarrassed about all my crying, nor did things seem as bad as they had when I arrived. I looked at Nina and Crispin, who beamed back at me, relaxed as ever.

"Um," I said. "What just happened?"

"What do you mean?" Nina asked.

"Well," I stammered. "When I got here everything seemed so bad and now I feel like nothing's ever been wrong in my life! How is that possible?"

Nina and Crispin exchanged a look and laughed.

"You just experienced Re-evaluation Counseling," Crispin said.

"It's a revolutionary peer counseling and liberation tool," Nina added. "I've been doing it for a couple years and it's changed my life. The theory in RC is that everyone is born inherently good and then everyone gets hurt, and those hurts grab on to us and make us act against our own best interests as adults—to develop addictions, to hurt others and ourselves."

I nodded, though I only somewhat understood.

"And in RC, we take turns listening to each other cry or yell or laugh, which liberates us from the hurt," Nina finished. "You cried off some early hurts just now, but you probably could spend thousands more hours doing this!"

"Okay!" I said, grinning. "Let's get going!"

Nina got me into a weekly class where I began to learn the theory and technique of RC. I started having one-on-one "sessions" with other co-counselors, and got to share my story, over and over again, even more fully than I had been able to in twelve-step meetings. There was space to feel all that was coming through my body, not just the good and the bad, but the *very* bad, the seemingly impossible.

I got to know and love people from a variety of backgrounds: a British Jew whose mother had been in a concentration camp, a recent immigrant from India who was a mother to three young children, a white American in her late fifties who'd grown up in the South where she had witnessed the lynching of a Black man, and a young gay man whose mother recently committed suicide. The beauty of the practice was that we took turns listening and being listened to, and I learned as much from being the "counselor" as I did when I was the "client."

One day Mary, the white southerner, and I were having a session. She was in my fundamentals class, and we'd hit it off and started doing regular sessions.

"I can't tell you what I'm thinkin' about right now," she said in her southern drawl. It was her turn to be client and I was the counselor. We sat in the living room of her flat in Chelsea, on an old floral love-seat. "It's just too bad."

I promised her that there was space for whatever she needed to share, and that I wouldn't't leave her alone no matter how bad it was. Then I listened for thirty minutes as she told the story of the lynching she had witnessed. We faced the suffering of racism and death together, and when her time was up, it was my turn to receive her attention.

I started with a few yawns. I had learned that yawns, like crying or laughing, can serve as an emotional release. "Hi, Mary." I looked into her eyes and felt tears in the corners of my own. To see a loving person gazing back with benign attention melted my heart. Someone knew the real me and liked me as I was—and she wasn't the only one.

At that thought I sobbed for several minutes, while Mary patted my hand and murmured softly, "Go ahead, darlin'. I'm right here."

I paused to blow my nose, thinking about what I wanted to focus on in this session. "I've been feeling really anxious all week," I began. "Like, when I leave my house or in my classes, I have this tightness in my chest that won't go away. I feel like I'm going to mess everything up, or something really bad is gonna happen."

"Could you try to shake a little with me?" Mary asked.

I shook my shoulders, opening my body to the familiar feeling of terror.

"Somethin' was really scary back there," Mary said in a light tone.

"Back where?" I asked.

"Back when you were little. If you're feelin' scared and anxious in the present, it's an indicator that you're bein' reminded of somethin' scary when you were very young. It's a re- stimulation, or reminder, of some early terror."

I continued trembling as she spoke, my insides clenching. What could have happened? I tried to picture myself as a baby. An image flashed across my mind: I was in a crib. I could hear my father shouting, then I saw my mother fall to the ground.

"Don't hurt her!" I yelled, as if at my dad.

"Take me back there with you, honey," Mary said, and her face swam into view. All at once, I was back in her living room, the image of the crib merely a newly unoccluded memory.

I continued shaking and crying as I told her what I had seen. "Do you think that really happened?" I asked.

"Well, your brain showed it to you for a reason," she said. "But let's take a minute to notice that you're not back there anymore. You are safe. You are in charge. You're not alone."

"Okay." I continued to sob until the timer went off.

As I stepped out of Mary's house that day and into the crisp, London air, I felt myself moving into a body I had never met before, a body that could hold suffering but was not determined by suffering.

I was becoming myself.

—14—

Trauma victims cannot recover until they become familiar
with and befriend the sensations in their bodies.
—Bessel A. van der Kolk, The Body Keeps the Score

Over the years, through counseling sessions and conversations with my parents, I've gained a clearer picture of the generational trauma I've inherited and the early experiences that shaped my life.

The story begins in 1961 in the Midwest, America's Breadbasket. Steve, my father, was sixteen and worked at the Eskin Theatre in Richland Center, Wisconsin. One day, as he took tickets for *West Side Story*, he noticed seventeen-year-old Carol circling the block with her girlfriend. They were driving a blue four-door Dodge Dart.

"Your mom never looked in," Steve told me years later, "but she had beautiful brown hair and the sexiest profile. When she took her foot off the gas, I had to cover up the rise in my pants. I didn't want to lose my job!"

I stifled my laugh and took notes.

My mom had heard rumors about Steve "Buck" Cook, that he took girls down to the theater basement and laid them down on a dingy mattress, that he would sneak into Sally Haskins's house at night. My dad's lifelong friend Mark Miller, who lived across the street from

Sally, has confirmed this story. In 2021 at my dad's annual Christmas party, Mark told me about sitting on his front porch one night when Buck pulled up in his black Ford and wobbled up to the back door. Mark heard a scream, then saw Buck fleeing the house—he had mixed up Sally's bedroom with her parents'.

Mark also told me about the time Buck totaled his parents' brand new De Soto sedan, "a gorgeous, yellow two-tone with fins and a 330 V8 engine." His narrow, lined face took on a dreamy expression. "Buck's dad was proud as hell of that car. No way he woulda let Buck drive it, so Buck took the car without permission."

Mark and Buck were only fifteen and fourteen at the time, and neither had a driver's license. On a cold March night, Mark was home looking after his four younger siblings when Buck called.

"My mom and dad are out of town and I got the keys to the De Soto. I'm taking it for a spin!" Buck said. "I'll pick you up in ten."

"I can't, I'm babysitting."

"Come on, they'll be fine without you for an hour." He hung up.

Ten minutes later, Mark heard a horn blast out front. "And dummy me, I left my thirteen-year-old sister in charge and got in the car!" Mark laughed, shaking his head at the temerity of adolescence. "We drove to the other side of town and then headed back, down Park street."

The boys decided to drive by Pam Schmidt's house, a pretty girl two years younger than them who lived at the top of a hill.

"Buck laid on the horn and I think Pam waved from the window, so he stomped on the gas pedal to show off, rev the engine, you know."

According to Mark, this hill was very steep, and a winter's worth of melted snow had run through the intersection at the bottom of the hill and frozen into a sheet of ice. "As soon as we hit that intersection, the car fishtailed and flew off the road, first into a row of mailboxes and then straight into the corner of a house. We must have been going over fifty miles an hour when we hit. It felt like the car was airborne for a minute."

I grabbed Mark's arm in shock. "You two must have been pretty beat up."

"Oh yeah. We didn't even have seat belts on, we were just sitting on top of them. That was the first car with seat belts either of us had seen, you know. My head just about went through the windshield, and Buck slammed his face on the steering wheel."

I shuddered. "That sounds terrifying."

"Well, it all happened so fast. One minute I saw the mailboxes going over the hood of the car, the next I was covered in glass and bleeding, and there was a forehead-shaped dent in the windshield above me—I must have passed out for a few minutes. And I look over and see blood streaming down Buck's face. He had broken his eye socket and his nose."

"Was there anyone in the house?"

"Oh yeah, a man had been sleeping in the room right on the other side of the wall we crashed into! He was unharmed. He came out and called the cops. And when the ambulance came, they had to pull me out the window. The car was destroyed. It was dented in the front in a sharp V shape that cut all the way back to the engine, which was smoking like crazy."

"Were you mad at my dad?"

"Sure. I was like, 'You fucking asshole!' He was always so reckless, didn't seem to care who got hurt so long as he had a good time. He never learned. But I wasn't mad for long. They had us in the same hospital room and, of course, when Buck's parents got to the hospital the next day, his mom says, 'There is no way that these two are going to stay in the same room and enjoy each other's company.' So they split us up."

Mark's lip had been torn up by the windshield glass and needed over forty stitches, "inside and out," he said. "I picked glass out of my lip for a year, and your dad's left eye was yellow for some time after that."

* * *

Even knowing what she knew about my father's ways, my mother still wanted him. She finagled him a job working for her father one summer, and they got to know each other while stacking hay in the hot sun.

My dad still remembers their first date. "Well, I can't say I remember much from the date itself." He gave me a sly look. "I know I took her to town and drove her home afterward. It was late and I walked her to the door."

Carol pulled Steve inside the front door into the mudroom, where Steve pushed her up against the chest freezer and kissed her hard. They pulled at each other's clothes in desperation in the dark, the sounds of heavy breathing and wet smacking interspersed with the rustle of fabric, the clink of a belt buckle. "I remember looking at the clock above the freezer and seeing it was 11:30 p.m.," my dad said. Quickly and quietly, he pulled her dress up and covered her mouth. Through the dark kitchen window behind them, he caught sight of my grandmother Margaret.

"I was still inside your mom and I panicked!" He laughed as he shamelessly recounted the story. He finished immediately, his orgasm frantic, cold sweat dripping from his forehead as he scrambled to pull up his pants and sneak back out the door, pecking my mom on the lips as he left.

I wish I had more of my mom's perspective in these stories, but I imagine her standing there, heart pounding in her chest, whole body pulsing. She had waited so long for something that lasted only minutes.

Two years later, a summer evening in 1963, my mom and dad finished milking forty Holsteins, shut the lights out in the barn, jumped into Steve's car, and drove up to an empty field to watch fireflies.

"She pointed to the Big Dipper," Dad told me. "She said something funny, like 'It's calling me.' I never knew what she was talking about, but I loved the sound of her voice."

He kissed her then and laid her down in the long, waving grass. She lifted her dress. The moon crept fuller and higher, soaking their bodies in rays of silver light. Fireflies lit up and faded, rising and falling, surrounding their merging bodies.

That was the beginning of me.

Thirty-six years later, my mom told me about getting up the courage to confess to her mother. We were playing cards one afternoon during my pregnancy with Rayna, which had opened up space for such a conversation.

Mom shuffled the deck, eyes narrowed in focus. "I remember Mother was scrubbing the kitchen floor. I just stared at her, terrified, unable to speak, watching her scrub."

I pictured Grandma Margaret, a stern, strongly built woman, on her hands and knees.

"After I said, 'I'm pregnant,' she didn't speak, just kept scrubbing away at the floor around my feet." My mom stopped shuffling, her gaze distant, perhaps envisioning her mother's tan arms pushing into the stiff-bristled scrub brush.

I could almost hear the brush's rhythmic shushing.

She started dealing the cards. "After what felt like ages, your grandmother just said, 'When's the wedding?'"

My mom didn't want a wedding, but her only other option was the life of an unwed, single mother—not a *real* option, as far as her parents were concerned.

Following the September wedding, with dreams of having a career, my mom entered nursing school at St. Mary's Hospital in Madison. Since my dad was about to join the navy, my mom thought it best to move into the nurses' dormitories. My dad helped her move, already feeling trapped in a life neither of them wanted. While dropping her off, he became angry and threw her suitcase forty feet up the street while my mother stared at him, eyes hollow and fists balled. I picture them now as a pair of lions at the zoo; one is furious, wild, lashing out at anyone who would try to control him; the other lies still, broken, having accepted her fate.

Under the disappearing light of a setting quarter moon, seven and a half months after Steve left to join the navy, my mom gave birth at her hometown hospital. Her older sister Ruth was a nurse there and caught me in her sister-hands.

With a full head of soft brown hair, I was a beautiful baby girl, everyone agreed.

A day later, the morning after my birth, as the USS *Sierra* (AD 18) crossed the Bermuda Triangle, my dad was informed, "It's a girl!" To this day, my dad thinks my birthday is March 19.

My mom's milk didn't let down, so she had to feed me formula from a bottle. Perhaps the formula wasn't enough nutrition, or perhaps I hungered for the comfort of my mother's breast. As the story goes, I was always hungry, always crying. It's something I've examined in co-counseling sessions many times, clued in by the fact that, all these years later, I still have feelings of scarcity where food is concerned. Once, while sobbing on Nina's couch, I unveiled a memory of myself as a baby, screaming in my mother's thin arms as we left the hospital. I'm confident that my baby body internalized what she was feeling: *What do I do now?*

Mom and I headed to her parents' brick farmhouse, where she tried to nurse me as she half listened to Grandma Margaret's farm talk: " . . . and your father hasn't even taken his tractor out yet!" Mom was distracted by her swollen breasts, hot with infection. When she passed me off to Grandpa Winslow, he held me like a bad hand of euchre. I remember this. Babies have the language of touch, and I sensed the resentment in my grandfather's hands. As soon as he could, he passed me back to my mother and walked out to the barn, his rubber boots squishing in the puddled driveway.

My grandfather did not want to be a farmer, forced to milk the teats of thirty-one milk cows twice a day; he wanted to be a writer and English teacher, to share his thoughts with the world. For years, he had ridden a horse and buggy on muddy roads to and from the University of Wisconsin in Madison. But when Margaret's father had died, he had to take his place on his wife's family farm.

Still, he loved poetry and would recite it any chance he had to any willing ear—the boys who helped on the farm, sitting beside him on his tractor while he drove; his daughters looking up at him from stainless steel buckets as they milked the cows. His favorite poem was "Crossing of the Bar" by Tennyson, a poem that compares death with crossing the "sandbar" between the river of life and the "ocean" that lies beyond.

> For tho' from out our bourne of Time and Place
>> The flood may bear me far,
> I hope to see my Pilot face to face
>> When I have crost the bar.

Early in my journey as a writer, when I hadn't yet claimed that identity, I was awakened by my chocolate Lab barking. I found him in the kitchen, growling ferociously at a small red fox on the other side of the sliding glass door, standing several feet from us in the yard. The fox stared back at us unblinkingly. I met his eyes and gazed into their depth. I closed my eyes to breathe in the moment, and when I opened them, the fox had vanished. When I lay back in bed, I found my grandfather shimmering in the room across from me. He looked exactly how I remembered him, in his farmer's uniform of overalls and rubber boots. *Write,* he said. My immediate reaction was resistance to his request, but I let the night's magic eclipse my own reluctance, holding the fox's eyes in my mind.

When I was three weeks old, my mom decided to join my dad in Virginia. She packed me up, along with all our worldly possessions, and bravely boarded a train to the edge of the world as she knew it, the Atlantic Ocean. I can only imagine how a nineteen-year-old mother of a tiny infant must have felt leaving everything and everyone behind, the foreign smells of sea and sand soon replacing those of river and woods and cows.

For the next six months, we lived at Magnolia Garden Apartments on the second floor near the naval base. I spent long hours in my crib, watching everything. Dad was often gone for long stretches of time, working as a radar man on a destroyer service ship. When he was home, I observed him prioritizing certain activities—doing push-ups, making a military bed, drinking beers with his buddies, and shouting at my mother. He also prioritized spending time with the blond wife of a fellow navy sailor who lived downstairs. He spoke with me candidly about it, years later.

"I was an ass," he admitted, smiling roguishly. "All I wanted to do was fuck. I know your mother could hear me when I was in the apartment below, fucking that lady. I did it when she was home, for chrissakes!"

"Which would mean I was also home." My face must have conveyed some of the shock I felt, because he laughed.

"Listen, I'm not proud of any of it, I know I fucked up. If I was your mother, I woulda run too."

Looking back, I see my mother, worry and resentment aging her young face as she paced across the dreary living room carpet. I see my baby girl body, trapped in a crib while my father was free to do what he pleased. My mom once told me that, more than once, she

left me alone in the apartment while she went downstairs to find my
father. I see her small fist raised to the gray door. I hear her shrill
voice trying to contain a lifetime of rage, *"Steve, goddamn it! I know
you're in there!"*

"Did you and he ever, even once, hang out and have family time?" I
asked her nearly fifty years later. We were driving to North Carolina
to visit my son in college, retracing the path we'd taken on our way
to live with Steve.

"No." She didn't take her eyes off the road ahead, though I was the
one driving.

"Never?"

"Unh-uh."

"So, you were just always alone with me?"

"Yeah, um"—she dug in her purse—"unless he would invite all of
his buddies over to get drunk."

"What would you do?" I turned on my blinker to pass a semitruck.

My mom applied ChapStick, returning it to her purse before she
answered. "I can remember hiding in the back stairway . . . because
he was threatening to beat me up and I didn't want to get too far away
from you. You were sleeping."

She looked out her passenger window at a passing Walmart and
McDonald's. I was glad we weren't looking at each other.

"That's when his buddies were there?"

"Uh-huh."

"Really?"

"Yeah."

"Wait, I don't connect the dots on this one . . . In front of his buddies? He was saying he was going to beat. You. Up?"

"Uh-huh."

"Didn't his buddies interrupt this?"

"No. I just remember being scared out of my wits, hiding in the
back stairwell."

"Why the hell would he want to beat you up?"

"Because he was drunk."

I looked at her and she pointed to the road, a signal for me to stop asking questions. An image materialized in my mind, real or imagined. Rowdy men drinking around the table and crowded in the kitchen, a keg in one corner, my father's face twisted in an ugly frown, violence emanating from his tall frame as he stood over my mother. My mother gasping when he shoved her into a keg. His buddies laughing as they guzzled their Budweiser.

My mom finally decided to leave my dad the night she found him fucking someone in their bedroom next to my crib. She'd come in to see if I was asleep.

Several days later, a friend helped her board a midnight train to Chicago. "Your dad swore he'd kill me if we left," she explained. I had brought the conversation back up later in our drive to North Carolina.

"Did your mother know you were coming home?" I asked. "Or did you just show up at the door one day?"

"I called her from Ohio," she said, "and she picked us up from the train station in Chicago. She recognized you, but she didn't recognize me."

"What do you mean?"

"I was skin and bones. I had no money for food."

"No money for food?" I tensed as a semi edged up along my left side.

"I had money to buy cigarettes though." My mother took a deep breath, as if remembering the pleasure cigarettes had brought her. She had smoked for sixty-odd years before she'd had to quit.

"You only had enough for cigarettes?"

She laughed out loud. I had sped up and was now passing the same semi that had recently passed me.

"Well, I fed you."

So, despite my dad's death threats, she had sped away—with me—into the night while he was out at sea.

When I tilt my head toward childhood, I hear the sound of the train's metal wheels against the steel tracks, feel the swaying of the cars, smell the relief on my mother's skin as the train carried us away from my father. That train has become a totem.

My dad, of course, contradicts my mother's version. "Aw Kris, that never happened." He shook his head as he stood at my kitchen sink. "Come on, why would I wanna kill your mom?"

"Well, then why do you think she left?"

"Oh, you know," he shrugged. "I wasn't the best husband back then, I know that." He sponged off a plate and set it in the dish rack. "I was caught up in the navy life. Boy, that was a wild time."

"I bet!" I tried to echo his light tone. "Hey, I've been writing about that time—for a memoir." I could barely squeeze the last words from my throat.

Dad grunted in response.

"I'd like you to read it."

"Yeah, okay, go ahead and send it to me."

Days later, in the kitchen again, Dad grabbed my arm. "Hey, that story of you and your mother fleeing on a train in the night?"

"Yes?" I tried to keep my voice warm. I'd been hoping for this conversation and was thrilled that he'd started it. I opened the microwave and stuck my finger into the stuffed pepper I was heating up.

Turning back to my dad, I watched him wipe the last plate and noticed there were tears streaming from his eyes.

Later that same year, I ran into my father's younger brother, Mike, at the yearly family Christmas party, and we got to talking about his father, my paternal grandfather.

"He was a massive woman beater," Mike said. "He nearly killed my mother, Bette Mae, on more than one occasion."

As my dad's family opened presents wrapped in shiny red and green paper, Mike revealed that he and Steve had been in the kitchen the last time his dad beat his mom. "I watched from my high chair as my dad threw my mom down the basement stairs."

"Ouch!" I pulled the bow off the present my dad had set on my lap while Mike continued whispering.

"The next day, my grandfather came and I remember him saying, 'You aren't to be anywhere near Bette Mae again.' Then he took your grandmother down to the attorney's office and paid for the divorce. I don't think she ever got over the shame of it."

My face grew warm as a wave of love rose in my body for my father, and his father, and his father. For the first three years of his life, my dad had watched his father beat his mother. Shivering, I opened the present in my lap, a six-pack of Budweiser.

I struggled to integrate this new information about my grandmother. How could it be that a woman who was abused by her husband in the presence of her sons also denied her son's abuse of my mother?

According to my mom, Bette Mae said, "We don't believe your stories, Carol, and we don't want to hear from you or your daughter ever again." She wasn't the only one who blamed my mother— when Grandma Margaret met us in Chicago at the train station, she snatched me from Carol's arms without even looking at her.

"Where's all your stuff, the wedding dishes?"

"I couldn't pack all that."

"We are going back to Virginia," my grandmother commanded, eyebrows narrowed and thin lips tighter than usual.

So that's what they did—headed back to Virginia without me—for dishes. (They would return two weeks later, bringing souvenirs from Washington, DC, along with the china.)

Despite my screaming protests, my mom left me at the farm, in the care of my great-grandmother Eliza, whom everyone called Nanny.

For the first few years of my life, Eliza was my primary babysitter. I have a blur of memories of those endless hours we spent—together, though very much apart. She would sit in a gray La-Z-Boy recliner, staring out the window and gripping a flyswatter, her wrinkled skin hanging loosely from her arm. Without another mind to engage or body to cling to, I burrowed deeply into myself, observing the world around me.

I remember crawling toward the cuckoo clock, looking up to see the bird come out, sing, and go back in. I must have been old enough to have been left sitting on the floor but young enough not to be able to wander far.

How does it do that? I wondered. *Where does the little bird hide away? Why does the clock tick?* I came to understand that the cuckoo bird came out to mark something mysterious—when food arrived at the table, or when grandpa put his mud boots on, or when Aunt Ruth came by the farmhouse to hold me.

Cuckoo, cuckoo, cuckoo.

Swat! The flyswatter cracked the air, startling me, squashing flies between its metal mesh and the glass window. I picture Nanny now, murmuring under her breath, "I hate those goddamn things."

A fly landed on my hand, crawled up my chubby palm, onto my thumb. There the fly lifted its legs, one at a time, to rub each wing. When the fly stayed too long, I shook my hand to send it somewhere else.

Cuckoo, cuckoo.

—15—

Facing death activates our inner knowing.
—Dr. Marc Gafni

As space continued to open for sharing and investigating truth, I felt closer to Jay. He came up in many of my sessions, and I got to tell my co-counselors his story. Sometimes I would scream with rage. Other times I would sob with guilt. It was the first time I had really felt safe to show other people the degree to which I held myself responsible for his death.

My counselors would always remind me that I was not to blame. "You did not kill your brother," I remember one man saying to me, staring into my eyes as I cried. "I'm so sorry he's dead. It is *not* your fault, Kris."

In one session with Nina, I found myself laughing hysterically about Jay's premonitions.

"I mean, what thirteen-year-old *knows* they're going to die young, and is perfectly okay with it?" I cackled. "How is that possible?"

Nina smiled.

"How did he know?" I shook her arm, my laughter turning into sobs. "How??"

I was obsessed with this question but eventually gave it up. It was just one of those unfathomable truths of the universe, like gravity, or the speed of light. It became a myth, a family ghost story. I never spoke of it with my mother, or anyone who had known Jay, but I would tell it to friends near the end of a dinner party, to my children and stepchildren when they were old enough. "He dreamed he would die young, and it happened exactly as he said it would."

The gasps and wide-eyed stares were gratifying, confirmation that this tale held magic. Perhaps some of it had rubbed off on me. I stopped questioning how he knew, chalked it up to forces unknown, and found comfort in the mystery.

Then came that day on the ice with Stevie, nearly forty years after Jay's visions began, when he told me the story Jay had told him about envisioning his death while tripping on acid. In the chaos and heartbreak of my fleeting interactions with Stevie, I momentarily lost this thread. Then, weeks or months later, I remembered Stevie's story and began to wonder: Did Jay lie to us when he told us he dreamed his death? Had he really been tripping?

I rejected this possibility at first—it was hard for me to imagine Jay getting his hands on some drug I had never tried. Then again, Jay was doing a lot of things I didn't know about. I recalled a conversation I had in 2012 with Phillip, who'd lived next door for fourteen years. He was one of Jay's many close friends, beginning when his mother babysat Jay. We met up at a cafe, and I was shocked to see a grown man when, in my mind, he was still a gangly fourteen-year-old. I shivered. The power of memory.

We had been talking for about an hour before he told me that, at one time, Jay provided marijuana to the entire neighborhood.

"He sold pot?" A train of thoughts raced through my mind: *How could I have missed that? I was older. I smoked pot every day. I smoked pot with Jay. I mean, we lived in the same house. Yet my kid brother got into dealing?*

"Yup." He spun a piece of ice in his water glass, creating a small whirlpool.

"Where did he get the pot?" I asked, a part of my mind riding the whirlpool's edge.

Phillip pulled his finger from the glass and stuck it into his mouth. "Jerry Mueller."

I picked up my mug and took a sip. "What did he do with the money?"

"Bought BMX bike parts." Phillip's face took on a dreamy expression. "Everyone wanted to ride Jay's bike. It was red and silver, with very expensive wheels, expensive rims. Riding it was like riding a cloud." Phillip gazed upward, his eyes unfocused.

I pictured Jay, shining with sweat, grinning at me, speeding past our house on his pride and joy. If he could sell weed without my knowledge, perhaps he could get away with using LSD.

Though not evident to me as a young person, our childhood was greatly influenced by the antiwar movement. I have a clear memory from autumn 1970 when I was six years old, a first-grader sitting on the floor in the kitchen, tying my shoe. My mom stood at the kitchen sink while Jay, two years old, chattered away in his playpen. Dick was still at work. Outside, a cardinal whipped notes off the silver maple tree on the hill. I needed to tell my mom a story.

"Something happened at the university, Mama."

I didn't feel scared about what I was trying to tell her because I was concentrating on sounds—the birdsong, water running into the sink, a fly buzzing by my head.

"Can you hear me?" I untied my shoe.

"Yes, honey, I can hear you." She turned off the faucet and walked over to the back door.

"Some people blew up a building."

My mom froze. "What did you say?"

"A building. Downtown." I brushed a fly off my leg.

She went back to the sink.

"It was because of the war."

"Kris, how do you know about this?"

"Mrs. Sugar." I held the two shoestrings up like rabbit ears and crossed my right hand over my left hand.

Mrs. Sugar was my favorite teacher. She had taught us about the war in Vietnam, how the American government was killing women and babies. She told us about the marches and protests for peace. When she talked about the bombing at the university, her face became fierce and solemn, eyes watering slightly as she said, "Those honorable young men are now on the run from the law."

But after Dick made my mom call the principal, Mrs. Sugar wasn't allowed to teach her first-grade class anything else about the Vietnam War protests. I didn't care. The damage was done. I knew about the war and I knew killing could be protested. In my six-year-old eyes, those bombers were heroes.

At the time, I didn't understand the whole story of Karl Armstrong and his brother Dwight, two of four young men who had been so committed to ending the Vietnam War that they'd bombed a wing of a University of Wisconsin building where the Army Mathematics Research Center was located. I've since learned that they planned the bombing for the middle of the night to be certain no one would be in the lab and made an anonymous call warning Madison police to evacuate the building, which was ignored. Several departments were housed in Sterling Hall, so although the bomb barely even touched the Army Math lab, several floors up, it caused extensive damage to other departments as well as to the hospital across the street. The explosion killed a physics researcher and injured three others.

The bombers got away, though three of four were apprehended years later. Rather than take a plea deal, Karl Armstrong decided to go to trial, to use it as an opportunity to amplify his message:

the U.S. government had committed far more violent and criminal acts than he and his comrades and continued to do so. The hearing consisted of a series of testimonies from experts in biology, history, and international law, as well as several Vietnam veterans, one of whom said, "I've killed many more people than Karl Armstrong and would gladly serve next to him in jail." Karl was sentenced to twenty-three years in prison, seven of which he served before being paroled.

I learned all this much later, when I met Karl as an adult. We both owned food carts that we parked downtown, less than a mile from the site of the bombing. By then, he lived a quiet life, and despite the unintended consequences of his actions, I was honored to know him.

The values, the music, and the drugs of the 1960s and '70s had become mainstream by the time I was a teenager. Jay and I listened to psychedelic rock and started smoking weed young. It was possible that Jay had gotten access to LSD as an eleven- or twelve-year-old. But could acid really lead a person to learn about and be okay with their own death? I did some research online and found that, though psychedelic experience can be risky—you can have "good" trips and "bad" trips—there are countless examples of people using psychotropics to reach transcendent or heightened states of consciousness. Brain scans corroborate these stories.

Stevie's story was beginning to seem more plausible, though I still doubted him as a reliable source.

The week after our dog walk on the frozen lake, I decided to bring it up with my mom.

"I hung out with Stevie Anderson last week," I began.

"I see."

"Did you know at the time that Jay and his friends were doing acid?"

"No. I don't think that's true," she said flatly.

I dropped the subject. For though I was a full-grown adult, though her viewpoint was limited, my mother still held some place in my mind as the authority on Jay. At any rate, she was more reliable than an unstable, drunken Stevie.

How did my mom think Jay could have known? I wished we could investigate these questions together, but I knew enough to keep quiet.

—16—

The bravest thing I ever did was continuing my life
when I wanted to die.
—Juliette Lewis

On a sunny morning in the fall of 1994, I drove my clunky gold van to the doctor. Something had been wrong with me for months.

It all started when my mom, my three-year-old son Eli, and I were in Isla Mujeres, off the coast of Cancun. The trip had been beautiful. We snorkeled in the Caribbean, trekked through Mayan ruins, and sat by the ocean listening to the waves. We were even invited to a Mexican birthday party after making friends with some children we met in the street.

We crowded into the living room of a modest home, neighborhood children shrieking and squealing in anticipation of the piñata. Women in full makeup with aprons covering fancy dresses bustled around the kitchen, from which emanated a strong smell of meat. My stomach clenched. Was that in reaction to the smell? Perhaps I'd had some bad street food. I tried to ignore my discomfort, directing my attention to Eli's delighted face.

He stared open-mouthed as a song began while the first blindfolded child swung a bat wildly in the air. When the song finished, her turn was up, and she handed the bat to the next person. I tried to figure out the words to the song but was distracted by the odd, pulsating pain again. I pressed my fingers into my belly and looked around the room. Each wall was painted a different bright color. On one wall was a picture of a glowing saint framed by ornate gold. To either side of the frame were two white skeletons wearing orange sombreros. On the opposite wall hung wooden crosses bearing the names and, I assumed, birth and death dates of ancestors. It struck me as fascinating that this family put death at the center of their daily life while my family hid from death.

A loud cheer filled the room, interrupting my thoughts. The piñata had broken and hundreds of brightly colored candies were showering the children who stood below with outstretched hands. Before I could stop him, Eli had sprung from my lap and was on his knees, shoveling candy into his pockets. This was one aspect of Mexican birthday culture he was familiar with. I laughed as he turned back to me, grinning and shoving a lollipop in his mouth. He was going to have a serious sugar crash if I didn't interrupt this frenzy, but I felt another spasm in my gut. What was wrong with me? Why was I in so much pain? Pressing harder and moving my hand a bit lower, I closed my eyes and listened to the mariachi music blast from the nearby record player. I wanted to enjoy this once-in-a-lifetime experience with my son, but it was all I could do to keep from falling out of my chair.

At a tug on my shirt, I opened my eyes to see Eli in front of me, licking the last bit of chocolate from his fingers as he stained my shirt with gooey brown prints, an expression of concern in his eyes. I tried to smile. "That's your last piece of candy for today."

The next day, with two days left in our trip, I found myself sitting in front of a solid oak desk that filled almost all the space in a tiny doctor's office. The doctor sitting across from me leaned in, elbows on the desk, listening to my broken Spanish.

"In the bathroom all day. My stomach hurts. I can't eat." My eyes filled with tears.

He leaned back in his metal folding chair, opened his top left desk drawer, reached in, and pulled out a white plastic bottle. I shifted in my seat, adjusting Eli on my lap. Eli stared at the doctor with rapt attention.

"Toma estos antibióticos," the doctor said, handing the pills to me over the desk.

Sitting on my lap, Eli grabbed the bottle from my hand and began trying to open it. I set him down. "Leave the lid on, honey," I said. A fresh wave of pain stabbed my gut and I winced.

"Es . . . esto . . ." I gestured to the bottle. I wanted to ask, *Are you sure this will work?* But I didn't know how.

He patted my hand. "Va a estar bien. Is okay. Is okay."

It will not be okay, I wanted to argue back, but I didn't. Instead I said, "Gracias," and pulled Eli out to the street.

The antibiotics did nothing. We returned home to Wisconsin the next day, my gut throbbing like a third-degree burn for the whole flight. I dropped Eli off at his dad's, then crawled into bed and curled up in a ball, holding my bloated abdomen. I faded in and out of consciousness, the next few days collapsing into one long fever dream in which I careened toward death. I had cancer or some other terminal illness.

My stomach twinged in pain as I pulled into the doctor's office parking lot. *I'm dying.* This had become an unintentional mantra. Over the weeks since returning from Mexico, my digestion had gotten even worse. I ignored it for a while, but then I started noticing frequent heart palpitations. When I found blood in my stool, I made another appointment. I had spent hours in waiting rooms to get a variety of tests. Now I was meeting with my primary physician to review the results. I dreaded what I would learn.

I checked the red digital clock on my dashboard. I still had a few minutes until my appointment, so I decided to give myself a pep talk. I turned off the engine and made a list in my head of things going well:

I was seven years clean and sober.

I owned a food cart and ran a successful business selling falafel. I made enough money working part-time three seasons of the year to support myself and Eli.

I played a leadership role in a community of peer counselors.

I had learned to treat my emotions as reliable guides instead of sensations I needed to fight.

I had solid relationships with people I could depend on. Even my relationship with my mom was better than ever.

A cramp spasmed in my belly. None of that even mattered if I was dying. I was going to die just like Jay died, and it was my fault. How poorly I treated my body all these years. Death was unavoidable. It was following me. And the world was dying too. I'd just read an article about extinct whales and melting ice caps. Before I could work myself into a full-blown panic, I noticed the clock. So much for that exercise. I wrenched the door open and got out.

In the waiting room, I sat on my hands to keep from fidgeting, but my leg jiggled uncontrollably. I hated doctor's offices. They reminded me of hospitals and hospitals reminded me of death. I picked up an issue of *People* magazine. On the cover was a photo of O. J. Simpson emblazoned with the words, "The Prisoner: The Full Story of O. J.'s Grim Life in Jail." On his face was an expression of utter defeat and resignation.

A nurse's voice jolted me out of my misery.

I followed her back to the exam room where she took my vitals and asked a few questions. I answered in a monotone.

"Okay, everything looks normal." She smiled and rose to leave. "The doctor will be with you shortly."

I had seen this doctor once before. He had been marginally more helpful than the others. The first doctor I'd gone to after Mexico had briskly asked me a few questions, then written me another prescription for antibiotics. In response to my faint protest that I'd already tried antibiotics, he told me to make an appointment with a dietician, then turned and walked out the door. The dietician recommended that I adhere to the food pyramid and sent me on my way. The next doctor suggested a different antibiotic, which again didn't work. It was only thanks to my peer counseling practice that I found the will to keep trying.

After the first appointment I had called my co-counselor Lucy for a mini session.

"Lucy," I wailed. "My belly hurts so bad. I can't live like this. What if I'm dying?"

"Keep telling me," she said. I could hear the loving smile in her voice. Her relaxed tone reminded me that I was not dying in this exact moment. Still, terror flooded my body.

"What if it's cancer? What if my liver is failing, or my heart?" My sobs became heavy as the image of my brother's bloody corpse swam into view.

After a few minutes, Lucy said, "Tell me what you're thinking about."

"I'm so scared," I whispered. "I think death is following me. All of a sudden I'm seventeen again and my brother just died."

"I know it feels that way, Kris. But look around you."

I did so. I sat in my dim bedroom. I caught my outline in the full-length mirror next to my bed. Outside, the sun was setting, and the sky was streaked with orange and pink.

"You're not back there anymore, honey," Lucy continued. "You survived that heartbreak. You're an adult now, and you're incredibly capable and resilient."

I continued weeping.

"You're dealing with some really hard stuff, but it's not bigger than you. And you know what else?"

I sniffled "What?"

"You don't have to figure it out alone."

That was what pushed me on in my quest for an answer, the knowledge that I didn't have to face this by myself. I pushed on, interwoven with my community, following up every appointment with a session, deciding again and again to call another doctor. I even brought one of my co-counselors with me when I had a colonoscopy. My doctor had also ordered blood work, a stool sample, and a CAT scan.

And now he was knocking on the door.

"Come in," I squeaked, my throat suddenly dry.

"Hi, Kristina." He smiled slightly but didn't waste time with pleasantries. "So. I reviewed your test results."

Just say it.

"The CT came back normal, as did your blood work."

But? BUT?? I gripped my thighs.

"I'm a little concerned about the results of your EKG. Seems you have an irregular heartbeat."

My heart was pounding in my chest. "How serious is that?" I stammered.

"We don't yet know. It could be that it's a symptom of some yet undiagnosed illness. More likely it's something we can just shock back into place with a catheter ablation . . ."

An electric shock? That sounded bad.

"Miss?"

"Sorry."

"That's all right. Now. Your colonoscopy."

My gut clenched, as if aware that it had become the focus of the conversation.

"Along with the symptoms you've described, the colonoscopy has led me to an initial diagnosis of irritable bowel syndrome, IBS. Have you heard of that?"

I shook my head.

"It's actually quite treatable, with diet changes and some combination of laxatives, antispasmodics, and painkillers. We're gonna start you on these three medications"—he handed me a list—"and take it from there."

I read three unpronounceable names. My heart sank. Not more pharmaceuticals.

"Nothing so far has worked. I think I even tried this one."

He shrugged his shoulders. "I'm sorry, all there is to do is keep trying. And at some point if you still don't have relief, the next step would be a colectomy."

"A colectomy?"

"Removal of part or all of the colon. It's a pretty involved surgery. So let's hope it doesn't come to that, eh?" He winked and walked out the door.

I tried to keep from crying as I walked back out to the car. Then I sat slumped in the driver's seat and let the tears fall.

"What the FUCK!" I screamed, banging on the steering wheel. Part of my colon? Shocking my heart? A nonstop string of pharmaceutical drugs, each less effective than the last? And I hadn't even had a chance to tell the doctor about the newest development: a sensitivity to strong smells. Anytime my housemate sprayed perfume or I went into a recently cleaned public bathroom, my head ached and I became nauseous. And what if the tests had missed something? What if the doctor was wrong? What if all this was pointing to something far worse than IBS, worse even than a colectomy?

"No," I said, shaking my head and wiping my eyes with my sleeves. I needed a session. It was the only thing that would help. I started the car and headed home, hoping someone would be available when I called.

I cranked the radio and focused on the road in front of me, singing at the top of my voice to R.E.M.'s "Losing My Religion." I noticed my empty light had come on, so I pulled over at a Citgo station. As I opened the door and stepped down from the van, the familiar smell of petroleum hit me. I gagged, unable to take a full breath.

I pulled my pink tank top over my mouth and nose. My head began to pound, intensifying with each inhale.

I didn't normally mind strong smells. In fact, I loved odors that others usually hated—cow manure and tractor fuel. I found them reminiscent of my grandparents' farm.

It took every bit of my will to stand and pump the gas. I wanted to vomit, but I made it back to the safety of the van, gasping for breath. I started the ignition, turning down the radio to ease the pressure in my head. Was it the gasoline? As the throbbing faded to a dull ache, I drove home on autopilot.

This headache and nausea felt similar to what I'd experienced the other day with my housemate's perfume. Was I allergic to smells? I didn't usually mind the smell of gas, but I really hated strong chemicals. I'd always hated that scented crap—lotion, detergent, shampoo. It smelled like death.

I pulled into the parking lot of my apartment building. Everything felt fuzzy. I staggered inside and fell into bed, burying my face in the cool, musty pillow. I let the familiar odor lull me to sleep.

Hours later, I woke to find the room dark. I looked around, confused, unsure for a moment where I was. Then I noticed a dull ache near my temple, a low, constant buzz. *Water,* my brain said with a pulse of pain. I stumbled into the kitchen to get a glass. The clock on the microwave said 11:30 p.m.

"Eleven thirty," I said aloud, feeling a tug at my memory. Eleven thirty was the time of my appointment. I looked at the calendar on the wall, confirming this fact. My appointment. Irregular heartbeat. Irritable bowel syndrome. Colectomy. It all came rushing back and I slid to the kitchen floor. Suddenly I was a baby and there was not enough food and my head was pounding and I didn't know if I'd make it to the next day. *I am dying.* I pressed my face into the cool tiles and saw my brother's face. "It won't be much longer." He had seen death coming. Now I saw it too.

I woke in the morning, stiff and with the imprint of the kitchen tiles across my cheek. I stretched, glancing at the clock, then the calendar. I had a counseling session planned with Lucy in thirty minutes. I changed my clothes and brushed my teeth. I couldn't handle eating breakfast, but I grabbed a Diet Coke from the fridge on my way out the door.

On the drive over, my stomach communicated its opposition loudly, but I ignored it, clinging to the sweet, caffeinated soda.

Lucy greeted me at the front door, beaming. "It's so good to see you, love!"

I fell into her arms and we stood, hugging, for a whole minute. I didn't want to move.

"Want some water?" she asked, stepping back. Behind her, the kitchen was brightly lit with sunshine, full of hanging plants.

"Sure," I said, heading into the living room to sit on the futon couch with Max, her black toy poodle. I glanced around the familiar surroundings—her bookshelves, her road bike leaning on one wall, the faint cobwebs in a couple of the ceiling's corners—and breathed a sigh of relief.

"How's Max doing after his surgery?" I called into the kitchen, scratching the dog behind his ears.

"Oh, much better!" She walked in carrying two green glasses full of water. "He seems to have most of his energy back and his post-op checkup went well." She plopped down on the couch next to me, her blond hair still mussed in the back from sleeping. "I think I have time for us to do thirty minutes each, you wanna go first?"

I started the timer on my watch. "Lucy?" I looked up at her loving face.

"Yes, sweetie?"

For the first time in days I considered that maybe I was okay.

I sobbed for a full ten minutes, looking back into her eyes every now and then to remind myself I was not alone. Images of my childhood popped up faster than I could follow them—my parents screaming at each other; trying to nurse from my mom; Jay's bloody head. I remembered how, when I was a baby, my grandmother used to lock me in the cold attic room. I thought about what my mother had told me about the years when she couldn't afford to feed us.

"It's too much," I sobbed, looking desperately into Lucy's eyes, wishing she would just put me out of my misery. "I don't know how to heal. I've already tried so many things that haven't worked. I give up." I was going to have to have a colectomy, I realized. What had been the point of quitting drinking; I was going to die anyway or live a miserable existence with half a colon. Maybe I would qualify for disability. I could quit my job and watch TV all day. Bill would have to take care of Eli; maybe he would get primary custody. Maybe I would start drinking again.

Lucy nudged my shoulder. "Where'd you go?"

I ignored her and began to consider leaving. She couldn't help me. No one could.

"Kris? It seems you're a little stuck." I buried my face, but she persisted. "I want to remind you that as hard as things are in the present, they're no match for you and me."

I barely took in her words, beginning to feel resentful that I was not home in my comfortable bed.

"The discouragement is old, sweetie," she whispered. "You had to give up long ago."

Lucy's living room faded away and I was a little girl at the dinner table, staring at my plate. Mashed potatoes and gravy. Flowers on the tablecloth. Dick's fury bearing down on me and my mother and Jay. I sat, silent, unable to move. Was he going to kill us this time? I started trembling.

"Tell me what you're thinking," Lucy prompted.

My eyes snapped onto hers. "I was back at the kitchen table, Dick was yelling." We'd worked on this memory before in past sessions, so Lucy was familiar.

"Okay, Kris, I want you to remember you're in charge here. What do you see?"

"Dick's at the head of the table," I sobbed. "And I'm on one side— frail, certain of death."

"How old is that little girl?"

"Three or four? Maybe less. She says we are dying. "

"No." Lucy's voice was firm. "She is not running the show. I know it was bad back there, but you are the grown-up now, you're not that little girl."

Her words caused something to rise from within my body, a dandelion burst of potential. I found that I could hold on to my young self. I could comfort her and know that I wasn't a victim anymore. I cried hard for several more minutes, clinging to Lucy's hand.

"Oh, my goodness!" I said, taking a deep breath and blowing my nose. It was all so heartbreaking. I knew in my bones that my grandmother wasn't bad, nor my mother, nor my father or Dick. "I feel their goodness in my body right now, Lucy," I said, yawning so wide I thought my face might split open. One long yawn after another rolled out of me. "I forgive them and I forgive myself!" I yelled, laughing now because I felt silly saying such things.

"Yes!" Lucy cheered.

"I'm in charge and I want to live!"

"Go, Kris!"

The timer went off. "Wow!" I continued to tremble. "I came in here so discouraged!"

"You did great. Any reflections?"

I took a sip of water. "Well, I can tell that this situation is not as impossible as it feels. I survived the impossible part, the part where I had no agency. I'm not back there anymore. I'm ready to commit to healing, however long it takes."

"And you've got a whole team around you!"

"Thank you!" I wrapped her up in a hug.

—17—

Your birth is out there in space-time.
Your death, too, is in space-time.
Every moment of your life is out there,
somewhere, in space-time.
—Kristie Miller

Through my healing journey, I rediscovered my love of learning, seeking out new alternative protocols as well as natural medicine teachers. I would try something, see what helped and what didn't, and use that to propel me onto the next attempt. Though my pain continued—and with it, crushing discouragement—I was able to keep moving through the hard feelings with help from RC sessions and even found satisfaction in the process. I was a detective solving a mystery, each clue bringing me closer to my goal. One thing I learned about was colon hydrotherapy. Though it was many years before I would fully heal my chronic digestive symptoms, colonics brought relief and, along with diet changes, helped me manage my multiple chemical sensitivities. I was still underweight, but I had gotten myself back up to 120 pounds.

The colon hydrotherapist I found, Mildred, was in her eighties and lived a few towns away. She wouldn't be administering colonics much longer. Perhaps hers was a niche I could fill. This career change excited me, because I saw how I could put to use my passion for study and research in continuing to develop expertise in my own and others' healing. I was beginning to feel the toll of working in the service industry as well, so, after six years of owning a falafel cart and selling food I could no longer eat, I embarked on a new chapter.

In fall of 1998 I opened my colon therapy practice, Optimal Health Center, which I operated out of a small two-room office I rented on the east side of Madison. About a year later, the *Isthmus*, a local paper, published an article about me and my practice. I was described as "an energetic and sprightly east-sider with long hair and little glasses." I was tickled by the reporter's account of my scholarly appearance and that I seemed the picture of good health. And about my office she wrote, "There is a bed covered in flannel sheets next to a colon therapy machine . . . There are diagrams on the walls, a scale on the floor, yet it doesn't feel overwhelmingly medical. The walls are pale purple . . . There are books to read, from the children's classic *Everyone Poops* to Mother Teresa's autobiography. The vibe is pleasing."

I had an influx of clients. People of all kinds walked through my door and lay on my colon therapy table wearing nothing but a mint-green gown: women with irritable bowel, fibromyalgia, and depression; men with cancer, prostatitis, constipation. While I administered colonics, I would listen to their stories of sickness and healing, constant pain, sleepless nights, juice fasts.

While I massaged their abdomen or examined their rectum before inserting the nozzle, some would also share personal life stories—of loss, heartbreak, or near-death experiences. One client would change my life.

The morning started off bad—I woke up shivering uncontrollably, an unbearable pain in my gut. My mind began to spiral into questioning what could have set off this new bout of pain and how I could possibly face my day, but I tried a new tactic. I shut my eyes, willing myself to go underneath the worry and find other feelings. I pressed my tongue against my teeth, felt the smoothness of each tooth. I listened to the faint traffic noises from the street that wafted gently through my window. I pressed my arm across my face and inhaled the sweet, soapy musk of my own skin. I let go of the future. I could hear a whisper of the universe vibrating throughout my bones. Death wasn't coming. Or, if it was, I could handle it.

I could continue my day.

I warmed up sea bass soup, a new regimen I was trying that, despite the soup's gelatinous texture, made me feel better. While I slurped, I checked my schedule. Fortunately I had only a couple of clients: first a regular, who I always enjoyed, then a new client, a man named JP Bowman.

JP was middle-aged, tall, with slightly graying hair. His smile was warm and somewhat puppy-dog-like, and he carried an air of mystery. He followed me down the blue carpeted hall to the colon therapy room. I pointed to the chair in front of the dark wooden folding table, noticing his dapper attire—including a tie and black patent-leather shoes.

As I took the chair opposite him, I said, "I see you came all the way from Chicago. How was your drive?"

"Not too bad. The drive is worth it as it's so hard to find a good colon therapist. I first learned about colonics from a doctor I was seeing in Denver, the first person who didn't just prescribe me laxatives. Now I do daily enemas, but I need to have colonics every so often in order for my colon to work. When I found your clinic on the internet I was so excited. I'm hoping to come up here a couple times a month."

"That's great to hear! We just put that website up last month. Isn't the internet amazing?"

"Oh, yes! The things you can do. I work as a private investigator and it has absolutely opened up my detective work." *So, that was why he reminded me of Sherlock Holmes!*

We talked more about his symptoms and diagnosis, and then I left the room so he could change into the gown. I returned and sat down next to where he lay on the table, connecting the tubes as I picked up on our previous conversation. "So, you mentioned this all started with a car accident?"

"Yes—well, I was on my bike and I was hit by a car."

I almost dropped the nozzle. He didn't seem to notice.

"It was a terrible accident, put me into a coma for a few days." A coma. "But then I woke up. When I got home from the hospital, I started to realize my colon didn't work anymore."

And here he was years later, still alive. A miracle.

"I was so grateful when I learned about enemas and colon cleansing," JP continued.

I had started the colonic machine, my body relying on muscle memory to go through the motions. "I'm so glad they've helped you," I managed to say. "And I'm so glad you survived that accident." I paused. "My brother was hit and killed on his bike when he was a kid."

JP craned his neck around to gape at me. "I'm so sorry."

"Thank you."

I felt a buzzing in my stomach unrelated to the pain from earlier or the machine gently humming beside me. Something tugged at the edges of my memory. The same accident, but alive. Jay. JP. "What does *JP* stand for?" I blurted out.

"It's my first and middle name, Jay Phillip."

"Oh my God," I said softly.

"What is it?" He jerked his head toward the machine.

"Sorry, nothing wrong with your colonic. It's just . . . My brother's name was Jay. Jay Phillip Amelong. The same middle name."

"That's a crazy coincidence."

JP returned only a few days later, since it had been a while and he needed extra treatments. The combination of his personality and the synchronicity we shared made me like him instantly, and we got along great. Little did I know, he was forming his own conclusions about me.

"I have this idea," he began, midway through his second treatment. "I use daily enemas and I know I'm not the only one, but colon cleansing has been cast out by the medical community and it's hard to access the products. Do you know the history of enemas?"

I didn't. In colon therapy school they had taught us enemas were dangerous. I told JP this and he smiled grimly, proceeding to educate me. Up until the 1960s, doctors administered colonics, and enema equipment was widely available in drugstores. Then pharmaceutical companies had realized they could make much more money selling laxatives, and through their control over the medical community, colon cleansing, especially done at home, began to be viewed as a health risk.

"It's absurd," JP said. "Enemas and colonics have literally saved my life. But the only place I've been able to buy decently made enema equipment is sex toy shops, and I'm sick of shopping there. I always feel worried someone in my apartment building will find out."

I chuckled, pausing the flow of water into his body and massaging his belly.

"So here's what I'm thinking. Someone needs to open a reputable online company selling affordable, quality enema equipment. And I think you might be just that person."

I was taken aback. I hadn't known where he was going but I had never expected him to pitch me a business proposal. I flipped the machine from fill to release.

"I'll help you get this thing off the ground," JP continued. "I've actually already sourced all the companies we would need to work with."

"You've sourced the companies?"

"Well, investigation happens to be my specialty." He grinned. "With my research and your enthusiasm, we can make this happen."

I felt a rush of excitement. The sensation reminded me of something that had happened a few months prior, when I met my webmaster, Janet. She was a new client of mine. I'd felt drawn to her, and after learning that she shared a birthday with Jay, I'd decided to hire her on the spot. Another synchronicity. And surely, we'd need a solid webmaster if we were going to launch an online store.

I told JP about Janet and he smiled. "Okay then. Looks like the stars are aligning."

A chill traveled down my spine. Was it the stars? Was it Jay?

"What do you say?" JP asked.

I didn't give it another thought. "Let's do it."

Despite the rashness of this decision, I felt little doubt in the following days. I had been curious about the healing potential of enemas for some time, despite what I was taught in my program. I knew only too well how mainstream medicine has been co-opted by capitalism and the pharmaceutical industry, so it was easy to believe JP's direct experience. More than anything, I was trusting in the universe, following the signs. I was a bit nervous about the implications of taking on such a big project without discussing it with my fiancé with whom I co-parented three young children, but my mind raced with the possibility. Besides, he could understand following synchronicities—that had been something we'd connected about early in our relationship.

During my years canvassing for Greenpeace before Eli was born, I had been the top earner of donations in the country for an entire year. Even before then, I had had great success renting apartments, my first full-time job. Perhaps this store was my calling! I had to follow these threads.

In 2002, on Super Bowl Sunday, JP, Janet, and I launched EnemaBag.com. JP didn't take any money, he merely wanted to aid in the creation of this resource for himself and the world. Twenty years later my business is still thriving. It has gone through many forms over the years, supporting my family through the recession. I've been able to provide work to friends, family, and community members. And the website (now OptimalHealthNetwork.com) has grown to offer alternative guidance on a wide range of health issues. Every week I speak to people with anal fissures who thought they would need surgery and use my protocol to avoid it. I have a protocol for prostate issues that has helped many men, and my website hosts hundreds of informational videos and articles combining everything I've learned over the years. Thank you, Jay.

Part III

—18—

We die. That may be the meaning of life. But we do language.
That may be the measure of our lives.

—Toni Morrison

In 2009, at the age of forty-five, I got it into my head to go to Guatemala. My marriage was on its last legs and I wanted some space from my husband. I'd loved my previous travels to Latin America, and since my business sold fair-trade coffee, there was an opportunity for me to visit the farm where the beans were grown, a cooperative of ex-guerillas-turned-farmers who had survived the civil war.

Searching the internet, I read of the dangers of travel in Guatemala, especially Guatemala City. Yet I felt a physical pull. I had to figure out a way to visit Finca Santa Anita. Rayna was eight and went everywhere I went, so bringing her was a given. I decided to invite my stepdaughter Johannah as well, then seventeen and in her last year of high school. She spoke Spanish and loved to sing and entertain her sister. But would we be safe, a woman and two girls traveling alone? I asked around for advice, and in the end, it worked out to bring along a young man named Jonah, who taught at Rayna's Waldorf school. He was adventurous and well-traveled, and his presence would bring me peace of mind.

Our trip turned out to be safe. We spent as little time in the capital as possible, favoring small tourist towns on our way to the farm. Guatemala is still wildland that spans a mountainous slice of Central America, filled with wonders ranging from thriving wild herds of howler monkeys to ancient Mayan ruins. Finca Santa Anita is nestled deep in a mountainous jungle, overlooking a smoking volcano. Our first night there, the guest services manager showed us a documentary, *Discovering Dominga*. The film follows Denese Becker, who, having survived the Guatemalan civil war as a child and been adopted by white Americans, was on a journey to find her people and her history.

Jonah, Johannah, and I sat in a crowded room, along with a church group of high school students, watching the tragedy unfold on a projector screen. (Fortunately, Rayna had already gone to sleep.) Johannah and I sat close on a couch, grabbing hands as Denese remembered witnessing her parents being murdered and when she spoke of escaping and carrying her dead infant sister on her back for miles. I learned that the thirty-six-year civil war was in fact a genocide of Indigenous Guatemalans at the hands of their own government. It had been funded by the United States and aided by the CIA and had resulted in the deaths of two hundred thousand people, 83 percent of them Mayan. By the time the war ended in 1996, over one million had been displaced, entire towns wiped out, and the country torn apart. As the credits rolled, we all sat in stunned silence.

I looked over at Johannah and saw a hollowness in her eyes that I'd never seen on her young face.

"Whoa," I offered, shivering. It occurred to me that however shocked I may have felt, it must have been even more earth-shattering for one so young. Her features were frozen into a shell of numbness, but it barely concealed what I suspected was a flood of emotion. I pulled Johannah out into the cool, humid night.

"How do you feel, sweetheart?" I asked.

Her face crumpled and she started sobbing, burying her head in my shoulder. "I can't believe that happened," she choked, her voice barely audible. "It's just so terrible."

I knew from my years of experience with Re-evaluation Counseling that the first thing to do when confronted with such heartbreak is to mourn. I held her close, breathing deeply, feeling the heartbreak. I wanted to give as much space as possible for her to grieve and heal, thinking about the tragedy I faced at her age and wishing I'd had someone to hold me then. I sent a prayer out into the night, for healing for us all.

"Yo quiero ver una serpiente, por favor," I said to our young Guatemalan guide the next day. "I want to see a snake!" Johannah and Jonah rolled their eyes, unable to understand why I would invite danger on our trek through the jungle.

"No," our guide replied, walking away from me toward the jungle. "No es posible ver una serpiente." *It's not possible to see a snake.* He pulled his machete out of his rope belt and beckoned us to follow.

We headed off into the woods to see the plantations of coffee and banana trees. Our tour had begun with a viewing of the mural painted on the side of La Casa Grande, the building where we were sleeping, a homestead that had been converted into our hostel. Every surface of the house was covered in intricately painted scenes depicting in vivid red, blue, and yellow the history of the farm and its people, the beauty and the trauma. The guide pointed out the story of the founding of the farm after the war. We learned more about the war's backstory, how greed, hatred, and racism had led the United States and the United Fruit Company to create the conditions that preceded the genocide. It was a story of wealth and power I'd heard again and again throughout my life, yet every time it shocked me.

As we walked on, my head pounded. So much violence in the

interest of profit. A mother hen and her flock of chicks scurried ahead of us on the path, causing our guide to pause near a shed where workers separated the green coffee beans from the red coffee shells. I took a deep breath.

"I'm so sorry," I said, doing my best to translate the fullness of my sincerity into an unfamiliar language. "Your blood, your babies . . ."

He turned back to me, his face soft but solemn. "Gracias." We held eye contact for a few moments. Above us, small white clouds floated in a bright blue sky past the cone of the Santa Maria volcano in the distance.

I suppressed the urge to bolt, to run from the pain in the young man's eyes. Rayna grabbed Johannah's hand and both girls skipped ahead along the path, as the same mother hen and her chicks scurried under a pile of brush. Jonah followed behind them, and I took the opportunity to connect more with our guide. "Have you lived here your whole life?" He seemed very young, and I couldn't remember the founding year of the co-op.

"Since I was a small child. My father fought in the war."

Despite the language barrier, we were able to muddle through a conversation, and I learned more about his life, how hard he and his family worked for very little money, despite recently switching over to the fair-trade structure. He paused at a particularly striking vista overlooking the volcano.

"It's hard to live here, but I can't leave the land." He set off again and I stood, in awe of the volcano and the relationship the people here clearly had with it.

At last I followed him, walking fast, scratching a bug bite on my arm. Catching up to where the group had come to rest, I noticed Rayna holding a dark purple object the size and shape of a small football.

"Que es?" I asked our guide. "What is it?"

"It's a banana flower, Mama," Rayna said, her eyes wide. She pointed to the thick palm leaves and clusters of green bananas. "He cut it off this tree for me. I'm going to bring it home for show-and-tell!"

"Great idea!" I doubted we'd be able to get this coconut-like object onto the plane, but why disappoint her in this moment of discovery?

"Wanna hold it?" Rayna asked.

"Sure." I took the flower and turned it over, feeling its fleshy firmness.

"El corazón de banana," said the guide, brushing his black hair away from his dark eyes with the back of his hand.

"Banana heart," Johannah interpreted.

Just then, a large iridescent butterfly flew over our heads—a blue morpho. I followed its path until it disappeared into the trees, then turned back to stare at the flower. I felt completely at ease as I contemplated the evidence of life all around me.

The guide led us deeper into the thick, green jungle, chatting with Jonah in broken Spanish and English as I floated behind them. I couldn't see the girls but could hear them chatting and singing somewhere up ahead. Around a narrow corner of the steep mountain path, we came upon a group of workers—ranging from young children to elderly people—sorting coffee beans on the side of the mountain. We greeted each other, smiling shyly and exchanging brief eye contact, then our party continued down the path. At last, we reached a waterfall deep in the jungle. I put my hand on my heart. It was beating hard.

Jonah, Johannah, and Rayna stripped down to their swimsuits and jumped into the falls, screaming and letting the force of the water pound against their backs. Our guide sat on a rock chewing on a leaf while I captured the moment with photos. After my daughters and Jonah had dried off, we grabbed our things and headed back to the farm in single file, our guide pulling up the rear. It was hot, and we were all tired and ready for lunch.

A family of parrots crackled in the distance. The wind rustled through the canopy of trees. Behind me, I heard Rayna making up a story about a snake. She stopped and grabbed a vine hanging high from a tree. "Jonah! Look! It's a snake!"

Jonah laughed, poking her in the stomach.

Johannah and I kept walking. Was that a *hisssssss* in the distance? Probably just the wind in the trees.

Suddenly Jonah screamed, "Snake!"

I whirled around to see he had pushed Rayna hard up the hill, and was standing with her behind his back.

"Snake!" he shouted again.

I followed his gaze and saw he wasn't joking. It was five feet long and seemed poised to strike, inches from where Rayna had been on the path. I took a step toward the snake, then froze. "Don't kill it!" I yelled, just as our guide brought his machete down.

I huddled with my daughters as he continued whacking the dying viper, sweat dripping from his brow. Rayna was shaking, her breathing shallow, so Johannah and I held her, stroking her back as the guide hacked away. Minutes seemed to pass before he stepped back, nodding with satisfaction.

"Can we see it?" I asked, moving toward his sweaty body.

Our guide picked up the bloody yellow-and-black snake with the tip of his machete, its limp body dripping blood. There was a yellow zigzag line along its body.

"What kind of snake is it?" I asked, taking out my iPhone to video the bludgeoned snake. Focused on my filming, I missed his response, so I asked again if the snake was dangerous.

"No hay problema. Serpiente de liga."

"A garter snake, I think," Johannah translated. "Seems like it wasn't poisonous."

"Why'd he kill it, then?"

She shrugged and followed him down the path.

As we continued walking, I tried to interrogate the guide further, but he insisted he had just killed the snake to be on the safe side. I turned it over in my mind, looking at the photos I had taken. I pictured it poised to strike Rayna. Why had I asked to see a snake? Who asks to see a snake in the jungle? And more importantly, how close had my daughter been to death?

When we got back to the hostel, I logged onto the internet to see if I could identify our snake—no luck. It wasn't until later, during a different leg of our trip, when we met a man who recognized the snake from my photos. He told us it was a barba amarilla, one of the most dangerous snakes in the Western Hemisphere, and he shared a chilling story of his wife's near-fatal encounter with one.

I found the Wikipedia page. The barba amarilla, or yellow beard, is an irritable and fast-moving viper, excitable and unpredictable, with a large head it often raises high off the ground. It can eject deadly venom over a distance of six feet in fine jets from the tips of its fangs. It is nocturnal. Meeting one in the middle of the day is highly unlikely. It may have been a mother protecting her eggs.

I couldn't get the snake out of my head—my closest brush with death in many years. On our plane ride home I marveled about my bizarre request for snakes mysteriously answered, our fortunate escape from tragedy. My still body buzzed with adrenaline. I opened the Notes app on my phone and started to write, fingers tapping feverishly on the small keyboard. I described Rayna's body trembling under my hand, the tension in the guide's arm as he brandished the machete, the snake's limp body. Jay's face crossed my mind, his crumpled form. It hit me that, for the first time in my life, I was writing about death.

Eight hours later, we arrived home after midnight. I had typed furiously throughout both of our plane rides and a three-hour bus ride from Chicago, and by the time we reached Madison, I had documented our whole trip.

"How was it?" my husband asked as he drove us home from the

bus stop. In the back seat, Rayna slept while Johannah caught up on texts from her friends.

"Amazing!" I tried to think where to begin, what stories I most wanted to share. Of course he'd be interested to hear about Rayna's near-death experience. What would he think of my newfound passion for writing? But I said, "It was a beautiful trip. We'll tell you all about it tomorrow."

—19—

Write what should not be forgotten.
—Isabel Allende

Four months later, I sat in a cafe with my writing teacher Miriam. We were discussing the prospect of my memoir, an idea I had only recently begun to take seriously.

She sipped her latte, the pattern of a heart made from frothed milk stretching and bending as it passed through her lips. "I think you should study with Natalie Goldberg. Register for one of her writing workshops."

Back home, I googled Natalie Goldberg writing workshops and immediately signed up for "Sit, Walk, Write," my first-ever silent writing retreat. Even as the voices in my head screamed at me for not first organizing childcare, I put my hand on my chest and felt my heart.

From the retreat reading list, I chose *Death in the Afternoon,* by Ernest Hemingway, and ordered it on Amazon. A couple of days later, when my package arrived, I ripped it open and sat down on the rooftop deck of my apartment building, five stories up. I closed my eyes and basked in the sun's warmth on my face.

A memory flashed.

I am thirteen; Jay is nine. We decide to ride our bikes to the Dairy Queen for chocolate-covered vanilla soft-serve cones, a way of saying goodbye before I leave on a school trip.

We race down our street, cross Forster Drive along the Warner Park lagoon. Jay is ahead, as always, even though he's three and a half years younger.

"What'll you do in Mexico?" he asks as I catch up.

"A bullfight."

"Cool! I want to come."

"I could pack you in my suitcase." I imagine hiding him amid my clothes.

"Let's do it!" He throws his hands in the air, his handlebars swiveling slightly. We turn right out of Warner Park and pedal toward Ryan Funeral Home.

"Watch out!" I yell. "You almost crashed into me."

"Sorry." He stands up on his pedals, speeds forward, and heads over a curb.

I follow him, but my bike tire gets wedged in a rut between the sidewalk and the grass and I fly over my handlebars, slamming into the cement below. Shooting pain in my arms. Then Jay's face above me.

"What happened?"

My smashed watch has cut into my wrist. "I don't know."

We head home, missing out on the Dairy Queen cones, blood streaming down my arm.

Thirty-four years later, as if no time had passed, I held Hemingway's novel in hand and gazed at the watch-shaped scar. I had crashed in front of the building where Jay's funeral would be held. The history of that afternoon was embedded in my flesh, and now the memory had returned. I opened the book and began to read. On page two, I read, "I was trying to learn to write, commencing with the simplest things, and one of the simplest things of all and the most fundamental is violent death."

Simple?

I didn't know about that. I put the book down. The image of Jay's mangled corpse on the grass crossed my mind. I didn't know if I was ready to take on the task of describing something so gory, but the hand holding my pen itched to try. Just then my phone pinged with a reminder to pick up my daughters. Violent death would have to wait.

Johannah was eighteen and home from college for the summer. The minute she got in the car, I felt her comfort in being part of the daily activity of the family, and it soothed me. Thrilled to have her sister home, eight-year-old Rayna climbed into the back seat next to her. As we started our drive, the girls leaned into each other, straining against their seat belts, laughing and singing along with Adele to "Rolling in the Deep."

Aligned with all that is family, all that is good and moving forward, I drove past the exit to Seminole Highway.

Then I stopped singing.

To my right, earth and tree branches were strewn about as if a tornado had hit. I slowed to fifty-five, remembering the storms that had come through the previous night.

"Look, girls!" I pointed. "Did a tornado come through here?"

Their heads turned quickly to the right, straining for only a second, until their own interests overcame their momentary curiosity. I looked in my rearview mirror.

"Oh, shit."

Now I had their attention. "What?" they asked.

"Oh, my God."

Even as I drove, the open highway behind my car seemed to widen. Two cars crested the hilly curve behind me, then appeared to pause. I glanced at the girls, who were singing again, their eyes tightly shut, *"Rolling in the Deeeeee-eeep . . ."*

In my rearview mirror, I watched a mother mallard duck lead her brown-and-yellow ducklings onto this stretch of eight-lane highway.

Ten or fifteen baby ducklings, one after the other, now evenly spaced across the entire four eastbound lanes.

Still peering into the rearview mirror, I witnessed a car run over the last two ducklings, scattering their bodies. The mother duck seemed to know instantly. The highway was again empty of cars. I watched as she turned to gather her remaining ducklings, now following her in a circle, back to the side of the highway they'd started from.

Again she began to cross the road. The last ducklings slowed, and the duckling directly behind her sped up, until once again the entire family was equally lined up across the highway. The two cars that had already hit ducklings were now somehow ahead of me.

A wall of cars, semitrucks, school buses, and delivery trucks crested at the hill. Again, each vehicle seemed to pause at the top, the drivers seeing the duck family and wanting to stop, but unable to. When the mother duck had reached the median and was stopped by a concrete barrier, the traffic scattered the entire family into feathers and blood.

I felt sick. I turned down the radio and exited the highway. The universe was showing me something other than the denial of death. Only later, after I had told this story a few times, did I realize the date of the duck massacre: May 27, 2011, the thirtieth anniversary of Jay's death.

—20—

You will be whole again but you will never be the same. Nor
should you be the same nor would you want to.

—Elizabeth Kubler-Ross

I continued to point my attention toward facing death head-on, with a goal of having the deepest relationship possible with its mystery. I attended Death Cafes, unstructured discussion circles for people interested in exploring and processing death. We would meet and drink coffee. Everyone was invited to share freely on any topic related to death and dying. After attending a few meetings, I decided they weren't for me (a little too stiff), but at one of them I learned about an evening workshop: Death 101, taught by Reverend Bodhi Be. I was immediately drawn to the idea of "befriending dying, grieving, and death as allies to deep, sacred living and strong community."

The following Thursday, I showed up at Unity of Madison, a modest, modern brick church. A few minutes late, as usual, I tiptoed into a large sanctuary with pews full of people and found a spot near the back, joining in with the applause as a woman introduced the speaker. A man who looked to be in his fifties walked onstage. His skin was tan and wrinkled, as if he had spent a lot of time in the sun, and his long gray hair was tied in a low ponytail. He began by inviting us to be grateful that we woke up again today, as many did not. I inhaled, focusing on my aliveness.

Bodhi's next words crashed over me like an ocean wave: "I want to invite you to notice death. Death is always with us, everywhere we look."

Around the room, people turned to their right and left. Some were tearing up. The expressions of relief and awe mirrored what I felt.

"We tend to ignore death, or make it something that's out there, over there." He pointed as if referring to some place far away. "But I encourage you to invite death in."

I began to relax.

"Everyone is grieving," Bodhi said. "Everyone has experienced loss. Part of facing death is facing grief."

I saw nods around the room and experienced profound comfort in large-scale mirroring. Maybe the grief I'd felt all these years from losing my brother wasn't weird or outsized. I wished my mother were here.

When Reverend Bodhi Be said, "Does anyone have a story of death that they want to share?" this was my chance, but I couldn't move. There must have been over one hundred people in this room, maybe two hundred! I couldn't remember the last time I had spoken in front of such a large crowd—if ever.

Before I could stop myself, I threw my hand up in the air.

"Please." Bodhi gestured to me.

I tried to keep my voice loud and clear as I summarized the story of Jay's death and premonitions, how I was left alone to grieve, and how I was looking for healing and meaning. Finally I sat down, trembling, staring at my lap. The shame of sharing publicly drowned out all the voices around me until I heard a woman's voice coming from somewhere in the crowd say, "That story she shared about her brother really moved me. So beautiful, so magical."

I craned my neck to see who had spoken, but my view was blocked. Instead I looked up at the high ceiling of the sanctuary and drifted in and out during the reverend's closing words. I felt a residual tightness in my chest. What had I said? Did it make sense? After the applause, people began milling around, a rustle of murmurs filling the large room. I stayed seated, my mind floating high above. A short, pale, friendly man with a beard and a green, yellow, and red yarmulke came over and shook my hand, thanking me for sharing Jay's story.

"You're welcome," I said shyly.

"I agree with what Julie said," he continued. "The way you told it was so moving."

"Who?"

"Oh, Julie's the woman who just spoke at the end." He pointed at a small cluster of people deep in conversation.

I felt a flutter of excitement. "Which one is she?"

"Come on." He led me toward them. "That's her," he said, pointing to an older white woman who looked to be in her seventies, wearing a pastel floral shirt.

At first, I stood awkwardly outside the circle, waiting to be noticed. When one of the women looked at me, I spoke. "Excuse me."

All eyes were on me again. Something awakened along the edges of my bones. I narrowed in on Julie. "Can you tell me why my story moved you?" Like a movie on fast-forward, the sensation sped along my neurons. *I shouldn't have said anything.*

Then Julie smiled. "Hi!"

I was able to take a deep breath. Julie sat on a beige metal folding chair between two other women. She had long, gray-blond hair and merry blue eyes.

"Thank you so much for what you shared," Julie said.

"Thank *you*," I responded. "If you don't mind, what did you like about it?"

"Well," she began, "I was sitting here, feeling all the pressure I put on myself, picturing that my death would come before I did many, many things that I thought I should do."

I nodded, familiar with such concerns.

"When I heard the story of how your brother was at peace with dying so young, I started to think that maybe I've been too fixated on what I haven't done. Clearly your brother . . ." she raised her eyebrows.

"Jay."

"Jay. Clearly Jay can't have made this up. He knew what most of us do not: that we are perfect as we are, no matter how messed up we may be."

I started to feel goosebumps on my arms.

"This story is so important, so magical. It's just healing, you know?"

I nodded again, beaming at her.

"So keep telling that story. Tell it over and over again."

"Thank you," I said. "I'm actually thinking of writing a memoir about it." I felt my cheeks burn.

Her smile broadened. "That's great!"

"For so long, I've been afraid to talk about Jay's death. I've felt totally shut down and abandoned by my mom and by anyone else I might have grieved with." I looked at my feet.

"But look at you now," Julie gestured around us. "Look at all the people you've connected to!" I felt her tossing me a life jacket.

"You're right!" I said.

"You've come so far! And you have a ways to go, probably. I don't think you are going to die before you write this."

"I hope not," I laughed.

"And Jay's on your side." She laughed, too, but her eyes were solemn.

"I hope so."

"He's given you a gift. You had to feel both sides, or it wouldn't be any use to you."

"Right," I said, still somewhat unclear.

Julie patted my arm. "I'm grateful to have met you."

I grabbed her hand. "You too, Julie! Thank you."

We parted ways and I walked out of the church, my body buzzing with possibility. I wrestled with the contradiction of a loss becoming a gift. The argument played out internally:

I paid such a heavy price, but maybe it was worth it?

No! I would rather have my brother than spiritual enlightenment!

But it wasn't your choice.

Do you really believe that?

I believe in Jay. I believe in his life, in his story. I believe death can be more than trauma.

At that moment, a memory eclipsed my inner dialogue, so strong and clear that I couldn't believe I hadn't thought of it in over thirty years.

I am seventeen. My brother is dead. It feels difficult to breathe, as if I'm in a cave with no air.

My friends take me to Devil's Lake State Park to get stoned, climb boulders, and swim in the lake. I stare at the ancient rock outcrops. A friend says, "Kris," and I burst into tears. I don't want to swim. I'm afraid I'll close my eyes under water. Every time I close them I see Jay's head, bloody and swollen. I keep them open, inspecting the boulders that form the valley.

"The water's great!" one of my friends calls to me. "If you get tired of staring at rocks, come find us!"

I no longer see rock. I can see 1.6 billion years of sand being compressed by water, heat, and gravity. I imagine the glacier that passed through here, rerouting ancient rivers and depositing dams of earth at the two open ends of the Devil's Lake Gap.

A rumble begins in the distance, a train on the tracks below me. My losses pour back into my body like sour whiskey, and the pain throbs. I feel poisoned. From my perch on a boulder, I crane my neck, smelling juniper on the air. I run to the start of Balanced Rock Trail, a steep, boulder-strewn five-hundred-foot climb to the top of the quartzite bluffs. I take off my shoes and socks and watch a green dragonfly hover over a batch of jewelweed flowering blood orange. Barefoot, I head up the narrow rock path built into the side of the boulder-strewn hillside like a long, winding staircase.

The soles of my feet meet smooth stones and I worry I might slip. But my toes grip the ground and send strength throughout my whole body. The screaming emptiness quiets when I notice how the sparkling sun quilts the rocks in patches of amber, red, yellow, and orange. I stop and pick up dead pine needles with my toes, grab a handful, and toss them over the sheer edge. I want to jump.

How did Jay know he would die?

I reach the last part of the path that rises to the top of the bluff. Through the cool, worn stone, I sense the footfalls of thousands of others who have journeyed this path. Crows fly over the black waves below me. For a moment, I hear a million voices telling their stories. I lower my body, stretching out on a rock that's been warmed by hours of sunlight. I want to be closer to the voices. I let the sunshine burrow into my face.

A man comes by, bursts into laughter, and says, "With that purple sweatshirt, you blend right into these rocks."

Without knowing it, this man gives me permission to be ancient, to be rock.

Can I live forever?

Two turkey vultures drift overhead, hungry and patient. I remember a dead raccoon in the road on the drive to the park. In my mind, the bloody animal morphs into a dead boy, red and glistening. I shake the image away and stand to walk toward a stretch of giant boulders hanging on the edge of even larger boulders. As I climb higher, I marvel at the ancient balance of purple-gray rocks, carpeted with greenish-white lichen. I study the patience of the path and the hundreds of boulders that create the bowl to hold the lake far below.

A blue jay shoots up out of a rock as purple as the darkening hue at the bottom of a rainbow.

I study the weight of my grief by taking the stone into my heart. I hear the far-off voices of people laughing and splashing in the lake. Something both old and immortal inside myself, beyond me and beyond death, works its way toward the steadiness of these rocks. I study a fly, its boldness, its ability to alight, come and go, and leave me behind. I listen to the flies' conversation. Voices break into my experience.

Man: "We're almost there!"

Woman: "You sure?"

Man: "Yes, you are doing a good job."

Woman: "I'm scared!"

Man: "I've got your back."

Not noticing me where I'm standing, they continue to the top, huffing loudly. Clouds stand like snow-covered mountaintops above the southern ridge of the bluffs. I long for someone to say to me: *I've got your back.*

I peer closely at a few rocks that are fully clothed with dirty lime-green lichen. Green and gold sweat bees land on my arms. I flick them off. I hike upward again, touching the soft, white bark of the birch trees, trying to engage in a process of making meaning without a brother.

I study silence and its interruption. The breeze through the trees . . . The voices rising and falling . . . The distant roar of a motorcycle muffler . . . A tongue-loose dog panting up the rocky trail . . . The "Whoa, that's slippery!" from someone coming down the trail. "Be a long way down if you slipped." Laughter.

I look out over the edge. Vultures soar in circles against a blue sky, defying the gravity that for me is deadly.

I reach the top of the East Bluff and stare off the cliff. The wide-open space again calls to me. I step closer to the edge, dangle one foot. I want to die. Instead, I become the turkey vulture.

As I fly over the lake, my eye is drawn to the changing blue of the water—navy to white to brown to black—and the wind rippling across. When the wind eases, the lake becomes smooth, then puckered again. The temporary patterns on the water mirror the seemingly permanent patterns on the stones. I learn the lake as a She, as a mother I do not understand, as a god of the open future. Staring at the water feels like watching an ancient sea. I hear poetry rising off the waves in sprays.

Someone passing by calls out, "Is it easier to go barefoot?"

I step back from the edge.

I close my eyes until the retreating footsteps have faded. I stretch out my toes, take one step, then another. I feel every pebble, every speck; the contrast between rock, pine needles, sand. Then I start back down the path, my awareness still in the soles of my feet. The ground shifts: one step on smooth stone, the next rough sand, followed by cool dirt. I move slowly, steadily, muscles prepared for sharp or uneven ground.

Sweaty and fatigued, I reach the bottom. I see my friends lying on their towels beneath a white pine, laughing, wet from the lake. I think about how the trees found themselves a home here after the glacier melted. Each moment goes on forever.

I beg for the courage of this place to stay with me as I throw off my clothes and wade into the cold water.

—21—

Death is when you become the world.
—Bernardo Kastrup

During this time of increased exploration of death, the universe sent me Denise.

We met in 2011. While attending the art opening of a friend, I was introduced to a stocky Latina woman with spiky gray hair and deep brown eyes. We spoke for a few minutes, though I remember nothing that was said. I was busy trying not to lose myself in the depth of her eyes. I continued circling the room, looking at the quilts hung on the walls, but the whole time I felt eyes watching me. I chanced a glance around the room, but the woman was nowhere to be seen. I looked back to the quilt in front of me, the largest in the room. It was divided into four quadrants, each containing a quarter of a circle. The quarters came together in the center like slices of pie. The result was a series of concentric circles in a variety of bright, hand-dyed fabrics. In one quarter of a circle the fabric had been dyed to convey a yellow sun in a blue sky.

I don't know how long I stood there, but when I looked away, the gallery was noticeably less crowded. Only a few individuals still meandered around, and I noticed my friend had begun cleaning up.

I went to the kitchen to see if I could help and found myself by the sink with the brown-eyed woman. She was washing dishes.

"I'm Kris," I said, approaching her side. "What's your name again?"

"Denise," she said, smiling. This time I let myself fall into those dark pools. She did not look away. As we gazed, I felt a train of thought flowing between us: *Who am I? What is love?*

Then another voice interrupted this exchange: *Jay is dead.* I looked around to see who could have spoken and immediately realized that the voice belonged to Jan Anderson, back in 1981, calling me to tell me the news.

My mind frozen, I turned toward the sink, washed a wineglass under the steaming-hot water. Denise walked away silently and came back with forks and more wineglasses. I grabbed the dish soap and squirted it into the sink where bubbles erupted instantly. *This woman is going to change my life*, I thought with a rush.

On the first night we hung out, I learned that Denise had recently followed a message from a dream telling her to move to Madison. She had had many versions of this dream over the past few years, a dream wherein she was a Native American man, riding a horse, leading a large group of people behind her. The fact that the dream kept coming back made it significant, but the thing that haunted her was the quality of the light and shadows. As she later described to me, "The shadows were in the wrong place." The dream kept her up at night, and she had taken to swirling a flashlight around her dark room, trying to duplicate the shadows she had seen while asleep. From this shadow play, she formed a conclusion: she was being called to go northeast. She lived in Austin but had a friend in Madison (the fabric artist who made the quilts) who would be able to connect her to the metalworking community here.

"It was a bit impulsive, perhaps, but I felt like the universe was pulling me here." She looked up and I felt goosebumps along my arms and legs. "What about you, what's your story?"

I told her about growing up in Madison. I talked about my children and explained the current situation with my ex-husband. "Things got complicated. We were separated for a while and then earlier this year we tried to make it work again. We had been together over fifteen years, I think our souls had to finish the journey they were on together, and it took me a while to get clarity on that."

Denise nodded. "So that journey is done then?"

I smiled at her directness. "Yes. I made a decision to focus on my inner life. I wasn't able to access that depth with him." For years we'd been stuck in a stale, dusty rut, and I sought a rushing river. Gazing into Denise's eyes was like plunging into that freezing water.

"Want a strawberry?" I asked, a bit self-conscious at how much I had revealed. I got up and walked to the refrigerator.

Denise finished her last bite of dinner and wiped her lips with her napkin. "Sure," she said. "But just one, I'm stuffed."

I opened the refrigerator door and reached for the bowl of fresh berries. I picked out two of the prettiest ones, rinsed them, and handed one to her. As I watched her mouth close around the red fruit, I took a bite, savoring the sweet, cool flesh. I became mesmerized, and before I realized it I was speaking.

"I don't want to die." That's what I had said. I swallowed the strawberry, unsure what had prompted those words.

The next thing I knew, Denise had gotten up from the table and walked over to where I stood by the sink. "Death isn't something to fear," she said lightly, picking another strawberry from the bowl.

"How do you know?"

She moved closer and I thought she might kiss me, but she reached past me to rinse off her berry. As the water flowed over her hand, the berry gleamed and her hand seemed to disappear as it mixed with water and light.

I looked up to find her staring into my eyes, and I felt like she could see past my skin, way back through my memories and DNA to my ancestors.

"How do you know?" I said again, in a whisper.

"I know because I've died before."

Shocked into silence, I picked up another strawberry and held it under the faucet, feeling the cold water rush over my fingers. In that moment, I felt loosened from the arrow of time.

F. Scott Fitzgerald could have been writing our love story when he said, "They slipped briskly into an intimacy from which they never recovered." Anchored by the gravity of our connection, I luxuriated in Denise's willingness to share spiritual and emotional depth. Before long, we were spending every moment together and sending romantic texts and emails when we were apart.

One night, a few months into dating, we were taking a bath together at my apartment. As Denise rubbed my back with a bar of soap, it slipped through her fingers and splashed into the water beside me. I could feel her hand fumbling for it under the water as she said, "I don't have any more money to pay my rent."

"What does that mean?"

"Well . . ." She paused in her search for the soap and looked up at me, her frown a slash of pain across her face.

"No!" I said. "You can't go back to Texas!"

"I don't know what else to do," she said. "I haven't been able to find work here."

"Move in with me and Rayna!" The words were out before I even thought about them. I dug the soap from beneath my thigh. "I mean"—I held it out—"if you want to. You know, until you figure something else out."

A smile slowly spread across her face, warming my naked skin like the sun.

"Are there any smells?" I asked Denise one night as we lay in bed.

She laughed. "What do you mean?"

"You know, does death smell like anything?"

"No."

"Well, were there any sounds?"

She laughed again. "These are silly questions, you know."

"I want to write about death."

"The only sound I heard was when my life went backward, like an old-fashioned tape recorder rewinding."

"What?"

"I heard the tape rewind, and on the tape was my life, in reverse." She lay on the bed on her right side, half covered with a white sheet, head propped on one arm.

"Really?"

"Yep. And then I heard, 'This is how you are going to die.'"

I shivered. "Are you okay if I put your story in my memoir?"

"I think that would be great."

"Okay, tell me again." I burrowed into her chest, looking down at our arms and noticing the gold color of my freckled skin next to the warm, darker brown of hers.

"What is this, the fourth time I've told you this story?"

I laughed. "You mean the eighth or twelfth?"

"Yeah." Her eyes closed as I kissed her. "Every time I tell you the story I figure out a little bit more."

I beamed with the knowledge that I was one of two people who knew the story of her near-death experience. "You could tell me this story every day and I'd never get sick of it." I continued kissing her as

I spoke, my lips following the geography of her jaw, then her ear, my hand caressing her hair.

"How come?" She opened her eyes.

We fell into silence.

"Why do you like it?" she repeated. "I don't get it."

"Oh, baby. You died and came back to tell us about it. You experienced the continuity of consciousness."

She kissed me. "Okay." She licked her lips. "It was New Year's Eve, 1986 . . ."

Denise was twenty-seven and worked as a welder and pump mechanic at the municipal wastewater treatment plant. That night it was her turn to change the two-ton chlorine cylinders.

"I should've called in sick," she said with a chuckle. "But I had used up all my time off skiing in Colorado."

When she arrived at the chlorine building, she found to her surprise that the large sliding doors were jammed open. Since the room had to be warm for the chlorine to work properly, the workers from the last shift had rigged a canvas sheet across the doorway. In order to access the hoist that lifted the chlorine cylinders, she had to remove the canvas, which was hooked to the beam where the hoist traveled. She needed to climb a twelve-foot ladder to access the beam and then reach past the wire that ran the hoist—a live wire carrying 880 volts.

"It was a stupid-ass thing to do in the dark," Denise said—the same thing she said every time she told the story.

Milliseconds before she touched the wire, she knew it was a mistake. *YOU ARE GOING TO BE ELECTROCUTED*, her brain screamed, seemingly in slow motion. As her pinky touched the wire, her eyes rolled back and her jaw clenched.

"There was a struggle between my body and the current. Then I went out of my body—that was when my mind rewound. I saw my mother, my whole childhood. That's when the voice said, 'Oh, so this is how you are going to die.'"

I pressed my body against hers.

"But then another voice said, 'Wait a minute. Is there a way out?'" Her eyes looked far into the distance and her voice grew soft. "I think it was that question, that voice, that saved me—the universe really likes questions, you know."

"Whose voice was it?" I asked.

"It seemed that the question came from a place," Denise pondered, as she had several times before, "a *Below*, from the earth, from where I had come from. It was my voice but it didn't come from me."

I squeezed her hand, itching to write it all down.

"This isn't really how it was, but it's the best I can do . . . Okay, imagine this. It's as if this big computer screen was above me—grids of light against a black sky. A red dot appeared on the grid right after the question arose. My awareness went to the red dot and clicked on it, as you would with a computer mouse. Awareness did it all. It was me but it wasn't me. I clicked on the red dot and a voice said—to the body that was being electrocuted, to the soul that was leaving the body—*relax the knee*. That voice was not me. I am not sure what that voice was, but I think it was God."

I loved when she talked about God.

"And then I came back, and everything had changed." She closed her eyes, brow furrowed in concentration. "I felt like hell. Everything seemed so heavy and there was a burnt taste in my mouth. I heard a beeping noise. I opened my eyes and I was in the hospital."

She was told she shouldn't have survived, that it wasn't possible with the intensity of the current. "I had an entrance wound on my finger and an exit wound on my foot, where the current went in and out of my body," she said. "They were really bad burns. And apparently I was incredibly fortunate that the current missed my spinal cord, or any vital organs. I shoulda been a goner." She opened her eyes to stare at me and continued. "But the voice—call it God, call it the universe—that voice saved me."

I felt tingling all over my body.

Here was further confirmation that death could bring more than pain, that it could bring me to the guts of truth, to radical transformation.

In 2012 I wrote almost every day, about God and death and mystery. I contacted people from childhood and continued to unearth memories of Jay. The more I searched, the more questions arose. I mapped a path through the past that wound toward my present. I became an archeologist of my own mind, and contemplative writing was my trowel and brush.

—22—

They share a lot, astronomy and childhood. Both are voyages across huge distances. Both search for facts beyond their grasp. Both theorize wildly and let possibilities multiply without limits. Both are humbled every few weeks. Both operate out of ignorance. Both are mystified by time. Both are forever starting out.
—Richard Powers, *Bewilderment*

I was three when Jay was born. I remember watching him sleep in his car seat in the living room, nestled under a pale blue blanket. The afternoon sun slanted through the big picture window, catching the dust motes that floated around him like glitter. I thought Jay brought the dust. In my mind, Jay was a magnet that the whole world—my mom, Dick, the sun—revolved around. He pulled us in.

Mom had met Dick in a bar when I was two. She liked him. I didn't scream when I met him, which was unheard of for me. After my mom and I had returned from Virginia, I screamed anytime a man came near me. I screamed when mailmen came to our door. I screamed as Mom wheeled me along the aisles of the grocery store past men shopping for Frosted Flakes. I feared men coming near me, feared they would slap me and my mother, throw things at us.

But not Dick. So Mom married him. For the rest of her life, when she told the story, I was the person who picked her second husband.

Dick wore stained white T-shirts. He would sit in an orange-and-green flowered chair in the green-shag-carpeted living room of his house on the edge of the Warner Park marsh where he invited my mom and me to move in with him. He'd set his cigarettes down in the groove of the green glass ashtray that by the end of every evening was leveled with crumpled butts. Dick favored Huber beer. He bought tall, brown bottles—forties—by the case, and I can still picture the labels, covered in condensation.

I never heard the story about "picking" my mother's mate until I was older, and as an adult, I've come to understand its absurdity, but I've also begun to consider that it may hold a shred of truth. I can't say why I didn't cry when I met Dick, but I know that he played an important role in my life: for eleven years, the better part of my childhood, Dick was Dad, the only dad I knew. Mom and I had a family, a structure. For a while, there was less violence too. And without Dick, we wouldn't have had Jay, the glue that held us all together.

Jay was beautiful, almost angelic. He had blond hair and big brown eyes, and he didn't scream when our mom was gone like I did. After he was born, Mom went back to the hospital and didn't come home again for a few weeks. Unbeknownst to me, she'd been sick and had almost died of a blood infection in the ICU. They removed her uterus. Dick's mom, Hulda Puttkamer, came to care for us. She taught me to love warm coffee and milk. It tasted like my mother.

There's a photo from that era of Dick and Carol and their new baby. It's dated November 1967, when I was three and a half years old.

I study the aging photo, the postures of my twenty-three-year-old mother and her new husband, leaning against a 1965 yellow Ford Galaxie. Dick is holding my brother, Jay Phillip, swaddled in a white blanket crocheted by Grandma Winslow. In the pocket of Dick's light burgundy T-shirt is an open pack of Camels. On his tan face is a huge grin, framed by his equally huge ears. My mother gazes down at her sleeping son, a deep adoration apparent in her smile.

I know what she felt.

I can still picture Jay as a boy, tilting his head, letting his long blond bangs fall away from his eyes. Mom and I loved everything about Jay.

By marrying Jay's dad, my mom had given us a home. Even Grandma Winslow began to accept her daughter again. They now had things to chat about—gardening, pot roasts, cleaning products. Before that, there had been no discussions about the Budweiser keg incident, the roar of laughter from the drunken sailors, the shame of leaving my father.

Jay was my mom's salvation, her ticket to stability. In the morning, she first found her glasses, then her black coffee, and then her smile. Once she had these in place, she'd sit awhile on Jay's dark blue bedspread and watch him sleep, his heavy breathing rustling his bangs.

I remember passing by the room as I got ready for high school. I could see the love in her gaze. I would already be mostly done brushing my teeth by the time she finally, reluctantly, stirred him awake.

In one of my earliest memories, I am five years old, sitting at the dinner table. Jay babbles in his high chair. Mama walks around the dining room table serving gravy from a skillet. I watch as Dad presses his spoon into his mashed potatoes, making a crater to receive the made-from-scratch gravy. I follow Dad's motions, pressing my spoon just deep enough so the gravy won't leak out. This is one of our favorite meals: turkey, green beans, mashed potatoes and gravy. I don't want to waste a drop. I still always feel hungry, even after eating. As I pull my spoon out of the potatoes so my mom can ladle out the steaming gravy for me, she stumbles and the boiling drippings of gravy flow like lava down my back.

Mama plunges me in a tub of cold water, with my clothes on. Dad is yelling at her to pull off my clothes. She lifts up my shirt but it sticks to my back. She stops.

"Take it off!" he yells again.

"The skin will rip!" my mom screams. I can hear two-year-old Jay crying, still in his high chair in the kitchen. I imagine him with mashed potatoes covering his face. I imagine Dick's furious mouth and ruddy cheeks, barking orders at my mother. I see her frightened eyes, feel her urgent hands tugging. Now my flesh is leaving.

As my mom lifts my shirt, I feel that she lifts me all the way to the sky—the ceiling of the bathroom is sky, birds, clouds—and then drops me toward the water. When I hit the water, it is not her hands holding me but the hands of the sky. Time slows. I watch my breathing. Gently, the hands drop my big toe into the water. A ring of circles radiates out into the tub, and I can observe other things besides the searing pain of my back, besides my parents' anger. I can observe something that holds me tenderly, with only my big toe in the water; the circles expanding; the infinite waves. For a moment, I am only waves.

Then a metallic taste returns to my mouth and I am screaming again, immersed deep in my burning body, in skin and bones and ice water, looking into the missing eyes of Mama. Where is my Big Bird shirt?

The next day, while Dad is at work, my mom removes the back of a chair so I can sit without screaming.

When Dad gets home, he yells at Mama for ruining the chair. I have to wear a shirt with the back cut out for three weeks. My mom moves my special chair between the dinner table and our television. Watching *Sesame Street* and *Mr. Rogers*, I concentrate on keeping my attention out of my body. My back throbs, but I keep my tears inside so no one will yell at me.

My mom was never able to put the chair back together, and Dick never forgave her for wasting his money.

I am eight. I hear a hairball arise in my cat's throat, then turn to watch as the soft, brown Siamese hacks in the sunshine. Jay, five years old, pushes his Tonka dump truck on the shag carpet, running over the plastic green army men, moving toward the cat. The day before, her claw brought blood to Jay's small hand. I see the scab from the wound as he throws the green army men into the back of the truck. I hear a clatter as my mom starts the dishes. I know that they must be cleaned or there will be a fight. It is Saturday morning—usually a bad morning. Later there will be card playing and more dirty dishes from Dad and his friends.

I look outside. I see falling yellow leaves and hear my mom turn off the kitchen faucet. I leave the house, quietly closing the screen door, stopping on the porch. I look up, see a water droplet hanging on the gutter, glistening against the crisp, blue September sky.

A drop falls on my forehead, and I touch it with my finger, examining it. I see wet. I see water attach itself to me. I touch my wet finger to my nose. I feel connected to something. I skip down the quiet street, cross the road, and sit at the edge of the lagoon. My fingers search the dew-drenched grass, finding a small, smooth, black pebble. I lift the pebble over my head. A chickadee sings "chick-a-dee-dee-dee," and I put the pebble in my pocket for another time. I feel desired, like the whole world wants me. I feel my body is the same as the grass. I stand up from the shore's edge and head back home.

It was almost my tenth birthday. Jay and I were riding to the liquor store in Dad's blue Ford truck with the white camper on the back—he was out of beer. Instead of focusing my attention on Dad's drunk swerving, I focused on how the motion made things around me seem to blur. When I looked back at Dad, he had parked in front of the liquor store. Jay and I ran into the fish store next door.

"Look, Jay!" I pointed to the long-finned, silver angelfish gliding through the water.

"How do they float like that?" he asked.

"How do they breathe under water?" I pointed to blue neon tetras.

Driving away from the liquor store, Dad cracked a cold one, ran a red light, and drove up onto a lawn. What would his boss at work think? Jay and I begged to be let out of the truck, but Dad refused, waving his beer, the gold liquid spilling onto Jay's bare legs. When we did arrive home, we ran to Jay's room and watched three episodes of *Gilligan's Island*, waiting until Mom got home from work. When we heard her car pull in the driveway, we shut off the TV and crept down the hall toward the living room.

Dad sat slouched in his chair in front of the TV, his expression vacant. He didn't look up when my mom walked in the front door and crossed to the kitchen, where Jay and I waited for her.

"What's the matter?" she asked, seeing our wide eyes.

"Dad ran a red light and almost crashed!" Jay blurted out before I could stop him.

Mom looked at me for confirmation and I nodded.

"What the fuck are you talking about?" Dad thundered. "You little shits made that up." He looked at my mom. "They're trying to turn you against me!"

Mom pressed her lips together in a thin line and said nothing, turning toward the kitchen to start dinner. As she began to chop broccoli, Dad lurched into the kitchen bellowing, his face red, spit flying from his mouth. Jay and I cowered in a corner, but my mother ignored him, continuing her dinner prep. Perhaps she forced the knife blade through the broccoli with greater force now.

The phone rang, and my mom picked up the receiver. Dad grabbed the green handle of the phone from her hand, slamming it back into the cradle. She lifted the knife above her head, facing his back. As he turned, so did she, returning to her place at the cutting board.

Dad eventually yelled himself hoarse and passed out on the couch, and the three of us ate our chicken, rice, and broccoli in silence. Then Jay and I put ourselves to bed. I fell asleep watching fish chase each other around across my eyelids and longing for my own tank, with blue and red neon tetras, black and silver marble angelfish, and sucker fish that keep the algae off glass and pebbles and plants.

I was twelve. Jay and I were playing TV tag outside with some neighbors, while Mom sat in her favorite orange paisley armchair, smoking and reading her mystery novel. I never interrupted her when she sat in that chair. But that day as I passed her on my way to the bathroom, she asked me to sit down. I paused. I didn't want to sit down. I wanted to pee. But I knew better than to argue, so I stood, watching as my mom carefully inserted her bookmark, set down the book, and snuffed out her cigarette. Then she motioned toward the matching orange chair across the coffee table from her. Squeezing my legs together, I perched on the edge of the chair, watching Mom light up a Virginia Slim. She took a long drag, seemingly oblivious of me sitting with my jiggling legs, wishing I could go.

Finally, she said, "I am leaving Dick." She was crying. Or I was crying. Smoke rose from her cigarette, sitting in the crowded ashtray.

"I hate him," was all I could say.

"Anyway," she said, "Dick isn't your father."

I did not know how to feel. Time stopped. She kept talking, telling me the story of when I picked Dick as a two-year-old. I looked out the front window. I saw Jay and the neighbor kids in our driveway, stacking up discarded pieces of cut wood. They had moved on from tag and were trying to build a ramp for their dirt bikes.

"Is he Jay's father?"

"Yes. He is Jay's father." She picked up the newspaper. "You picked him. Now go outside and play."

I did as I was told.

Anyway, Dick isn't your father. The words echoed inside my head. The next day, I kept flashing on a vision of tractors and cow pies and myself sitting on a rock in a pasture. I could make out my Grandpa Philip driving a tractor along the pasture fence, turning over the hard spring soil, howling out poetry over the tractor engine rumblings.

Who was my father? Who did I hate and who did I love? Who loved me?

A dusty, cold wind was blowing through the house, telling its own story. I couldn't stop shivering. Gone was the incessant stream of yelling, its place filled by the silent shockwaves of divorce. Jay, Mom, and I found ourselves not knowing who we were. We sat deep in our chairs, staring at the dinner table as if it were a hot, dry summer's bullfighting ring. A space between us had been lost and our only language was silence.

Dick and Mom had gone to court, and all four of us had to be interviewed. I told the truth, motivated by the terror of losing my mom. When the courts ordered Mom to stay in our home with Jay and me and for Dick to move out of his house, sadness washed against me like an angry ocean.

I could see that Dick did his best. I weighed both sides as carefully as a twelve-year-old could. My heart told me it mattered that Dick was broken, that he was losing his family and his home.

Reality with Dick as Dad had been built up like layers of sedimentary rock, had been collected as parts of me and, through the pressure of our home environment, become denser, more compact. Now that Dick was gone, I was cracking open. I saw how Dick's goodness had lived side by side with his rage and dominance.

For weeks after he left, everything reminded me of him. I saw his smiling brown eyes as he won at euchre, or as he sang "Happy Birthday" to Jay on his ninth birthday, or when I delivered him that last beer. I remembered our family camping trip when I was eleven, and how he always gave me his last marshmallow. I remembered the pride in his eyes when he brought me and Jay to work and introduced us to his coworkers. I missed existing through his eyes; when he left, a part of me disappeared with him.

Simmering on the stove, my mom's homemade pasta sauce sent pillowy clouds into the slants of late-afternoon sun. I breathed in the smells of fresh-picked tomatoes and oregano as I set the table, comforted by the soft sounds of my mother humming and bustling around the stove. Jay hunched over a math worksheet at our round wooden dining table.

I watched the steam rise around my mom, a sense of calm moving through my body. I observed my family locating the new steady ground of our lives. *We're gonna be okay.*

"Mom?" Jay asked.

"Uh-huh?" She dropped spaghetti noodles into the pot of water boiling on the stove.

Jay pushed his pencil across the paper. "I had a dream last night."

"Yeah? What was it about?" Chopping broccoli, she nicked her finger. "Ugh!"

"Are you okay?" Jay asked.

"Yeah. I just cut myself a little." She sucked her finger. "What was your dream about?"

I finished setting the table and sat down in one of the four floral-patterned vinyl chairs. Dick had taken the other table and chairs to his new place, but I didn't mind. I felt better sitting on flowers.

"I'm riding my bike." Jay shifted in his seat, lifting his pencil above his head, and turned to watch Mom.

She dropped the broccoli into the steamer, stirred the spaghetti, and turned down the flame on the bubbling pasta sauce. Jay just watched her juggling the many cooking tasks. His soft eyes gazed in rapture, following her every graceful move.

Then he sniffed and started again. "I'm riding my bike and a green car is chasing me." Jay paused and so did my mom, wiping her hands on her apron and surveying the state of the meal.

"That sounds scary," she said absentmindedly.

"That's how I'm going to die," Jay finished.

My mom pulled three white plates from the cupboard and handed them to me. Other than the frown that settled onto her face, I saw no indication she had heard him. I wanted to speak, but after many such conversations, I had learned to be quiet. My mom dished out the pasta and the sauce, and while we ate I watched the sunlight, hoping I wasn't wrong about the steady ground.

—23—

Consciousness is a kind of weird presence that is human and not human at the same time. Consciousness is cosmic.
—Jeffrey Kripal

On the thirtieth anniversary of Jay's death, I posted a picture of him on my Facebook page with the caption, *I miss you, Jay.* One of the comments was from Michael Hahm, a classmate of Jay's: *Thank you for sharing. I still love him so very much. I think I will probably think of Jay at my own passing. And when I do, I will smile.*

I replied to his comment: *Michael! Good to hear from you! Please feel free to send me any other memories of Jay or the day of his death, I'm working on a book about him.*

Michael was generous with his response, telling in great detail his experience of that day. *One of the guys invited me along to skip school that afternoon. I was very flattered, shocked that they invited me—eighth graders are fickle, and I didn't think Kurt liked me much. Jay and I had been close in the past but had drifted apart. I felt that by going, I would have been part of the "cool" group, but I was petrified of skipping school.*

Instead, Michael had spent the afternoon daydreaming about how much fun they must have been having. By the end of the day, rumors had begun to circulate about Jay and an accident. *Something had happened and it did not sound good,* Michael wrote. *I went home heavy.* Later that night, Michael and his parents sat down to eat, watching their small TV in the kitchen as newscaster Rick Featherstone began the evening news: "A tragic accident today on Madison's north side. Jay Amelong was killed . . ."

"OH, JAY!" Michael had screamed, bursting into tears. *I just bawled for an hour. My family was dumbfounded at how to handle me.*

The next day, as Michael tells it, the halls of Jay's middle school were filled with weeping children. Jay had been universally loved, and the entire school was riddled with grief. The girls were vocal, howling and sobbing, while the boys were mostly quiet. Kurt, who had witnessed the accident, was the quietest of all. He kept to himself the whole day, a dull, ghostly expression on his pale face. School let out early—the teachers and principals were ill-equipped to deal with the inconsolable students. That evening, some of the students who'd been closest to Jay walked down to Cherokee to gather at a classmate's house.

The parents offered the group snacks and drinks, trying to wait on the eighth graders as the children did their best to digest Jay's death. They played games and someone brought out a stereo and put on "Stairway to Heaven."

It was a day of humility, Michael wrote. *Everyone was reduced to a numb blankness.*

The kids had gathered a stack of newspapers from that morning, with Jay's broken body on the front page, and they burned them in the fireplace. They discussed the upcoming eighth grade end-of-year dance, deciding on the spot that "Stairway to Heaven" should be the theme song. They knew Jay loved the song but couldn't have known that he had requested it for his funeral.

Michael's concluding thoughts brought tears to my eyes: *It remains an indelible event that made a profound mark on my life. It really did rock me to my core. I will always love Jay Amelong and I will likely always feel a measure of sadness when I think of him. It's so funny how so many people say "reliving" the past is futile. I am finding more and more that going back offers a sublime opportunity to heal. You know, I can picture that beautiful boy's face as clearly as I can my wife's and my children's. I really can.*

I composed a response: *Thank you so much for sharing, Michael, I so appreciate these memories! If you have contact with anyone else from that time, please tell them to get in touch.*

A few days later, I got a Facebook message from Billy Essling.

> *Kristina,*
>
> *Mike Hahm told me that you were writing a story about Jay and his passing. Kurt, Jay, and myself were together on the day of his death. I'm not sure if you have talked to Kurt Smith yet? I haven't spoken to him in years, but I remember the day well enough, even with years of trying my best to forget it.*
>
> *Billy*

My stomach dropped. This was closer than I'd ever been to the story of Jay's last day. It was too bad Billy didn't have contact with Kurt, but this was the next-best thing! I invited him to share as much as he wanted. One month later, he sent me several paragraphs of his memories. This is his story:

It was a gorgeous day in May, seventy-two degrees and sunny. Billy and Kurt helped Jay hatch a plan to ditch. *We were crafty little delinquents,* Billy said. *Since we were only in eighth grade, our hooligan skills weren't fully developed, but practice makes perfect and we practiced every chance we got.*

It just so happened that the hour they wanted to miss was the hour when Diane Zenze, teacher's pet, was responsible for handing in the attendance slips to the office. *She had a crush on Kurt, so we coerced her into scratching our names off the attendance slips so that it wouldn't appear that we were missing that last period,* Billy wrote. *It all came together so nicely, as if it were meant to be. If only we could have known.*

Jay, Kurt, and Billy ran to their bikes, fearful of being stopped by their middle school principal but glowing with their freedom. Lilac trees rustled as they whizzed up Esch Lane—Jay in front, Kurt in the middle, Billy pulling up the rear—lavender petals showering their heads with sweet smells. Up and up they pedaled, heads down, legs pumping, hair flying, outstretched hands tapping every blooming tree they passed.

Jay took them over curb jumps, down U-shaped driveways, through a backyard—any opportunity to defy gravity or to provoke someone to chase them with a broom. The boys lived for risk; they needed it as a pack. Fast, daring moves strengthened their unique bond, offered them a sense of power, fed their imaginations with the thrill of flight. Any pedestrians or cars they passed provided added obstacles, heightened precarity; quick saves were always followed by floods of adrenaline.

Atop Sanitarium Hill, the second highest in the county, they paused to admire the sun glistening off the Warner Park lagoon. Then they took off down the other side, swerving back and forth in lazy switchbacks, eyes watching Northport Drive for a window in traffic. They crossed seconds before a city bus came rumbling by, then raced up Goodland to Troy Drive, cutting through an alley to Novick Drive. They pulled into our driveway and threw their bikes onto the grass, dashing inside and downstairs to the basement.

Kurt got the bong going while Jay focused on the tunes. His new Van Halen album was already on the turntable. As he lifted the tone arm to set the needle on the spinning disc, Kurt started coughing from his bong hit.

"Kurt, cut it!" Jay and Billy yelled.

"We won't be able to hear Eddie," Billy said, buoyed by a small moment of unity with Jay. He had always felt like the odd one out with Jay and Kurt and as an adult had some guesses as to why: *Maybe it had something to do with the fact that my parents were still together, or that my dad made some money, or that I made the A squad hockey team every year, maybe a combination of all the above.* The other boys' families were broken and poor and didn't have money for private hockey lessons or equipment.

The boys didn't have much weed—*just enough for us to debate Edward Van Halen's guitar techniques for an absurd amount of time,* Billy wrote. As they passed the bong around, Van Halen's purest and edgiest guitar landed on the teens' ears, the drugs and the music conspiring to take them to another plane. They laughed and teased, crooning along with the music, arguing about who was the fastest biker.

"We should race," one of the boys might have said, eyes glazed.

"Yeahhhhh," said another.

"Wait!" cut in the third. "What if we started at the top of Sanitarium Hill, that way we'd really get our speed up."

The others cheered, thrilled by the prospect of crossing Northport Drive at breakneck speeds.

They planned out the race course, with a finish line at the Milk Depot, then scrambled back upstairs and out to the bikes, belting out the lyrics to "Unchained" by Van Halen. They couldn't be famous musicians at thirteen, but they could be daredevils. Racing straight down from the top of Sanitarium Hill and then blasting across the highway without stopping for traffic was about as close as they could get to an Evel Knievel stunt. Their own Russian roulette, a reliable high.

Up the hill they rode, their faces glistening with sweat. Pink and white crabapple, red and silver maple, yellow weeping willow trees shimmered in the strong breeze. A chorus of spring peepers rose and fell below the wind. They passed the church near the old Sanitarium and entered the cemetery, which lay along the western edge of the hill, zigzagging their bikes through the tombstones of those who had died of tuberculosis—and who now were said to haunt the graveyard as ghosts.

Billy thought he heard Jay yell something to Kurt over the wind but was too far back to make out the words. He accelerated to catch up, but the other two were silent.

The boys were neck and neck as they exited the cemetery, free and fast. Reaching the crest of the hill, they stopped to catch their breath. The familiar smells of the city rose on the wind and whipped across their faces. They stared down to the foot of the 1,017-foot hill where the highway separated them from the final stretch to the finish line, then exchanged a look.

"Let's do it," Jay said.

The other two nodded.

Billy remembers it clearly: *When the word "Go" was called, I shot down the hill like a bullet from a gun, never looking behind me.*

So focused on the goal, Billy raced across Northport at a fortuitous gap in traffic, not pausing to look behind him until he'd reached the other side. After Jay's death, Billy often wondered if they had let him race down the hill ahead to laugh at him or get rid of him for a few minutes. Perhaps they had hatched this plan while he was in the bathroom. Whatever the case, Kurt and Jay missed Billy's window and were stuck waiting for traffic to clear again. Billy coasted on ahead toward the Milk Depot, reveling in his certain victory.

But too much time passed at the mini-mart and Billy began to worry that the other boys had ditched him. Maybe *that's* what they'd been talking about in the cemetery. They were playing a prank. After waiting for what seemed like forever, Billy slowly rode back to Jay's house. *They're probably having a good old laugh at my expense*, he thought, picturing the pair cracking up down in the basement. When he arrived, however, the bikes were not on the lawn. Confused, he rode back to the mini-mart. Nothing. He remembered hearing sirens in the distance.

He decided to ride down to the BMX track the boys had built by Mottier's grocery, but the field there was deserted. He rode back to Jay's house. On a side street, as he neared the house, he noticed flashing lights, police cars, an ambulance, and a small crowd of people. Since he didn't want to be caught skipping school, he avoided the scene and made his way straight to the house. Still no bikes.

"Fuck them!" Billy said to himself, turning his bike around and heading home. He felt a lump rising in his throat as he rode, and he swallowed hard. His route again took him near the scene of commotion, and this time as he peered from a distance, he thought he noticed Kurt sitting on the curb, head hung down. It looked as if he was writing something. Billy coasted over.

Kurt's face was red and streaked with tears.

"What's going on?" Billy asked. "Are you busted for skipping school?"

"No, you fucking retard, look!" Kurt pointed toward the ambulance, where paramedics were loading a body into the back.

Billy turned to Kurt. "What?"

"Some guy passed out and ran Jay over." He wiped his nose with his sleeve and wrapped his hands around his head, staring wide-eyed at the ground.

"Is he going to be all right?" Billy asked.

"How would I know?" Kurt snapped.

Billy looked toward the ambulance again. He thought he caught a patch of white-gold hair amid the blood, but the body was that of a tall person. That couldn't be Jay, he thought. He stood in silence. He wanted to cry. Since Kurt clearly wanted nothing to do with him, Billy rode off toward home.

On the way, tears overtook Billy and built into great sobs. By the time he rode past Jimmy Foye's house, he was wailing like a baby. I got this part of the story from Jimmy, decades later, when we spoke on the phone. He didn't remember why he hadn't ditched school with the other boys, but his memory of the moment he learned about Jay's accident remained as clear as if it had happened yesterday.

"My neighbor Martin and I had cut class," Jimmy told me, voice strong with the excitement of having an audience for his dramatic tale. "We were sitting there by the living room window, just smoking a bowl, getting high. And down the street comes Billy, cruisin' past the house, bawlin' his eyes out!"

Jimmy had called out the window to him.

"Billy! What's the matter?"

Billy slowed to a stop in front of the house. "Me and Kurt and Jay were riding down the hill!" he hollered back between sobs. "And some guy passed out in his car and ran Jay over. I think he might be dead."

"What?" Jimmy cried. The only people Jimmy ever heard of dying were old people. "Don't worry about it, Bill. He'll be okay."

"I don't think so," Billy sniffed before biking off.

For the moment, the stoned boys shook their heads and shrugged off Billy's alarming story. But later that night they were bored and decided to check out the scene of the alleged accident. There they found the tree that the car had crashed into, a great gash cut in its trunk.

"Whoa," Jimmy said, looking at the damage. "If that's what the car did to the tree, imagine what kinda shape Jay's in."

"Yeah," Martin breathed.

Just then a woman poked her head out the front door of the nearest house. "Are you two friends with that little boy who was hit down there?" She gestured to the next block over. Jimmy noticed a dark stain on the curb in front of a house with a torn-up lawn.

"Yeah," the boys said in unison.

"You know," she said gently, "he died a little while ago. It was on the news."

Jimmy stood, rooted to the spot, staring at the blood pooling in the gutter next to the curb.

—24—

It seems that the laws of nature preserve information entirely,
so all the details that make up you are immortal.
—Sabine Hossenfelder

Everyone I've spoken to who knew my brother agrees: Jay was special. He was good at everything, an All-Star in both Little League softball and hockey. He was good-looking and popular and had tons of friends—a golden boy. Many people referred to him as their best friend, myself included. And then there was the whole "I will die young" thing.

He talked about it all the time—to Mom and me and, as I learned much later in life, to our cousins and even some of his friends. Despite everyone's discomfort, Jay seemed completely at peace with his impending death. Years later, our cousin Marty told me about a conversation they'd had.

"I'm going to die young," Jay had said.

The boys were sitting side by side on the white wooden swing of the Winslow family farmhouse where Aunt Alice and Uncle Orlen lived. Perhaps Jay gently pulsed the swing with his left foot, the two boys captivated by the floating and turning fireflies. Marty, not quite sure what Jay had said, swatted a mosquito on his arm and scanned his mind for thoughts of hockey, wrestling, or baseball.

"I'm okay with it," Jay said.

"Okay with what?" Marty flicked away the dead mosquito.

"Okay with dying."

Easter 1981, after the church service, when we were all looking forward to lunch at Alice and Orlen's dairy farm, Jay started badgering Mom.

"Can I go with Kenny and Uncle Neal to feed the calves? Real quick, before lunch?"

"Sure. Make sure you aren't late," she said, pulling her lipstick from her black clutch.

"Thanks, Mom, we won't be." Jay kissed her cheek while stealing a piece of gum from the open purse.

"Hey, that's my last piece!" Mom cried, but Jay was already out the wide church doors.

Mom and I headed to Aunt Alice's for a lunch of ham, homemade rolls, green beans with bacon, red Jell-O with mini marshmallows, and home-grown corn—frozen last summer, now smothered with butter. After polishing off Aunt Ruth's poppy seed cake, we rearranged the tables in the dining room for the euchre tournament.

Mom and all her sisters had learned to play euchre before they learned to read, and they raised their kids the same way. For all of us, there were few greater joys than being good at this game. We valued the tactics, the courage, and the antagonism.

Mom and Jay were partners against Cousin Kenny and me. Mom dealt first and turned up the ace of spades. Kenny passed.

"Pick it up." Jay declared. "I'll go alone." Spades would be trump and Jay needed to win three of the five tricks with no help from his partner.

"Alone? You sure about that?" Mom teased.

He nodded, face determined.

Kenny led with the ace of diamonds. Jay trumped his ace with the nine of spades and I followed suit with the ten of diamonds.

"Awesome!" Jay shouted, jumping out of his chair and spinning in a circle. Still standing, he laid down his remaining four cards one by one: jack of spades, jack of clubs, king of spades, and queen of spades, a perfect loner hand. He whooped. "There ain't no hand better!"

"Four points for the bad guys," I glowered.

After Jay and Mom had defeated Kenny and me three games in a row, it was time to go back to Madison. As the red sun set behind the hills of Ithaca, Wisconsin, Jay, my mom, and I entered the mudroom, which featured a gallery of family photos. We pulled on our coats and said our goodbyes. To the right of the door hung a photo taken from an airplane of our aunt and uncle's five-hundred-acre farm and its surrounding countryside. In the top right corner of the photo was a country graveyard, Neptune Cemetery. As Mom's hand reached for the doorknob, Jay pointed to the photo and said, "Mom, when I die, I want to be buried there."

Jay's comment hovered in the air like the silent aftermath of a bomb. Frozen in the act of putting on my Nike tennis shoes, I stared at my mom. For a few seconds, her face was blank, looking where Jay had pointed. Then she gave Jay a stern look, grabbed her jacket, and quickly hugged Aunt Alice goodbye before herding us out of the house.

One time Jay came into the bathroom while I was curling my hair.

"It's not going to be much longer," he said.

"Would you shut up? What are you even talking about?"

"I just want you to know I want 'Stairway to Heaven' played at my funeral. Mom might not like that idea."

I felt Jay's words burning through my body, as if I had swallowed a flame that now traveled into my gut. I noticed the hair I held with the curling iron was starting to smoke, so I quickly let it go. I heard the song's refrain in my head: *Ooh, it makes me wonder . . .*

"Are you scared?" I asked.

"No," he said. "I just want you all to be prepared."

Our black cat, Shadow, ran past Jay down the hall, her whiskers twitching, sensing possibilities. Jay turned and followed her, and I continued curling my hair, trying to ignore the hollowness in the pit of my stomach.

A typical teenager, I was self-absorbed, unaware that my mom was at her wits' end with Jay and his premonitions. I learned this much later from Marcy, the daughter of one of Mom's best friends.

She called me out of the blue one day in 2016.

"Hi, Kris! This is Marcy Strand, Wanda's daughter."

My mind flashed on Wanda—round body, big smile, and gray hair wreathed in a constant cloud of marijuana smoke. She'd been my mom's best friend for years until they'd had a falling-out a decade earlier. A deep, hungry curiosity arose in me.

"Marcy! Hello!"

"Hi. I'm calling you, Kris, because I found a box of yours at my mom's house. I'm going through her stuff. I wanted to make sure you got it back."

A few days later, Marcy and I sat in a sunlit room on the sixth floor of the YWCA, where she worked, overlooking the Wisconsin state capitol. We went through the box, finding a sweet collection of some of Jay's schoolwork and art. I appreciated these artifacts, but I was much more interested in talking with the kind woman sitting across from me.

"Jay loved you. He really loved you." Marcy gazed into my eyes. "I clearly remember going over to your house one day. I'm an only child, so I was jealous that Jay had a sister. I told Jay how lucky he was and he said, 'I know, I love my sister and I'm very proud of her.'"

Sitting across from this woman whose aging face I hadn't seen since she was a girl, I felt Jay's love, heard his voice.

Marcy told me she remembered my mother talking to Wanda about Jay in the middle of the night. "I could hear her sobbing. 'Jay won't stop talking about dying. What do I do?' she kept repeating. I was only twelve at the time."

From Marcy's timeline, I realized Wanda and my mother had started talking about Jay's premonitions a year or two after Dick left. Jay was twelve and I was sixteen. This means it was during those years when my mom was a single parent and we were living on her three-dollar-and ten-cents-an-hour job. No child support. I couldn't imagine how my mother coped. My heart ached for her.

In those days after Dick left, before I got distracted by boys and parties, Jay was my best friend. We did everything together. I remember when Jay got it into his head to get a dog. He was eleven, I was fifteen.

"Mom won't let us," I told him, passing him the pipe we'd just made from aluminum foil and a toilet-paper tube. We watched the smoke spiral up and into the rays of light pouring through our living room window.

"We could go to the pound right now," Jay said. "She's at work. She won't even know."

There was no way we could hide a dog from her, but the idea of a secret mission was thrilling. "How would we get there?" I asked, watching him flick the lighter and bring its flame to the tiny pile of buds sitting in the small, pin-pricked aluminum foil bowl. Flame in place, Jay lifted the paper tube to his mouth, inhaled, and winked.

A car horn sounded outside, startling me, and I leapt up to shut the curtain. We'd been caught; now we'd be thrown in jail for skipping school and smoking pot. A moment later, I sat back down, realizing my fear was silly—too much *Hawaii Five-0* and *Columbo*.

Settling myself, I breathed in the smoke from Jay's exhalation.

Jay said, "Let's take the bus. I've got fifty cents."

I grinned, feeling a rush of pure freedom. Stoned as monkeys, we ran out the front door, down our block, through the grassy expanse of Warner Park, and around the black swamp. The wind carried us. We looked at each other and laughed, never stopping. We passed the park where we'd played a thousand times. It looked sad and small, a world we'd outgrown. My brother and I were moving beyond our neighborhood.

As we ran past the Milk Depot, I felt a strong desire to run in and steal a candy bar, but Jay said we didn't have time. After three more blocks, we arrived at the bus stop, gasping for breath, holding our stomachs.

"What kind of dog, Jay?" I saw myself holding a black toy poodle.

"Maybe a cocker spaniel," he said.

The bus arrived and we jumped on, each grabbing a window seat. We slid the windows open and stuck our heads out. The wind sent my hair flying. I pointed to the McDonald's. "I'm gonna get a job there next year. After my sixteenth birthday."

Jay pointed at the baseball diamond. "Remember my grand slam last month?" I was there. I attended all his games.

Watching the world blur by, I was free with Jay, on the move, where life was fun, where we belonged to each other.

We arrived at the Humane Society and walked the rows of caged dogs, pointing, oohing, plugging our ears when it got too loud. I lingered in front of a buff toy poodle, but Jay only had eyes for the cocker spaniel puppy. I joined him on the ground in front of her cage. We reached our fingers through the holes in the silver fence, letting her lick and nibble them.

Jay convinced Mom to adopt the puppy. We named her Terra and glowed with the shared feeling of being part of a pack. Most dogs in our neighborhood lived outside, attached to chains on dog houses, but we kept Terra with us. My mom even let her sleep in Jay's bed, but only on top of the navy-blue bedspread. I saw him tucking her under the covers, but I didn't tell on him.

Eight months later, we locked ourselves and Terra in a tiny room with a white male pug. We squealed and cheered as he mounted her. We wanted to watch sex. We pointed and laughed. We were powerful, making life together.

One Sunday afternoon, three months later, while Jay and I hunched like turtles over the funny pages laughing at Beetle Bailey taunting Sergeant Snorkel, Terra's uterine contractions started. The puppies would come in two to twelve hours, we knew from a library book. Terra shivered and panted. I was worried when she bled on the floor. "Bloody vaginal discharge is normal," Jay quoted from memory.

Then Terra began pushing, yelping and grunting as she writhed. I caught the first puppy, and the second shortly after, completely in awe.

We nudged each puppy to a teat, thrilled when Terra licked a puppy and they peed and pooped.

I can still see Jay's delight as he gazed at the fruits of our labor, face shining like the sun.

—25—

Why is the universe? To shape God. Why is God? To shape the universe. I can't get rid of it. I've tried to change it or dump it, but I can't. I cannot. It feels like the truest thing I've ever written. It's as mysterious and as obvious as any other explanation of God or the universe that I've ever read, except that to me the others feel inadequate, at best.
—Octavia E. Butler

Thirty-seven years after Jay died, I stood on Goodland Drive, staring at the ground. I had come in search of Jay, in search of answers. Gripping my notebook and pen, I studied the sidewalk, not sure of what I was looking for.

Chickadees flitted about in the red-tinted maple trees that line each side of the two-block side street. I walked up to the closest house and knocked on the door. An old woman opened it cautiously, her eyes peering out from drooping, wrinkled skin. "I've lived here some forty years and there wasn't no accident," she said, scowling. I thanked her and walked to the next house.

Another woman around my mother's age answered, her hair dyed orange and close cropped. Behind her, I could see her husband in front of the TV, hooked up to a respirator, watching *The Price Is Right*. "We would have been on vacation just about then," she said when I told her the date of Jay's death. "But I ain't heard of any accident happening here."

Unable to tackle stories so different from my own reality, I skipped the next few houses. I walked over to the old red maple tree with the healed-over gash. I placed my hand on the rough bark, staring up into reddish buds just about to open.

I looked at the nearest house, where the garage door was open. A young man was working on a car in the driveway but had started watching me.

"Hi there," he said.

"Hi. I'm interviewing residents of this neighborhood about an accident that happened about thirty-five years back. A boy—my brother— was hit and killed by a car. Do you know anything about that?"

"No, I haven't heard of an accident. I've only lived here nine years though." As he spoke he rubbed grease off his hands with a dirty white rag. "It happened right here?" He pointed to the tree.

"Well, supposedly the car hit my brother down there," I pointed to the next block over, "then it hit this tree."

"Oh, wow. I had been wondering about that tree. I thought it had a disease or something." We both studied the gash spanning the bottom half of the tree trunk, and then he sighed. "Wish I could help. Good luck in your search."

I thanked him and walked away, frustration building in my belly. How was it possible that no one knew? As I trudged back to my car, I passed a man and five kids playing HORSE with a garage-mounted hoop. The man waved, and I decided to try once more. He let the kids continue playing as we talked, and I shared my story with him. "I've only lived here twenty years, but I heard stories—something about a boy being dragged, quite a ways, by a car. Is that what you are talking about?"

I felt his words in my chest. *Dragged quite a ways.* I nodded. My story had been corroborated, but I didn't feel any better. I looked up at the blue sky. Was this the last thing Jay saw?

I wished I could talk to my mom. I wished I could find Kurt. Instead, I went home and dug out the printout of the police report that I had stashed in a box of memorabilia.

I read the narrow, inky typewriter font. The driver, Robert, had reported eating lunch at VFW Post 8483 for about an hour, with a friend. A face swam across my mind: Mike Larson. A few years back, I had accompanied my mother to a funeral of one of our former neighbors. After the service, while my mom caught up with Char, I took the opportunity to speak with her two daughters. "I'm actually writing a memoir," I told them. "Do you remember anything about my brother or about the day he died?"

A man my mother's age who'd been standing near us broke into our small circle. "I remember that day," he said.

"Kris, you know my dad, Mike?" said one of the women.

I remembered hearing from my mom that he and Char had had a divorce many years back. At the time I couldn't picture him, but seeing his face now, I remembered him walking around the neighborhood in his cop uniform. "Hi, Mike! Good to see you. I'd love to hear any details."

"Well, Robert was actually a friend of mine."

"Oh really? The driver of the car that killed Jay?"

"Yep. He and I ate lunch together that very day, at the VFW."

"No way!"

Mike nodded somberly, taking a bite of a Hawaiian roll.

"That's so intense! Did he seem off in any way? We never got much information about why he passed out, though there was some speculation that he had a bad reaction to a new medication?"

"Huh. I don't know anything about that. No, he seemed totally normal when he left the VFW. And he had no history of diabetes or low blood sugar or anything."

"So weird."

"I know. I remember when I saw it on the news. I was shocked. You never think something like that would happen to someone you know. He was such a good guy too. It's a shame. It really ruined his life." He took another bite, chewing thoughtfully.

"And did you have much contact with him after the accident?"

"Not really. He kinda holed up after that. Maybe his family even moved, I can't remember. Such a shame."

I returned my focus to the police report. After lunch, Robert had climbed into his green Ford T-Bird, which was hot from sitting in the sun. He rolled down the windows and headed home around 1:00 p.m. Driving northwest on Highway 113, he started feeling woozy and faint.

Missing the chance to pull into the PDQ convenience store, he decided to turn onto Goodland Drive for a minute to regain his composure. He pulled into the left turn lane and waited for the southeast-bound traffic to clear. After that, the last thing he remembered was waiting for a red pickup truck to pass before making his turn. When he regained consciousness, his car had slammed into the tree.

I continued sifting through the pages of the report—an account from the officer who spoke with the first person to arrive after the accident, the official fatal incident report form filled out with an overwhelming slew of details.

On one page, a drawing caught my eye, which illustrated the path police believed the green car to have followed. It featured a basic sketch of the two blocks of Goodland Drive where the accident happened. A tiny square shape represented the car and was drawn both at the approximate impact location and then again at various points along the car's assumed path, which was diagrammed with arrows. Other spots were labeled such as "Bike," and "Juvenile Boy," both shown on the lawn some unlabeled distance from the curb. The distance between the impact location and where Jay was found was measured at twenty-nine feet. *Dragged quite a ways* popped back into my head.

So where had Kurt been in relation to Jay? Had he been far enough ahead that he didn't see it happen? Or did he watch it all unfold in front of him, unable to do anything? Below the diagram, a few sentences described the scene and what they assumed happened. Interestingly, it commented that the street was completely clean except for three bike parts, which is apparently how they estimated the impact location. There was nothing written about the blood in the street that I had heard described by multiple people. Had the blood pooled on the grass and sidewalk and run into the street? Or was it only a rumor, an image conjured up in the heads of those who knew of Jay's death.

While skimming an officer's report that seemed to mimic one I had already read, one line lodged in my heart: "The bicycle that was struck was . . . turned over to the older sister of the deceased boy." Me. That was referring to me. I traveled back to that moment, to the mangled bike deposited on the lawn. How strange to be reduced in an official document to "the older sister of the deceased boy." After that, each sentence I read carried greater magnitude.

"The driver was advised that the boy that he had struck on the bicycle had expired, and the driver stated he had nothing to hide and would answer our questions."

Under "Nature of Injury" for Jay it said, "Complete upper torso— waist up."

On some pages, large amounts of information had been redacted, making it even harder to understand. I could tell some of it had been the names and addresses of the minors involved, Billy, Jay, and Kurt. On one page, I read, "witnesses reported seeing the driver's head resting on the steering wheel before the vehicle struck the bike." Who were these witnesses? Who besides Kurt had watched this happen? From what I could make out, it seemed the police had tried to interview Kurt about what he saw, as the sole eyewitness. One of his parents had intervened due to Kurt's emotional state.

So, no one could give me the information I sought. *Kurt, where are you?*

—26—

*Death is like a mirror in which the true meaning
of life is reflected.*

—Sogyal Rinpoche, *The Tibetan Book of Living and Dying*

On the evening of May 26, 1981, I was in the kitchen cooking dinner. It was ten minutes to six and Mom would be home from work any minute.

"Jay!" I yelled out the back door. No answer. I cupped my hands around my mouth and angled my face up the hill to the Anderson house. "Jaaaaaaaaaaaaaay!"

I walked back inside, lifted the lid off the cast iron skillet, and stirred the sizzling hamburger meat, all the while listening for his footsteps. *Where is that boy?* Yesterday, he'd told us he thought his death was coming soon. Mom had sent him to his room without dessert and issued a week-long grounding, but Jay always managed to wriggle free. If she caught him, there'd be hell to pay, so I turned off the burner and stomped out to find him.

I stuck my head in the picture window of the Krauses' dining room next door. "Have you seen my brother?"

All twelve Krauses stared at me and shook their heads, seated quietly around their dinner table.

I wanted to swear but the Krauses were devout Catholics, so

instead I said, "Thank you," and ran off. I climbed the hill, jumped over the fence, and wrenched open the sliding glass backdoor to the Anderson house. "Jay?"

"He ain't here," one of the Anderson kids yelled over the theme song to *Gilligan's Island.*

"Where is he?"

"How the hell would we know?"

I glared at the backs of their heads and slammed the door shut, running off down the street toward the Henry house.

As I rounded the corner I spotted Jay, carrying a speaker out of Byron Henry's house and onto the front lawn, where he set it next to a record player.

"Jay, it's dinner time. I need your help setting the table."

He scowled at me. "I don't want to, we just did a fuck ton of work getting these mattresses out in the yard. I am not leaving now."

Only then did I notice the stack of mattresses piled on the ground just beyond Byron's mother's garden. "What the hell are you guys doing?"

Jay grinned. "Byron's parents aren't home, so we made this landing pad and he's gonna ride his scrambler off the roof for a crash landing!" Jay pointed to a second-story window where Byron grunted as he hauled his BMX bike out the window and onto the flat garage roof.

"And the sound system is for . . . ?"

Jay set a record on the turntable. "Van Halen."

"You guys are idiots," I said, crossing my arms. "A few mattresses are not going to break his fall."

Jay ignored me, turning to call to Byron, "You got this, buddy! Jump at the part that goes, '*I'm on fire*'!" He dropped the needle on the record and the first power chords of the song blasted out of the speakers like cannon fire. It startled a few crows in a nearby tree who flew overhead, cawing their disapproval. The sun was setting and the baby-blue sky was streaked with pink. The electric notes of Eddie

Van Halen's guitar riff hooked me, and for a moment I was lost in the sharp harmonics and crunchy distortion of "On Fire."

"Jam, Byron!" Todd and Jay shouted, bringing my attention back to the imminent stunt.

I shook my head and turned toward home, hollering behind me, "You better come inside, Jay. Mom's gonna be home any minute!" But I couldn't resist looking back as the boys on the ground wailed along to the speakers.

"I'm on fire! / I'm on fire!"

I turned just in time to see Byron soar off the roof, his front bike tire missing the mattresses all together, flipping his bike, and tossing him onto his head. I started to rush back when Byron sprang to his feet.

"Oh, man, shit," he said, laughing and grabbing the other boys, who collided in a huddle. As I turned again to walk home, I heard a car pull into Byron's driveway.

"Byron, what in God's name are you doing?" screamed a shrill female voice. "Did I just see you up on the roof? Get those mattresses off the lawn, what will the neighbors say? I think it's time for you kids to go home. Byron, in the house!"

As I arrived home, Jay came running up behind me. "I told you stupid idiots not to get hurt," I scolded.

Jay rolled his eyes. "He'll be okay."

Our pet pigeon swooped down, landing near the hose. Jay crouched down. "You wanna drink?" he asked. The pigeon strutted in circles, scratching at the grass beneath the hose. "Okay, I'll turn it on, but you gotta drink fast." He walked the length of the hose and gently turned the spigot, releasing a slow flow perfect for a small beak.

I shook my head and went back into the kitchen, letting the screen door slam behind me.

A minute later, Jay poked his head in the door and took a whiff. "Aw, not Hamburger Helper again!"

"Don't be so ungrateful. I don't see you helping out with dinner. You haven't even set the table."

Jay made a face and was gone again. "Will you turn the hose off for me?" he called through the window as he ran by. "I'll be right back!"

"You better not leave the yard, Jay," I yelled back, knowing it was pointless.

I swatted a fly away from my face and returned to the stove. I took the lid off the pot of meat and slammed it on the counter harder than I intended. I was sick of Hamburger Helper, too, but what choice did I have? With Mom working long hours at Dane County Social Services, I was responsible for dinner, and at seventeen, this was the best I could do.

I stomped around the kitchen, adding water to the skillet along with the sauce mix and the noodles from the box. As I returned the lid to the pan and turned down the heat, I heard the creak of the back door and my mother's strained voice and clattering crutches as she fumbled through the doorway. "The hose is running!" She hobbled past me and deposited her purse onto the counter. Mom had broken her foot a week earlier. "Where's your brother?"

"How should I know?"

"I swear to God, if he left this yard . . ." She turned toward the door.

"Sit down, Mom," I sighed. "I'll go find the twerp." I handed her the wooden spoon and strode toward the door.

"Grab some lettuce from the garden while you're out. We can dip it in sugar as an appetizer!" Mom called after me.

Our family tradition: Bibb lettuce with sugar and a pitcher of red Kool-Aid. I cranked the hose off, then skipped away. Jay was nowhere to be found in the front yard or out in the street, so I headed for the shed. As I walked past the garden, I noticed a storm of silver maple helicopters swirling down over the carefully planted and labeled rows: Boston Bibb and butter lettuce, beefsteak and cherry tomatoes, spinach, and sweet corn. The golden light cast everything in a hazy glow.

I approached the shed. "Jay! Where the hell—"

"I'm coming!" He sat on the gravel floor of the shed tightening his handlebars.

"Mom says now!" I glared at him. "Come on, she said we should pick some lettuce!"

"Cool!" Jay threw down the Allen wrench.

I shook my head, unable to keep a frown in the presence of Jay's grin, and we raced off toward the raised beds, laughing and shoving each other as we selected the biggest leaves.

Back in the house, my mom had turned off the stove and gotten out the orange plastic pitcher. Jay and I rinsed the lettuce while Mom mixed the Kool-Aid. We sat at the table for a pre-dinner game of euchre, dunking lettuce in sugar and drinking Kool-Aid until our lips were red.

"Okay, Mom. Jay only has three points to win, we gotta get him." I held out my hand and she shook it.

"Yeah, good luck with that," Jay smirked.

I finished dealing and contemplated my hand. Maybe I could get three points on this one.

"Five," Jay bid, staring me down.

"Ugh, no fair." I rolled my eyes. "What in?"

"Hearts." Jay smiled sweetly before proceeding to take every single trick.

"Well, I guess you showed us," Mom laughed, ruffling Jay's hair.

Jay raked the cards in, smiling so big I could see his artificially red tongue.

"Good game, Jay." I couldn't help joining in the laughter.

As we all sat slurping our Hamburger Helper, Mom said, "While you two clean up from dinner, I'm gonna run out to Penney's and pick up a new sprinkler. I can't find the old one and my tomato seedlings are wilting."

"I can go, Mom!" Jay cut in, and he couldn't quite control the edge of desperation in his voice.

I raised my eyebrows at him. His cabin fever must have been pretty bad if he was willing to run errands for Mom.

She wasn't fooled. "I already told you, school and home and that's it."

"But Mom, you should be resting your foot!"

She glared at him but said nothing. Her foot was probably killing her.

Jay seized the moment, taking on an injured tone. "Please, Mom? I'm so bored." He stood and started walking toward the back door, then turned around to reveal his perfectly practiced puppy-dog eyes, hands clasped in front of his chest as if in prayer.

"Okay, fine." She sighed. "But the store and back. Nowhere else." She stuck a piece of lettuce in her mouth and chewed slowly, staring Jay down.

"Yep!" Jay nodded, turning to open the door.

"Wait, I need to give you some cash!" She grabbed her purse and began digging for her wallet. "This is enough for the sprinkler." She handed him a ten. "And here's your allowance."

Jay's face lit up and I practically choked on my Kool-Aid. Mom never gave us allowance when we were grounded.

"Thanks, Mom! Now I have enough for the new Van Halen album!" He stuffed the money into his blue jeans pocket. "I'm gonna go see if Terry wants to come with me."

There was silence after the screen door slammed shut. I toyed with some food on my plate, annoyed at my mom bending the rules for Jay. *He's so spoiled!* I'd surely regret speaking those words, so I started stacking dishes and tried to think of another topic. "We dissected rats today in biology."

Mom stared absent-mindedly at the back door where Jay had vanished, munching on the last of the lettuce. "That's nice."

I frowned. "It wasn't nice, it was disgusting!" I pictured the gray, limp body. "I learned how to make the incision. It was so freaky. And our rat was pregnant! The tiny baby rat came out with all this blood and intestines and—"

"Okay, that's enough!" Mom cut in. "Jesus, Kris, I just ate." She took a stack of mail out of her purse and started to sort through it.

I brought the pile of dishes to the sink and ran the water. I could hear my mom behind me, tearing open one envelope after another with rhythmic rigidity. I could feel her anxiety lapping at my back, but I tried to fall into the water with my hands as they swirled around plates and cups and knives, wiping and rinsing. *Jay will be fine, Jay will be fine*, I chanted to myself, like a prayer.

But an hour later, he still hadn't returned. It was almost dark, and as we sat in the living room watching *The Dukes of Hazzard*, Mom kept checking her watch and looking out the window to the dim street.

"Go turn on the porch light," she barked at me.

I rolled my eyes and got up slowly, inching toward the front door while keeping my eyes glued to the TV.

As the program ended, Jay and Terry burst through the front door with the buzzing energy of two adolescent boys who have just been racing on their bikes.

Terry clutched a large flat package under his arm that was clearly the new Van Halen album, *Fair Warning*.

"Here's the sprinkler!" Jay said, dropping a plastic bag in Mom's lap. "And look what else I got!" He returned to the open door and hauled in a small yellow rose bush.

"Wow!" my mom said, looking surprised. "How on earth did you carry that on your bike?"

"It was easy," Jay shrugged. "It's an early birthday present!"

"That's very early. My birthday is a month away!"

"Yeah, I know," he paused, looking down. "Well, I wanted to get it now. Just in case."

Mom's face hardened. "It's beautiful, thank you."

They stared at each other in silence for a moment, the only sound a muffled ad for I Can't Believe It's Not Butter!

"Okay, well, we're gonna go listen to *Fair Warning*!" Jay said, breaking the spell. He and Terry dashed off, leaving me alone with my mom and the stricken expression on her face.

"Turn the volume back up," she said.

—27—

*For what is it to die but to stand naked in the wind and
to melt into the sun? And when the earth shall claim your
limbs, then shall you truly dance.*
—Kahlil Gibran

In 2021, after years of dead ends and several unanswered Facebook messages, I got a message from Kurt:

Hi

My heart leapt. I quickly responded: *Kurt! Is this really you?*

Hi Kris. Yes, it's me.

OMG! How are you? I've been looking for you for a bunch of years now! Are you open to talking with me?

He said yes, but that he first needed to check in with his girlfriend about talking with another woman. A few weeks passed with no contact, so I reached out again.

Hi Kurt! Just checking back in. Would love to talk sometime.

He responded an hour later: *Sure. Call me now.*

Our call was brief. He was at work and said he only had a few minutes to talk, but he could call me another time. We caught up a little and I learned that he lived in North Carolina, that he'd had a rocky past. His wife had died from alcoholism, but he was newly sober and in a good place, working as a carpenter. Then, remembering how hard it had been to reach Kurt once, I asked the question:

"Did Jay make a joke right before he was hit?" It was something another friend had told me once, that when the car was careening down the road, Jay had said, "Where'd this guy get his license, Sears?" as he attempted to get out of the way. It had always sent chills down my spine thinking of Jay joking around seconds before his death, relaxed about his fate even then.

"No, I don't recall anything like that," Kurt said, his tone defensive.

"It would be kinda weird if he was joking, right?" I played with a pen on my desk, worried I was moving too fast for Kurt.

"Yeah, I mean, I honestly don't remember stuff like that. I don't know. I don't know. Jay's death . . . to me it was just a fluke, you know? He was at the wrong place at the wrong time. And the man who passed out shouldn't'a been driving that day, he had a diabetic seizure or something. I remember running up to the car and scream-ing, 'You just killed my best friend!' And the driver was totally out of it, almost like he'd been drugged. They never…" Kurt paused. "No one ever figured out what happened to that guy or why he passed out but…I wish we would'a stayed in school that day. None of this would'a happened if we'd just stayed in school." He sounded agitated. Perhaps sharing the backstory of Jay's death would help.

"Well, did you know that Jay actually told us he was going to die young, that he would be hit by a green car? He even picked out the cemetery—"

Kurt interrupted me. "You know what, I will tell you something. That day, before we biked down the hill, we were riding through the cemetery up on Mandrake."

"Uh-huh."

"We liked to take little joyrides, get our bikes going fast and then weave around the tombstones. And that day as we rode we were kinda chatting, and Jay said something I'll never forget. He said, 'I don't care what happens to me when I die!' And then he was dead three minutes later, more or less."

"Wow." I felt chills. "That's fucking intense!"

"Yeah, and why he would say that, I don't know, unless he had some information about his death."

"So, he said that, and then you all rode down the hill and then what happened?" I could feel the time ticking away and I needed answers.

"So at the bottom of the hill, at Northport, there's a stop sign. And Billy blew right through it, didn't even look. Me and Jay stopped at that stop sign, and then we pulled ahead, but I stayed on the left side of the road and Jay stayed on the right." Kurt sighed. "You know, I wish . . . I wish I would have told Jay, 'Follow me on this left side of the road!' But I didn't know the guy was gonna pass out, make a turn at the exact same moment Jay's on the right side of the road. The guy's making a right-hand turn"—surely, I thought, Kurt meant to say left, as is documented in the police report—"and Jay's on the right-hand side of the road, Jay's in his path. So, that's how that all went down."

"Wow." A million questions were formulating in my mind, but I couldn't pick one. "Do you—"

"You know what, Kris, I need to get back to work, can we pick this up another day?"

"Of course! When would be good for you?"

"Anytime when I'm working is good. You know, my girlfriend wouldn't like us talking and I don't want to get into all this stuff with her. So anytime between seven and three thirty."

"Okay, great. And you're willing to give me more details from that day?"

"Yeah, yeah. As much as I can recall. It's been a long time."

"I understand. You know, I met up with Stevie Anderson a few years back, we went to visit the tree and he carved 'I love you, Jay' in it." For some reason I had to tell him this piece of information. I needed him to know that he wasn't alone in missing Jay, in losing his friend. "I know that day must have been horrible for you," the words tumbled out. "I really appreciate you being willing to talk about it. I feel so much relief talking to you about it, there's so few people who have been as close to this thing as you and I are."

"Yeah, you know, it's . . ." Kurt paused. "Lemme collect my thoughts a little bit. I'll mentally try to revisit it and next time you can ask me the tough questions, I'll see what I can do to help with your book."

Kurt and I never spoke again. I tried to reach him several times, but he was always too busy. He had put me in touch with other friends of Jay's and I kept him updated on my conversations with them, but he continued to put me off. Then one day I received this message:

> *I'm so glad you are connecting with all these people. Not everyone is nice and well liked. I'm a private person. I moved away from Wisconsin to be far removed from people, places and things. I'm not interested in verifying with you every story from all these people you mention who could give a flying fuck about me. I suspect there's not a whole lot of nice words about me anyways. I'm not the same person I was when they knew me anyway. I'm sorry that Jay is dead. I'm sorry, sorry, sorry. It was not my fault. It was a fluke accident involving a diabetic seizure. I hope your book is fulfilling and prosperous.*

A lump rose in my throat. How could he have misunderstood me? How could he not see that I in no way blamed him for Jay's death? I only wanted to connect with him! Kurt, more than anyone I had spoken with, knew how it felt to lose your entire community after Jay died, to have no one to grieve or remember Jay with. It must have been so painful to be the sole survivor of the incident, to watch Jay's gruesome death and then go on living. And now I would never know all the details of his experience. I would have to imagine them.

Having missed Billy's gap by a long shot, Jay and Kurt silently decided together against a suicide mission. They waited a few moments for the traffic to clear again, watching cars and trucks thunder by at speeds over forty miles an hour. The traffic from the left cleared except for a green Ford T-Bird waiting in the left turn lane, so the boys crossed to the middle. Then they stood up on their bike pedals to cross just behind the tail of a red Chevy pickup truck. On the other side of the highway, they noticed the green car had turned down Goodland Drive behind them, and was swerving dangerously close to their path. Kurt moved to the left side of the road to get out of the car's way while Jay started to turn right, neither boy noticing that the driver of the green car had passed out.

As the front bumper crested over the rear tire of Jay's red BMX bike, it pulled Jay and his bike underneath the car. The green car dragged Jay's body for almost thirty feet, up over the curb on the opposite side of the street, before crashing into a telephone pole and ricocheting off at a diagonal in the other direction, leaving Jay's bloody, mangled body and broken bicycle on the lawn.

Robert's head rested on the steering wheel as his vehicle continued some two hundred feet from Jay's body before slamming into the maple tree.

"Jay!" Kurt screamed, throwing down his bike and running to his friend. "Somebody help!" Jay appeared as a motionless jumble of limbs and blood in the green grass. "No!" Kurt yelled. Looking down the block where the green car had come to a stop, all he could think was, *You killed Jay, you son of a bitch!*

Kurt sprinted to the car and up to the driver's window, yelling,

"Oh, my God! You just ran over my friend and killed him!" Neighbors and passersby had started gathering.

Robert looked up at the furious, teary-eyed boy cursing him out. Blinking in confusion, he shook his head to clear the fog.

The police arrived. An ambulance. Paramedics began working over Jay, while Kurt paced along the sidewalk, hands balled in fists. An officer asked Kurt to fill out a form. Billy biked over, then left. The ambulance drove off, sirens blaring. Kurt sank to the curb and closed his eyes to block out the still-flashing lights from the ambulance. He couldn't stop reliving the scene, replaying it over and over: slipping behind the red truck before the green car crossed, noticing the car careening behind them, splitting off from Jay right before his best friend disappeared under the bumper, the car slamming into that post, then on down the road and into a tree, leaving Jay on the grass behind it. *If only we had just stayed in school. We all just should'a stayed in school.* The words kept repeating in his mind as he struggled to come to terms with the fact that Jay appeared to be dead, while he, Kurt, was alive and unhurt.

At 3:20 p.m. the bell rang at Gompers Middle school, and Jay's classmates began to speculate about his fate. Across town, in a cold white room at University Hospital, Jay was pronounced dead.

Part IV

—28—

I do not fear death. I had been dead for billions and billions of years before I was born, and had not suffered the slightest inconvenience from it.

—Mark Twain

On a cold night in November 2016, I sat at my computer, writing and listening to Jack Johnson. I paused to check a text, then looked back at the screen. A book of Rumi's poetry lay open on my desk. Johnson's upbeat, melodic voice spoke of sharing love with the whole world while Rumi invited me to sit with pain and sorrow. Out of nowhere, the driver of the green car crossed my mind. I'd been wondering about him a lot lately, even tracking down his phone number, but up until this moment I'd been too afraid to use it.

I pulled out the copy of the newspaper article detailing Jay's death, which I'd found in a box of his old stuff my mom gave me a while back. The Post-it note with the driver's number was stuck to the article, highlighter pink against the musty yellow of the paper. My breath shallow, I typed the seven digits into my phone.

Briiiiiiiing.

Maybe he wouldn't pick up. I couldn't tell if I'd be disappointed or relieved.

Briiiiiiiing.

"Hello?"

A thick heat rushed through my body. "Um, hello. Um, is this Robert?"

"Speaking."

"Well, um, this is a strange phone call . . ." I began.

"Well, I'm a strange kind of guy," he said, then laughed warmly. I tried to join him.

"I would understand if you hang up on me . . . I am Kristina Amelong. Does this mean anything to you?"

"Yes," he said softly. "Jay Amelong. An eye for an eye."

"What?"

"I lost my daughter in 2005."

I seemed to have stopped breathing. "How?"

"It was drug-related." His voice was a dull whisper.

"An overdose?" I asked. My chest tightened as I anticipated all the bad reactions he could have to my prying.

He hesitated. "Prescription medication."

"I'm so sorry."

Though we were on the telephone, I felt as if I were looking directly into his eyes. I resisted an urge to end the conversation, remembering how life kept nudging me toward something other than denial of death.

Robert broke the silence. "Well, like I said, an eye for an eye." His voice was louder but sounded detached.

I wanted to say, *Listen, you had a green car. My brother needed a green car.*

A Rumi quote appeared in my mind: "The wound is the place where the light enters you." I noticed Robert was speaking.

". . . May 27, 1981. I'll never forget it. I'll take it to my grave . . ." His voice trailed off.

As if hovering above my body, I watched myself nervously turning the corners of the newspaper clipping, Robert's pain palpable in my own heart. *I am sorry for making you remember,* I longed to say.

"Can I ask you a few questions?" I inquired tentatively. I knew I could lose him at any minute.

"What kind of questions?" His voice was high and wobbly now, spiraling like a top. "There was no alcohol or drugs. You can read the public records. I don't know if I should talk to you."

"I am writing a memoir. I am seeking healing and to tell my brother's story. Did you know that Jay knew he was going to die, knew he would get hit on his bicycle by a green car?"

I willed my words to embrace him. I felt as though I were straddling time, trying to open windows to forgiveness. *You and your green '76 Ford T-Bird did not kill my brother. Life killed my brother. Life!*

"No," Robert said. "But I think I can say I know how you feel, losing your son." Apparently, he hadn't heard a word I'd said.

"I am his sister," I corrected him, worried that we seemed to be getting off track.

"Well, it's a horrible fraternity to belong to, to lose a child. I can't . . . I can't put it into words." His voice sounded softer, more relaxed, but still halting.

I wondered if he wanted to say more but couldn't find the right words, if he, too, was searching for a new story. I imagined living in a reality where I had killed a child while blacked out, then lost my own daughter to the pharmaceutical industry.

I heard my mom's voice, remembered from an old journal entry I'd recently read, written a few years after Jay died.

"I've lost all purpose," she had told me. "I think about killing myself, but I don't think that would be fair to the rest of you."

Poor Mom. Poor Robert.

"It would be fine with me if you didn't want to talk," I said to him. "I could give you my number in case you change your mind."

Nothing.

"What happened to you that day?" My voice was becoming shrill. Why wouldn't he answer? I wanted to hide. I wanted to shake him.

Finally he spoke, voice tight again. "I don't remember. I don't remember any of it. It was a horrible experience. I was feeling sick and then I don't remember."

"Did you wake up when you hit the tree?"

"Yes."

"Did you see Jay?"

"No—I don't remember," he repeated, stammering slightly. "I don't remember anything after feeling sick and turning off the highway. I don't . . . what's your telephone number?"

I told him the number, knowing this might be the last chance I would have to speak with him. "I want you to know that I feel like you are family, that I have a tremendous amount of compassion for you, that my brother knew he was going to die and he was okay with it. He accepted his death and I do too. I love you."

"I'm not sure what to say about all that, except I appreciate your words."

"Goodbye, Robert."

There was silence on the other end. Then the dial tone.

A week or so later, I stood in my mom's kitchen, chopping cucumbers for a salad. "I spoke with the driver that hit Jay," I said, bracing for the worst.

My mom said nothing for a moment. Then, "Did you tell him I hate him with all my heart and I hope he suffers?"

I kept chopping. "Can you hand me a plate?" I heard Robert's words in my head—*it's a horrible fraternity to belong to, to lose a child.* I felt his misery and her hatred swirl together in a turbulent storm. It struck me that hatred had been the only way she could relate to the reality of Jay's death. In her story, Robert was responsible for killing her son, for plunging her into darkness, for ruining her life.

I have come to see things differently. In my mind, the cosmos

orchestrated countless unlikely events—Robert feeling sick and turning into our neighborhood, then blacking out at the exact moment
when he and Jay crossed paths, just long enough to change the world
forever.

Jay needed a green car.

His death did ruin my life, *and* it has transformed my life. The last
thing I would want is for the driver of the green car to suffer from
the belief that God took his child as payment for the child he killed.

Robert never did call me back. I've googled his name a couple
times over the years to see if there's been an obituary, but as far as I
know he's still alive. I think often about what he said, "an eye for an
eye," and then I think of Jay's eyes, blue like mine, full of fun.

One Easter in Richland Center, I sat eating lunch and talking with
my Aunt Ruth—the woman who caught me when I was born—about
my search for information about Jay. She told me that she had once
crossed paths with the nurse who had been working in the ER when
Jay came in.

"I was shocked to learn that he donated his eyes!" she said, her own
eyes wide, her face animated by the pleasure of an eager audience.

"He did?"

"Your mom approved the donation of all his organs, but the eyes
were the only things fit to be used." Her face darkened.

"Wow," I said, an image of Jay's bloody body pushing itself into
my mind. I didn't try to force it out; instead I kept my heart open to
the reality of what I was hearing: Jay's eyes had gone on to make it
possible for someone else to see. My brother's gifts just kept coming.

—29—

The evolution of our spirit is blazed on the dark background
of eternity by our individual wakes. Every person can, if he/
she wishes, leave a more or less brilliant wake behind them.
—Bertrand Russell

My relationship with Denise spanned five years, during which both my spiritual and writing journeys progressed. Though we were deeply in love, our connection dredged up both of our earliest traumas, and Denise moved back to Texas, though we continued our relationship from afar. I visited her several times. On my last trip to Texas, we got an Airbnb on South Padre Island.

Shortly after arriving, I began taking inventory of our food supply. "I don't know if we have enough food to last us till Thursday," I said.

It wasn't rational, but ever since I was a screaming baby on a train in my mom's arms, I'd been hungry. Even now, the threat of not enough food triggered panic. It didn't help that Denise laughed at my concern. She'd grown up with powdered milk and powdered eggs, while here, in our Airbnb fridge, we had leftover steak, sugar snap peas, smoked salmon, and four bottles of kombucha, not to mention a couple of bags of chips and a jar of salsa on the counter. So the idea of not enough food made her laugh.

"*. . . you will starve again, unless you learn the meaning of the* *laaaaawwww . . .*" she sang, but seeing her now for the first time in six months, I was not in the mood for *Les Misérables.*

"Would you stop?" I asked, fighting to cover my rising humiliation. "I'm trying to figure this out."

"What's the matter with you?" she asked, eyebrows raised—a warning sign. "I was just kidding."

"Okay," I said, attempting to keep the peace. But a story had already begun to solidify in Denise's mind.

"You are treating me like one of your employees," she said. "This isn't a business issue you need to assess. We're not going to starve. You don't need to control everything!"

"Okay," I said again, willing myself to stay calm. Knowing that horizontal reality often offered a safer perspective between us, I stretched out on the bed and tried again. "Would you lie down with me?" I asked, patting the bedspread beside me. I looked up at Denise standing over me. "Please?" I added.

Her hands were still balled into fists, and for a minute, I felt certain we would not spend the day together. Then the shadow energy that so often drove us into our separate worlds evaporated. Her face softened, and she flopped down on the bed next to me.

"I'm sorry for making fun of you," she said. "Thank you for making sure we are fed."

"I'm sorry for being grumpy," I said, putting my hand on her arm. "I don't want to be controlling, I just got a little anxious." Some of the tension in my chest was starting to clear.

"I know," she said, pulling my body closer to hers and kissing me lightly.

Before long, we had solidified our plans with the Airbnb host and managed to get our suits on and jump into the car. First stop, the Sea Turtle Center.

The problem was, I hated the place. I'd been with sea turtles before while undersea snorkeling at the Belize Barrier Reef. Those turtles had been swimming free, but here the scene felt like a metaphor for my own situation—tiny round blue pools housing sad-looking creatures with noses torn from repeatedly knocking against the aquarium glass.

I walked over to a placard explaining that the Kemp's ridley sea turtles were endangered and that this center was keeping them alive, preventing the species from disappearing altogether.

I watched Denise in a conversation with a small, three-year-old green turtle. As she took photos and looked into its eyes, it kept rising and falling right at her nose level. The joy in her face lightened my heavy thoughts.

I was much more excited for our next stop: the new South Padre Island Birding and Nature Center. As we entered the building, I bounded up to the elderly blue-haired volunteer at the reception desk.

"Where can we go to see lots and lots of birds?" I trilled.

She frowned. "Did you pay?"

"Don't we pay here?" I asked.

She pointed to the entryway. We retraced our steps and found a ticket machine. I could feel the tension in Denise's body. What was wrong now?

I took out my credit card and studied the machine's instructions, pushing buttons as the machine beeped unhelpfully. Behind me, Denise fidgeted, shuffling from one foot to the other.

"Just put the card in here," she said, scowling.

She was often triggered by my outsized enthusiasm, but in this case I felt that her irritation was inappropriate. After all, I was the one bankrolling the trip. I finished paying in silence.

Trotting back to the desk, I asked again, "Where do we see the birds?" I had read online that there were whooping cranes in southern Texas, and I was excited to see the birds that had inspired some of the first endangered species legislation.

The lady pulled out the map of the entire birding center with its movie room and gift shop and broken elevator. "You'll have to take the stairs up three stories to the lookout tower," she said, pointing to the mile of boardwalk behind the center that edged the Laguna Madre (one of five hypersaline marshes in the entire world, I'd read). I followed her wrinkled finger, trying to keep the directions in my mind.

As soon as we stepped outside on the new boardwalk, four light pink roseate spoonbills flew in for a landing. I raised my binoculars and gasped. I'd never seen the pink giants in flight, and they were stunning against the baby-blue sky. Necks outstretched, their stiff, shallow wingbeats alternating with glides, the four birds made a giant *U* and landed three hundred yards away. A sensation of fullness flooded my body. I dropped the binoculars, saw that Denise was a bit ahead, and ran to catch up. When I grabbed her hand, she smiled and I relaxed a little, noticing how much my entire body still sought her reassurance.

Back at the Airbnb, as we unloaded the food, I asked Denise, "What was your favorite part of the day?"

She shut the fridge and paused, closing her eyes. "I loved my time with toddler turtle. I became timeless, completely merged with her. And then when I looked up I didn't know where I was. It was a little scary. But you were there."

I hugged her. "I knew where you were. Go ahead and get lost. I'll look out for you."

She fell into my body, pushing me down on the bed, pressing her lips against mine.

Still, fighting continued, and I ended up leaving a day early. I called Nina from the Austin airport as I waited to board.

"It was so bad this time," I sobbed, ignoring the bustling travelers, staring as they passed.

"I wanna know, sweetheart." Nina and I had been loving each other in this tender way for thirty years, through her move to Madison, coparenting my son, Eli, and her eventual relocation to DC for her career in public health. We had known each other in so many stages of life. Even though we were on the phone, I felt myself curl up in my best friend's lap. I could sense her arms around me, buoying me.

"I don't understand it!" I vented. "We miss each other so much when we're apart, and then we get back together and we're at each other's throats! It's the same shit every time. Why is she so mad at me? I didn't do anything."

"Well, you did and you didn't."

"What do you mean?" I felt my hackles raise.

"You didn't ask for this trauma, and neither did she. She has inherited the trauma of generations of genocide and abuse, and you have inherited the trauma of people who dehumanized themselves in order to dehumanize others."

"But shouldn't we be able to find our way through it? I don't want to believe we can't grow beyond the patterns of our ancestors."

"You can. And you have. Look how far you've come! But you're swimming against a strong current. You come from violence and alcoholism and abuse, just as she does."

"And I want to work on it!"

"Think about it this way: when she looks at you, some ancient part of her sees the skin and the face of the oppressor. Forcing her into processing might be counterproductive."

"So . . . what do we do?"

"You haven't been able to get yourselves out of this pattern. It seems that if you stay together, you'll keep spinning."

"You're saying we need to end things."

"Ask yourself this: Is the relationship helping you become the person you want to be?"

I said nothing, staring out the window at a plane lifting off the tarmac in the distance.

After I ended things with Denise, I was single for the first time in almost twenty years. Though it was the right decision, the darkness in the world became too much for me. On top of my depression, Rayna had recently quit eighth grade due to severe daily headaches and nausea. She had gotten a concussion from a bad fall a couple of years ago and now spent most days in bed under the guise of "home-school." I'd tried everything from acupuncture and physical therapy to bringing home one new dog after another. Over time, we'd acquired a whole pack—a poodle, a shepherd mix, and most recently, a golden retriever puppy.

On a long, cold Saturday in February, the two of us had retreated to our separate corners of the house. Rayna hid on the other side of her closed bedroom door, buried in soft blankets and her puppy with only her phone and the TV to keep her company. I huddled at my computer with the other two dogs at my feet, sipping kombucha, reading depressing news, and crying all day.

I called Nina, the one person who always made me feel less lonely.

"I don't think I can do this any longer," I sobbed. "I feel like suicide is the only way out."

"Just keep telling me how you feel, sweetie," Nina said.

"Fuck you! It's too hard. And Rayna is too sick. I can't figure out how to help her. I'm so discouraged."

"Yes, you are," Nina affirmed. "But right now I will hold all those challenges. You just crawl into my arms and tell me about it."

Nina and I went back and forth, listening to the other shed her suffering. At the end of an hour I felt drained but ready to try again.

I fixed Rayna a gluten-free dinner, then turned my attention to my spiritual studies. I picked up Thomas Merton's *A Search for Solitude:*

Pursuing the Monk's True Life and began reading. I wanted to be a monk, a mystic, and a scholar too. Merton had set up his life within the walls of a Tennessee monastery, developed specific practices, and surrounded himself with people who held the space for his spiritual growth. This setup allowed him to go within, write, reflect, and find God.

I started to feel Thomas Merton inside my own body, and another layer of loneliness lifted. I began to consider that my solitude could guide me to deeper places within, a connection with humanity, and a relationship with cosmic consciousness.

I was jolted out of my reverie by a sharp bark. Sheeta, the shepherd mix, was asking for a walk. I tucked the book under my pillow, threw on my thick coat, and headed into the night.

The lake was frozen. The first quarter moon hung low and bright, beginning to touch the horizon. The whipping wind burned my face. The dogs ran ahead. I trudged after them, my feet keeping pace with my breath, plowing on toward the center of the lake. I had no destination in mind, only a need to move, to keep the blood pumping in my veins.

The wind had blown the snow into drifts, so I was forced to lift my legs to my chest, interrupting my rhythmic march. As I stumbled through a particularly deep patch, my boot caught and I almost fell.

Sudden anger surged through me. I screamed at the moon, the wind, the stars: "I don't care if I am alone!"

I listened to the gaping silence that echoed around me, broken only by huge gusts of wind.

The blue-black sky seemed to swallow all sound and light from the city. I closed my eyes and went inward, where despair, fury, and terror raged. It was all too much. A great, silent sob emerged from my throat and I sank to the ground, landing in a snow drift.

What if I just gave up? Froze to death out here? I opened my eyes. I could almost feel the sweet peace of surrendering to the snow.

Someone would find me out here, but I'd be long gone. I'd cease to exist. Wouldn't I? I wanted nothingness, a complete and utter blank. Was that what Jay had experienced?

No, said a voice somewhere in the dark of my mind. I saw Jay's face. He was still with me. I opened my eyes.

Ahead lay an open patch of ice, blazing with the reflection of the moon. I ran closer, lying down on the frozen water. I looked up to the night sky and found Orion, the Hunter, three pinpricks of light in the velvety black. I took three deep breaths, the heavy air pressing me closer to the ice. Then the dogs were above me, licking my face.

I sat up and pushed them away, reassuring them with ear scratches that I wasn't wounded, and they ran off again, chased by their shadows across the powdered tundra. As I stood up and pulled my hood back over my head, I remembered Thomas Merton and his monastery.

"I need a monastery!" I shouted over the bitter wind.

A new thought arose: *Why a monastery? Perhaps periods of solitude could be my monastery.*

At that moment, a snowflake hit my cheek. I looked up, opening my phone camera. A few clouds had rolled in and flurries made blurry streaks across a dark gray world. I pocketed my phone again and looked at a flake that had fallen on my mitten, holding it close to inspect the many-faceted fractals. I stuck out my tongue, caught one sharp, icy dot, then another, imagining the sparkling outline of the snowflake melting into my warmth.

Perfect. A monastery! On the lake. Within my body.

I continued tasting snowflakes, finding joy in my being.

Then I noticed the moon was gone. I called the dogs in high-pitched staccato. "Pup! Pup! Pup!" I turned and headed back to my quiet, lonely house and a daughter in constant pain. Trudging through the drifts, I thought about the night two weeks ago when her pain was so severe I had to take her to the ER. I thought about the day, months earlier, when she had decided to quit school, after being unable to sit through class three weeks in a row.

From within my new monastery, I could begin to interact with reality more intimately and stay emotionally centered.

I thought about how, on days when Rayna had enough energy, she would take the dogs for walks and take photographs and sing and play piano. Leaving school had enabled her to spend hours outdoors, learning from the natural world. She continued to be my fiercely independent, wonderfully creative daughter.

The darkness deepened. I spun in a circle, and all around me were open patches of stars overlaid by snowflakes. The three dogs wrestled at the lake's frozen edge. I clambered back to land and followed the dogs home.

I opened the back door and was met with a blast of warmth and light, the smell of roasting chicken. My cheeks tingled as they began to thaw. I shed my layers and hung them to dry, then I tiptoed to Rayna's door and tapped lightly.

The TV went quiet.

"Yeah?"

I opened the door a crack and peeked my head in. "I love you, Rayna."

"I love you, Mommy."

I closed the door quietly, then shuffled into my office. I sat down at the computer, picturing the endless dark sky, the open expanse of frozen lake, the snow making everything gray and sparkly. I began to write.

Something happened tonight. Life made me a monastery.

—30—

The irony of man's condition is that the deepest need is to be free of the anxiety of death and annihilation; but it is life itself which awakens it, and so we must shrink from being fully alive.
—Ernest Becker, *The Denial of Death*

In May 2018, I decided to talk to my mom about Jay. It was the first day her condo's pool opened for the season. Rayna, my mom, and I were sitting poolside around a white metal table playing a variation of euchre called dirty clubs. Bikini-clad, Rayna and I had arranged ourselves in such a way that we could attend to our cards while still exposing as much skin as possible to the hot midday sun—an art we had perfected over the years.

For the past six years, our once-a-month card game was the only time my mom and I spent together. We still had not recovered from my leaving my husband, or from the time in 2010 when I'd lost my patience during a long car trip and shaken her (which she perceived as my wanting to strangle her). Or, obviously, from Jay's death. A friend once told me that when some people lose a child, they cannot bear to lose another, so they simply "kill off" the living children in their hearts. I believed that was true for my mom.

Still, we could connect through euchre.

My mom dealt, her hands trembling slightly as she placed the cards evenly around the table.

I watched her, worry and guilt swirling in my body like cream in coffee: I was not taking care of my aging mother. I wanted to, and I know she felt I should, but she simultaneously left no way for me to be close to her.

In 2012, I'd listened to my mom cry about the Sandy Hook school shooting, a rare moment of vulnerability for her. She surprised me with an even more vulnerable statement: "I don't know how those parents go on living." After she'd dried her eyes, she added gruffly, "By the way, I've disowned you." The crevice created by Jay's death had widened a bit more. Still, I felt compelled to take care of the person who had taken care of me.

The wrought iron gate into the pool swung open with a screech and banged shut behind a loud family with three kids. My mom winced, pausing her dealing to press two fingers to her forehead.

"You feeling okay, Mom?" I asked.

She finished dealing and laid down the last five cards in a pile, turning up the top card, the king of clubs. "Headache," she said, picking up her hand.

"Aw, I'm sorry, Mom." I wished she would look at me, but instead she studied her cards, picking up the king and replacing it with a card from her hand.

My heart hurt. I wanted to leave, yet I picked up my cards, seeing a handful of red. "Shit." I hung my head, knowing I would not do well this round.

This my mom acknowledged with a smile. Though she tended to ignore or minimize all strong emotions, she made an exception to this rule with cards.

I led, tossing my ace of diamonds onto the center of the table. Since there was nothing I could do to avoid a bump—negative five points—I started contemplating how best to introduce the subject of the dismissive comment my mom had written on Facebook a few weeks earlier.

Rayna looked up from her phone and tossed out her king of diamonds. Maybe I would get this trick after all!

But then my mom played the king of clubs, winning the trick. She sat up straighter in her chair and tossed out her jack of clubs, the highest card. Rayna and I followed suit with our lowest clubs, both of us noticeably slumping in our chairs. Pulling in a second trick, her hands seemingly less shaky, my mom turned to me and asked how my second cousin Walt's graduation party had gone.

"Oh, great," I said. "Everyone told me to tell you hello."

"Great," she said. She laid down her last three cards, the highest remaining in the game, taking all five tricks, earning her five points, and bumping me and Rayna. We tossed our cards in.

"They all wondered where you were," I said, collecting the cards and beginning to shuffle.

My mom looked across the pool where two kids were shrieking and splashing each other. "I sure didn't feel well that night."

"Sorry about that," I said, wishing I could alleviate her pain. Instead I finished dealing and flipped over the ten of hearts. "Sherry talked about Grandma Winslow."

My mom's body tightened as she picked up her cards. "Yeah? Did Sherry tell you how Grandma Winslow used to lock the children on the sun porch? Isn't that terrible?"

"Three," Rayna said, shifting our attention back to the game.

"Five." My mother grinned, her own mother's abuse no longer on her mind. That's how powerful a good hand could be.

"What in?" I asked.

"Hearts."

Rayna and I both folded, giving my mom the five points without a fight, avoiding negative fives for ourselves.

I'd never heard my mom talk about her mother like that. How could I get her to say more?

Before I could speak, my mom said, "Well, memory is just memories." Her voice was tired now, as if speaking ill of her mother and then winning a hand had wiped her out. Her intention was clear: *this conversation is over.*

I had tried many times to get my mother to talk with me about Jay's death, about anything real or hard, and she had always fended me off. Once, while traveling together in Italy, I'd made a particularly ill-conceived attempt.

I had recently started co-counseling and had endless questions for my mother about my life as a baby, about my father, about our escape. I'd decided that our two-week tour of Europe would be the perfect opportunity to dig into these conversations, to force her to talk, but anytime I even hinted at something related to the past, she would quickly bury herself in a guidebook. And when that didn't work, she stomped off—left the hotel room for a smoke or even walked away from me in the middle of a foreign town. When I lost her in Paris and had to walk twenty blocks back to our hotel, I realized I had to take a different approach.

Our second-to-last stop before heading home was Pisa. The day started off fine, but before long we were completely lost. By the time we reached the Leaning Tower, we were both in foul moods, my mom chain-smoking while I chugged Mountain Dew. I could feel the anxiety radiating off her as she fidgeted with her lighter. I longed for a joint (I was less than two years clean and sober). She finally got the cigarette to light and took a sharp drag, looking up at the looming structure. I stood and watched her for several minutes. She seemed to calm down a bit. "Sure is something," she said, letting out a sigh of smoke and nodding to the tower. Perhaps the awe she felt was similar to the way I felt looking at her, a fragile structure likely to collapse at any moment.

"Mom?"

"What?"

"Remember that co-counseling thing I was talking about?"

"What?"

"You know, that peer-counseling thing. I've been doing it for a couple months now, it's pretty incredible."

"Neat." She threw the butt of her cigarette on the ground and tapped it with her toe.

"It makes me feel like a new person. I'm using the process to heal painful things that have happened—"

"What are you even talking about, 'painful things'?"

"Well—"

"I'm tired, let's go back to the hotel." She walked off to flag a cab.

"Mom, wait! I was in the middle of talking!"

A taxi had pulled right up to where she was standing, and she slid inside. "Let's go!"

I got in behind her. "Okay, but will you just listen to me? I've been learning a lot about myself and—"

"That's great, Kris, but I'm too tired to talk right now. I have a headache."

"You always say that! Why won't you talk to me? What are you afraid of? You think you're defending yourself, but—"

"ENOUGH!" she yelled, causing both me and the driver to flinch. "We are not discussing this now."

I crossed my arms and sulked the rest of the way back to our hotel.

Back in our room, my mom went into the bathroom and I turned on the TV. I sat on the hotel bed, flipping channels without listening to the content until I couldn't take it any longer. When I heard the toilet flush, I got up and barged into the bathroom.

"Why did you leave my dad when I was a baby?" I blurted out. "What happened?"

My mother glared at me, turning on the faucet to wash her hands.

"Mom!" I said, louder. "Was he abusive? Did he do something to me?"

"I'm not talking about this, Kris," she said, drying her hands on the towel and moving to push past me for the door.

I slammed it behind me and blocked her path. "Tell me what happened!" I yelled.

"I don't remember!" she yelled back.

I looked into her eyes and screamed until my face turned red, every cruel, honest, hateful, desperate thought I had had. She just stared at me in silence, face blank, shoulders hunched, until I unlocked the bathroom door in disgust.

This wasn't how I had wanted things to go. I was supposed to keep my temper, to remember that the goal was to heal from trauma, not create more. I had done it all wrong. After that day, I gave up on connecting with my mom.

Since then, we'd had one brief conversation a few years back while on a road trip to North Carolina, during which I'd learned a few details about the first year of my life. We had still never discussed Jay. Now, a few days after the thirty-seventh anniversary of his death, I wanted to try again.

The previous week, I'd felt brave enough to post a piece of my contemplative writing about the day my brother died on Facebook, for the first time. To my surprise, my mom had been the only person to leave a comment. *That is not what happ*ened, she wrote. I had decided to take this as an opening. But here she was, shutting me down again.

All at once, the heat from the sun and the game and my building frustration was too much. I stared at my mother's face, her skin wrinkled and sagging, her mouth set. Her eyes weren't visible behind her sunglasses, but she seemed to be gazing into the pine trees that stood beyond the pool fence. I glanced at Rayna, who was ignoring the pile of cards in front of her and instead rubbing coconut oil on her belly.

I stood up, walked a few steps to the pool, and dove in. The shock of the cool, chlorinated water cleared my snarling thoughts, stripping away some of the fear and frustration. When I came up for air, all that remained was a faint sense of hope. Yes, my mother shut down real conversations, but she had also mentioned memory, and she had engaged with my Facebook post about Jay. Perhaps the door was not shut completely. I swam to the ladder and climbed out of the pool.

Wiping off my hands, I picked up the cards Rayna had dealt.

"Dirty clubs again," she said, pointing to the pile of remaining cards. A club was turned up, and Rayna picked it up and added it to her hand. I saw a few black cards in my hand and felt slightly hopeful that I would not get bumped again.

"Why do you say memory is just memories?" I asked as my mom laid her ace of hearts in the middle of the table.

I trumped her ace with my ten of clubs, but Rayna dashed my hopes by taking the trick with her queen of clubs.

"One of my childhood memories," Mom began, her voice suddenly alive with a childlike, spunky edge, "is of sitting in an outhouse and Uncle Neil barging in because I was screaming. There was a leech stuck to my leg, just above my ankle. My sister Mary swears it happened to her. Every time we ask Neil, he just laughs."

"So who was it?" I asked, laughing too.

"That's the point," Mom said, taking the last trick with satisfaction. "You can remember something one way, but your memory might be wrong." She tossed the rest of the cards into the center, knowing she had ended the round.

"Who got what?" Rayna asked.

"I got a bump again," I said, irritation growing. A pair of middle-aged women in brightly colored swimsuit cover-ups entered the pool gate with a loud bang, complaining about the maintenance of the grounds.

As my mom dealt the next hand, Rayna tallied the score: "Okay. Gran has five to go out; I have eight to go out; and you have twenty-five to go out."

I picked up my new cards, a solid handful of spades, and bid four. Feeling renewed confidence, I turned toward my mother.

"I agree with you about memory," I said. "That's why I want to talk to you about Jay's story, Mom. There is so much I don't remember; and when I posted on Facebook, you corrected me." I offered this as softly as I could, reaching over to touch her leg. Her skin was smooth and cool, the flesh beneath soft, squishy. "Maybe we can find some healing together." I braced myself.

She looked down at the cards. "It's a bad time of year," she said softly. "Not today." Bringing us back to the game, she asked, "What in?"

"Spades," I called out stiffly, trying not to take her dismissal personally. I reminded myself that everyone I had interviewed about Jay had told me that my mom remained a sealed vault when it came to discussions of Jay's death.

Her cards were weak, so she dropped out, sitting quietly and watching a dad toss a small child around in the pool as Rayna and I played out the hand.

When we finished, my mom spoke. "Annette says you didn't tell her what had happened when you called."

Annette is my oldest cousin. Since my mom is the youngest of five sisters, she and Annette are quite close in age.

"What?" I asked, searching my mind for memories of calling Annette. I could not remember calling her once in my whole life.

Rayna penciled in our points on the pad of paper while my mom collected the cards.

"You called Annette," she said, her hands trembling again as she dealt.

"Huh. I don't remember calling Annette." I watched a young boy jump into the pool where his mother caught him in her arms. Then I picked up my cards.

"Well, that's what Annette told me when she and your grandmother came to the house." She studied her cards, ignoring my baffled expression.

We were talking about my grandmother again? What was happening?

"Two," Rayna said.

"Three," my mom overbid her. Then, mostly under her breath, she added, "Thank God she was there to run interference with my mother."

Seemingly out of nowhere, a memory I had completely blocked arose of Grandmother Winslow, stern as ever in her plaid house dress and stockings, walking into our house the day Jay died. A bolt of cognition surged through me. My mom was volunteering information on this forbidden topic! I played my hand on autopilot, trying to figure out how to respond. I worried that any reaction could shut her down, so I rolled with it as I followed her ace of hearts with my ten. "What did Annette say to Grandma?" I asked.

My mom put her last card on the table. "She explained why I was holding a sweatshirt and a flashlight." She seemed to sink deeper into her chair and clutch at the air in front of her, as if she were still holding the sweatshirt and flashlight.

"Were they Jay's things?" I asked, the words shards of glass leaving my body. I laid down my ace of clubs, taking the last trick and finishing that round. I pictured my mom, clinging to a random assortment of her dead child's possessions.

"Mother wanted me to stop holding them. I was glad when she left."

My hunger for story morphed into compassion for my mom's pain. Jay had been dead only a few hours. Even in the beginning, where could my mother have found a place for her grief?

"Yes, I was glad when she left too," I said.

I wished I could give that sweatshirt and flashlight back to my mother and encourage her to hold them for as long as she needed to.

—31—

*Death is someone you see very clearly with eyes in the center of
your heart: eyes that see not by reacting to light, but by reacting to a kind of a chill from within the marrow of your own life.*
—Thomas Merton, *The Intimate Merton:
His Life from His Journals*

It is winter. My mom opens the car door, slowly works her way into
the seat, and closes it behind her. She is breathing heavily. It's 2018
and she is seventy-four years old.

"Are you okay?" I ask.

While she gasps for breath, I calm myself. She will answer when
she can. This is the first time we've spent without the grandkids in
years, the first time we've been alone since she "disowned" me a few
years back. We are going to *The Post*, a movie about bravery, the
Pentagon Papers, and telling the truth.

"COPD," she rasps, finally. "And cold air."

"COPD?" I try to recall the acronym. It has something to do with
the lungs. Again, I wait, forcing myself to breathe deeply as my mom
attempts to do the same.

"Chronic obstructive pulmonary disease."

"Oh no, that sounds bad." My stomach clenches. Why didn't I realize it had gotten this bad?

"I'm okay." She pulls a white tissue from her purse and blows her nose.

I grab her hand. "Are you sure?"

She turns and smiles. "Yes, I'll be fine." For the first time in memory, she seems to be comforting me, like a mother.

As we drive, she points the directions, and though I know where we're going, I don't stop her. "How was Los Angeles?" she asks.

"It was wonderful!" I start with topics guaranteed to be safe: "The ocean was beautiful, and the weather was great."

"It was warm there?"

"Yes, well, to them it was cold, but to me, coming from the coldest week in Wisconsin, it was very warm. I waded barefoot in the Pacific at Venice Beach."

She laughs. "Yeah, it was twelve below zero here. Budi lifted his leg and his pee froze to the bush he was peeing on!"

"No!" I join in her laughter, which soon turns into a coughing fit.

When she's regained control, she asks. "What else happened?"

Even this slight bit of curiosity from my mom is thrilling. I want to tell her everything. She points right, and I turn down Hoepker Road, passing a red barn, not bothered by her insistence on driving from the passenger seat.

"I found myself going deeper into prayer." I work to keep my grip loose on the wheel.

"Really, how does that work? Who do you even pray to?"

I think about this for a minute, amused that my mother, who taught me to pray every night before I went to bed, seems to think that I don't believe in God. Does she believe in God?

"I pray to the universe," I say. "To reality as I understand it from studying physics. God, Outrageous Love, the Mystery. To me they are all the same thing."

She points forward, through the four-way stop sign, saying nothing.

I want to know what she thinks of my thoughts about God, but instead I ask, "Want to hear a story?"

"Sure." She points up the highway, then to the right.

"On Wednesday night I was on the phone with Nina."

"Oh, how's Nina doin'?"

"Good! Just got back from a work trip to Africa."

"Wow!"

"She asked about you. I told her I don't see you much lately."

"Yeah."

I glance at her. She is looking ahead. "Anyway, um, I'd been telling Nina about my decision to open up to miracles. And she suggested I could bring you into my prayer practice." I plow ahead bravely. "So, Thursday morning, I added you to my morning ritual. I pictured us sitting in a room together. I asked for more for us, without trying to change anyone." I decide to leave out that I envisioned us holding hands. "A couple hours later, you texted me to ask if I wanted to go with you to see *The Post*!" When I saw the text, I almost dropped my phone. Currents of power seemed to course through my body. Perhaps I haven't portrayed this moment with as much magic as I felt, because my mother seems unimpressed.

She says nothing and we drive the last couple of minutes in silence. I take deep breaths and let them out slowly, counting to ten each time. My mind travels back to the last time we were alone in a car together, more than seven years ago.

That fall, my mom and I drove from Wisconsin to Davidson, North Carolina, to visit my son Eli for his freshman year parents' weekend. It was my first time seeing Eli since he had left home in August. Something had happened that day, when he crossed the threshold of our home and got into his dad's car. His energy changed, from the son I had known and who belonged with me, to an independent entity. Watching the loaded gray minivan drive off, I knew something had been severed. It seemed to come from him, as if part of him had to shut me out in order for him to go into the world as his own person.

I almost didn't recognize Eli from across the campus lawn; he seemed taller and his dark hair was shorter, his jaw squarer. We yelled and ran to hug him, smothering him for a few seconds before he managed to push us off. He smiled warmly at my mom, but he flat-out refused to look at me, barely even saying hi. I tried to shrug this off, telling myself I must be making it up, but over the course of the weekend, his distance from me became more and more pronounced. He wouldn't respond to anything I said unless I asked a direct question, and then only muttered, frowning and looking away. Though frustrated and hurt, I intentionally swallowed my own feelings. I could see how much he wanted to be liked and to fit into the college community. And since the whole purpose of our coming was to support him, I fought to keep my temper under control.

Once during dinner when my mom had gone to get another plate of food from the buffet, I attempted to broach the divide. "Are you mad at me?" I tried to get him to meet my eyes but he stared resolutely past me.

"No."

"Well, then why—"

"I'm gonna get more too. Want anything?" He stood abruptly and walked off.

I stared after him, my blood boiling. I wanted to confront him right there in the middle of the dining hall. Instead I went out into the cool autumn night and waited for my breathing to return to normal.

Somehow I kept it together for the weekend, and my mom and I started our fifteen-hour drive back to Madison. Yet as we got onto the highway, I couldn't help thinking, *I've lost him. I've lost my son.* I wasn't wrong; this was the beginning of Eli's disassociation from the family, starting with me.

Several hours into the trip, we stopped at Starbucks. What

followed isn't clear in my mind. I can remember opening the door to my black Prius, one of the few cars in the sunny parking lot. We both got in, and only then did I realize our cups had gotten mixed up in the store. My mom had been drinking my coffee for the past five minutes, and it was over halfway gone. I felt a sudden rush of days'— probably years'—worth of rage and disappointment tear through me and hone in on my mom's narrow frame next to me in the passenger seat. *Everything is her fault!*

"Goddamn it!" Blind to any rational thought, I placed my hands on her neck where her wrinkled skin sagged and shook her viciously.

"Kris!" she yelled, pushing me away.

The shock and fear in her eyes jolted me out of my rage. I quickly started the engine and began driving, hands shaking as I clutched the wheel and headed back to the highway. I couldn't look at my mom, could only feel her presence next to me, buzzing with outrage and terror. Neither of us spoke. As the hours wore on, I wrestled with my thoughts, trying to figure out what had come over me.

Perhaps it was a result of suppressing my sadness and anger around Eli, or perhaps I simply couldn't handle another loss, even one so small as a cup of coffee.

Now, I relive this memory with a combination of sympathy for myself and deep regret. I have paid a steep price for that loss of self-control. Since that day, my mom has told me many times about her nightmares of being strangled by me. When her health first started to decline, she announced to me that she didn't want me to be her power of attorney or to care for her on her deathbed—she didn't trust me not to kill her.

As I pull into the theater parking lot, I wonder if she, too, is thinking about the moment when my hands circled her neck. My knuckles on the wheel are white, my chest tight. I want to be brave, to bridge the divide of silence between us, but all I can do is stare straight ahead.

"Drop me off at the front, I'll get tickets," she says, offering an escape for us both. I pull over and she clambers out. I am shaking.

Now it is spring, and though the world bursts with new life, my mother is dying. I stand at the top of her hillside garden amid the lime green of young bee balm stalks. "Can I dig up some of this bee balm for my yard?" I call down to her.

"Sure," she replies from the base of the hill, her voice faint as she wheels her oxygen tank toward the hostas. Worry rises in my gut. My seventy-four-year-old mother has been diagnosed with lung cancer. She fell the other day, and since she is no longer steady on her feet, I'm helping her in the garden. I kneel, my bare knees nesting into the soft grass, grounding me in the way that only touching wild things can.

The bee balm's root system consists of tiny, delicate threads shooting off a mother plant, with no central root core for me to dig. I reach my hand into this green, growing community of plants, asking where I can safely harvest without causing damage. A clumping of six or seven young bee balm stems catches my eye. I shove my trowel into the ground, lifting and thrusting it several times until I've worked my way around the clump. I feel a twinge of pain with each snapped root. I lift the cluster of stems and roots and soil into the plastic bag my mom gave me. I sprinkle water from my water bottle on the tiny threads, then stand up and brush dirt off my knees. A fly lands on my face, and I swoosh it off. I look down the small hill, across arching hostas, pink bleeding hearts, and purple vinca vine to catch my mom's eye. She waves. I collect my things and head toward her.

My mom is heartbroken. Creating expansive gardens is one of the few art forms acceptable for the women in my lineage—perennial flowers mixed with vegetables, color and geometric shapes to nurture the soul and feed the body.

I reach my mother and can hear her breath, loud and ragged. "You okay, mom? You don't sound well." I touch her bare arm with the back of my mud-stained hand.

"I was up all night throwing up," she says. Her throat sounds raw. I hug my mom, trying to keep the mud away from her skin and clothes. I look into her brown eyes. "I love you, Mom," I say. "Let's go into the house and drink some apple cider vinegar water. Maybe that will help your belly."

As we sit at her kitchen table, grief, joy, and longing surge in my body. She is my first love, and I'm not ready to lose her. I reach over to touch my mom's hand and feel her asking me a question she won't voice, seeking answers with her golden-brown eyes. I think I know what she is looking for.

As I deal out the cards for a quick game of two-handed euchre, I gaze at my mother. Then I say, "I will help you die. I will come here every day."

One morning in August I lie in bed texting with my mom. "And how do you feel emotionally?" I ask her.

"Numb," she replies. "But it's quality of life I am going to focus on, not quantity."

I look out the window at the hot, blue summer sky and cry for a solid fifteen minutes.

Then I scroll back on my phone to find my mom's first text of the day, where she tells me about seeing her lungs via a CAT scan. Each lung had four black nodules, she explains, cancerous octopi with tentacles escaping her lungs and wrapping around her spine.

The radiation isn't working.

I google the statistics for the third or fourth time. Small cell lung cancer—the overall five-year survival rate for both stages is only about 6 percent. Without treatment, the average life expectancy is two to four months; with treatment, it's six to twelve months. What

I don't yet realize is that these estimates don't account for my mother's additional complication of COPD. She won't live to see another spring.

It's quality of life I am going to focus on, not quantity.

I can hear my mom's quavery, hoarse voice uttering these words aloud, attempting to convince everyone (including herself) that she's at peace with her fate. But is she at peace? Has she lived a quality life?

As far as I know, she never truly recovered from losing Jay. Perhaps she saw no option other than to keep waking up, going to work, and feeding herself. She stayed at her job at the Dane County Social Services for many years until she retired, working her way up the ladder and becoming financially stable. She has loved being a grandmother to my children and stepchildren, playing a large role in raising both Eli and Rayna. She's pursued a passion for travel, taking trips around and outside of the United States with family and friends and even solo. She has spent retired life gardening, playing euchre in tournaments, and caring for her dog, Budi, and from the outside she has seemed to live a fulfilled, if a bit lonely, last few years. But I can't help thinking about that thing she once confided in me: *I think often of ending it all, but I know it wouldn't be fair to the rest of you.*

Have all her hobbies, her career, her pursuits, been nothing but a performance?

Now, with her body in such decline, her quality of life has decreased even more. I want to help her find quality, even if the quantity is waning.

"Can Rayna and I bring you dinner again tomorrow night?" I text her. "We can play a couple rounds of euchre if you're up for it!"

It is winter again. My mother is in her last month of life, and I am meditating.

Outside my wide living room window, a thick snow falls.

Uncountable numbers of unique flakes pelt the glass. I feel my body melt along with the snowflakes cascading down the windowpane. Through the melting snow I see car lights blurring into fractals. Watching the world through water is my most frequent meditation on the deep nature of reality. I love how water distorts and exposes the world. As my mother's condition has worsened, I've found expansiveness through grounding in reality.

A horrific gust of wind shakes my two-story house, pulling me out of my reverie, and causing my four dogs to bark.

"Hey!" I yell, silencing the dogs. They are eager for their evening walk. Any minute the meditation timer will go off—*BEEP. BEEP. BEEP.*

Time to walk the dogs so I can return to my dying mother.

I drop two pieces of gluten-free bread into the toaster, press the black handle, watch the coils turn red. I grab an overripe avocado from the fridge, saw it in half with a dull steak knife, and spoon out the green meat, which I smash on the steaming toast before walking out the door, all four dogs trailing me frantically.

After our walk, as I drive through the snow to my mom's house, I get a call from Johannah.

"How bad is it?" she asks. She's trying to figure out if she should take off work and come home now or wait a little longer. "How long do you think she has?"

It's the question on everyone's mind, the one no one has an answer to.

"I don't know, sweetheart," I sigh. "If you ask Gran, she'd say not to worry about it, to just come home in summer when you're planning to—she's in total denial."

"But what do you think? What is she like?"

"Well," I pause, picturing my mother's pale skin, vacant eyes, and gaping mouth. "The nurse I talked to said that once they start morphine, most people don't last more than a couple of weeks. So, really

I think she could go any day now." I've said the same thing to other family members who have been asking me, even encouraging my aunts to drive to town and play euchre with us, thinking it might be their last chance. I feel the burden of being the only one acting on the reality of my mother's death, but this is the role I am meant to play.

Johannah is silent. I want to invite her to open up to her grandmother's death, to face the feelings coming up. But I'm pulling into the driveway and I'm late for the next shift with my mom.

As I walk into my mom's bedroom, two hospice nurses are helping her sit up. Though her eyes are open, my mom is nowhere to be found—I can tell the morphine is having its way. She doesn't notice I am here until they lift her up and I am right in front of her. For a moment, the fogginess in her eyes clears, and she glares at me. Her next words are like an exploding star. "Stop telling people I'm dying. That's *your* thing."

Even with death right outside her window, hitting the pane like millions of relentless snowflakes, she refuses to look at it.

Two days later, my mother is dead. I crawl up onto her bed and stretch out beside her. I touch her body, pressing my palms along her cold face, feeling how her skin is still soft on the surface while underneath she is becoming hard, like stone.

I experience a tinge of shame, from breaking a taboo and lying with the dead. The truth is, I hadn't planned to keep her body with me after her death, but it is good and right for me to be with her, so close to her now.

I feel my mom with me more now in death than she ever was in life. I talk to her about her death, touching her cheek, her hands, in a way I never could when she was alive. She is changing me, healing me from the pain we caused one another. Tears fall down my cheeks and drop onto her fleece pajamas.

I grab her hand, close my eyes, and reflect on the final months. First there was the doctor's visit when my mom was advised to consider hospice, and afterward she yelled at me in the parking lot, blaming me for the doctor's prognosis. Then, after hospice had started, I supported her reluctance to start morphine, both of us knowing it would be the beginning of the end.

I watched as her struggle to breathe worsened. It got especially bad in the night, when her breath rattled and caught in her throat, and her eyes widened in panic. One night around 1:00 a.m., she awoke with a violent fit of coughing. I rushed to her bedside with water and the pulse oximeter, but the coughing subsided. The deadly silence that followed it seemed to last for many minutes. The hospice nurse had come in and was fiddling with some machines, preparing to replace the nasal cannula for a full mask. I clutched my mom's hand and felt her grip back firmly, shaking and sweating as she fought to inhale, eyes locked on mine in terror. Her oxygen levels had plummeted to 50 ppm and her CO_2 was dangerously high. The following night, she accepted the drugs.

I invited various family members to visit, letting them know she might not have many more days. Her sisters, nieces, brother-in-law, son-in-law, and grandson took turns gathering in her room, squeezing into folding chairs around her bed to play games of euchre. She continued to grumble at me, rehearsing the same story right up until her death: she didn't want to die, she wasn't dying, she would be better soon.

I spent every day with her, undeterred by her anger. I learned to stay present both to her desires and to the story her body was telling me. I learned to look into her eyes and be true to her. I learned to track the subtle changes in her personality. I learned to continually question the statements of other family members and the hospice nurses.

"It could be weeks," they'd say. "Move her into a care facility. It's too much to take care of her by yourself."

But my mom wanted to die at home.

I was with her all night before the morning she died, holding her hand, reading to her, posting on Facebook, meditating, crying. In the morning, the hospice nurse came to relieve me.

"I don't want to leave her," I said, certain the end was near.

"Just go home and shower, maybe get some food," the nurse encouraged me, taking in my rumpled clothes and tired eyes.

"Okay," I said. My mom was sleeping, looking as peaceful as if she had died already. I bent down and kissed her forehead. "Bye, Mom," I whispered. "I love you."

One hour later I got a call that she had died.

Now I lie next to her in her bed. I lick the salt off my lips, feeling more open as I write and cry. I think about what the nurse told me, that mothers rarely pass from this world to the next when their daughters are present. Perhaps she said this only to comfort me.

I examine my mother's face. *We did it, Mom! You died at home.*

The shadows outside lengthen. Snowflakes fall. I call my friend Beth who comes over and suggests we bathe my mom. "It's tradition in some cultures to bathe the dead," she says, seeing the grimace on my face.

Would you want this intimacy, Mom? I don't want to violate you. Her face tells me nothing, so I look out the window and am reminded of a line from James Joyce's "The Dead": "His soul swooned softly as he heard the snow falling faintly through the universe . . ."

"Okay, let's do it," I say. It's time for me to engage with death, to touch it in a way I've never been able to. I think of Jay's body, bloody and distorted on that stainless steel table, cold and alone. I want more for my mother.

I find a ceramic bowl in the kitchen that my step-daughter, Taran, made for her grandmother for her last birthday. I turn on the faucet and watch the water pour into the bowl. Then I sprinkle a few drops of lavender in the bowl and head to her bedroom, careful not to spill. The surface of the water ripples and rises near the edges.

Stay.

The air in the bedroom shimmers; my mom's skin has grown gray; my heart hurts.

I kiss her cheek. *I love you, Mom. I've always loved you.*

My friend goes to the bathroom to get washcloths, and I take selfies with my mom. I smile. She continues to turn to stone. Parts of us are agreeing to always go forward together.

I pull the covers back. Slip off her clothes. I dip the cloth and wring it out. Her chest is hard, her face a rock. She has only been dead a couple hours, yet she is already becoming Earth.

I hover over her feet, studying each toe, the contours of her ankles, the rise of her legs. *You are dead.*

I feel myself being squeezed, as if this death ritual is a birth. My mom's dead body. Jay's dead body. *I am touching you both.*

In the golden light of the early evening, I leave for the airport to pick up my daughters, who are arriving home early from a trip. I fold them each into my arms, holding them tight and trying to radiate the healing I received from my mother's body. Rayna holds on to me for a couple minutes, sobbing softly into my shoulder.

"So," I say as we pull away from the curb, "want to go see Gran?" I tell them about the time I spent with my mom's body, how important it felt for my mourning process.

"I want to see her," says Johannah. "It still doesn't even feel real that she's dead. I think it would be helpful for me to see her body before it's cremated."

I look at the other two girls. Taran appears unsure but Rayna shakes her head, laughing nervously.

"I don't think I want to, but I'll come there with you guys and wait in the car."

We decide to drive over and feel things out. By the time we turn down my mom's street, Rayna is considering at least coming into the house. "I just don't want to go into her room, that would be so creepy!"

We all laugh, though I don't agree. I'm glad we're all here together, laughing, missing Gran.

As we pull in at my mom's condo, Rayna screams from the back seat and drops to the floor behind me.

I jerk my head around, crying out, "What's going on, Rayna?"

"Gran!" she screams, curling her body into a ball. She is both sobbing and laughing. "Look!" She points toward the windshield.

Taran, Johannah, and I follow her finger to my mom's bedroom window, directly in front of our car. When I left my mom, it was still light out, so I never thought to close her curtains or turn off her bedside light. Now that night has fallen, Gran's body is framed by the window, on display as if someone had staged the scene. She lies as I left her—on her back, head propped on pillows, tucked peacefully under the covers. Her face is turned up to the sky, mouth parted, skin pale. Her cheeks are noticeably more hollow than they were when I left, but otherwise she could be asleep.

"Whoops," I say. "Sorry, Rayna!" I laugh at the beauty and the absurdity of this moment, the fact that I've unwittingly traumatized my daughter with my decision to keep my mom's body in her bed.

None of my daughters has ever seen a dead person before, and they grab each other's hands, laughing hysterically. "Oh, my God!" Taran cries. "I was *not* expecting her to just be lying there like that!"

I know how important this emotional release is for all of us. I feel relaxed, having spent the afternoon lying peacefully with the dead.

The next day, the people from the funeral home arrive to take my mom's body. I wish we could keep her with us, but we help them put her in the van, then wave as they drive away. "Goodbye, Mom," I whisper, bending down to comfort her whining dog.

—32—

We live in an intimate universe.

—Dr. Marc Gafni

On a windy day in November 2021, I met up with Todd Schantz, Jay's eighth-grade locker mate, at Governor's Island. It's a teardrop-shaped peninsula dangling off the north shore of Lake Mendota, and it's my preferred spot for a dog walk.

"So," I said, following the dogs through a corridor of black raspberry patches and pine trees. "Kurt tells me you knew Jay." During our brief correspondence, Kurt had recommended I talk to Todd.

"Oh yeah," Todd's feet crunched through the leaves behind me. "Well, Jay knew everybody, which was lucky for me. I was new in school."

I turned to look at Todd and tried to picture him as a boy. Todd the man was tall and broad with laughing eyes and a matter-of-fact smile like a straight line across his face. His short, dark hair was balding only slightly and he wore it in a crew-cut. And as I'd begun to discover, he was a natural storyteller.

"I had been in Catholic school, but I was sick of the routine and the fascist structure." Todd laughed. "So I convinced my parents to let me go to public school, and when I showed up the first day I was totally lost. I was a shy kid, and I didn't know where to go or who to ask. But Jay just walked right up to me and said, 'Hi!' I told him I was new and that I needed a locker and he said, 'Come with me, we'll get one together,' and marched me down to the office. It was super funny, this short kid leading me down the hall like he owned the place!"

We both erupted in laughter.

"And just like that, I had my first friend. I don't know what I would've done if Jay hadn't picked me up. He was just real affable. He had so many friends. He ended up introducing me to the people I would hang out with in high school. There was a core group of us— me, Jay, Kurt Smith, Jimmy Foye—those three were like a trio."

The path we walked on followed the shoreline around the peninsula. Though much of the southern side was elevated on a cliff, we began on the western side. We paused near an algae-free area of a sheltered beach, where Sheeta dropped a stick like a fat *L* at my feet. I tossed it into the lake, watching the wood break the water's surface.

Todd looked out across the lake, observing the mostly smooth water sprinkled with whitecaps. Seeing his warm eyes glistening with memory, I started to sense the boy I barely knew.

"Jay really brought me into my teenage years," he reflected. "We did so many things that I'd always thought about but had been too chicken to do, or didn't know how to do, lots of rebellion."

"Like what?" We started walking again, Todd leading the way.

"Well, the first time I ever smoked pot was with Jay," he chuckled. "We did it at Gompers."

"You smoked pot at *school*?"

"During recess! I didn't even know we were gonna do it. Kurt and Jay and Jimmy told me to come with them up the hill. And we sat there and then Kurt pulls out this pipe. When it got to me I was nervous, you know, but I did it. I mean, these are my new friends, I don't want to be a sissy!" Todd was gesturing with his hands and turning back to me every now and then so I could see his facial expressions. "I got so stoned! I was just like, wheeew, and Jay's like, 'Are you okay?'

And I'm like, 'I think so?' But I was like a cat on a hot roof. And Jay was laughing his ass off—he'd obviously smoked pot before. Him and Kurt were just cracking up." Todd and I started cracking up too.

"So then the bell rings for the end of recess and I'm like, ahh!" Todd gasped and clasped both hands to his face, eyebrows raised and mouth wide. "So we went into science class with Mr. Beecher, a total jackass, square jerk," he added as an aside. "And we sat down. I was two seats behind Jay, and I just remember sitting there in class, just holding on to my desk for dear life. And Jay kept looking back at me with this evil grin." He imitated Jay and we both exploded with laughter. It was a spot-on impression. I had forgotten about Jay's evil grin.

"That's such a funny story!"

"Yeah, we had some hilarious times. Speaking of Mr. Beecher . . ." Todd launched into another story about being shown in science class the process of distilling alcohol. Later that day, the boys had wanted to smuggle alcohol into a hockey game. "We said, 'Wow, I bet if we took this wine and boiled it and put a rubber hose here and into this jar with ice water, we could make hard liquor. So we took Mr. Beecher's teachings, and we turned this wine into high-powered liquor!" Todd laughed, eyes twinkling with mischief and pride. The boys had poured their moonshine into tiny sandwich bags secured with twist-ties. "So when they patted us down at the entrance, it was squishy and they couldn't feel it. Then we poured it into our sodas and got a nice buzz!"

I raised my eyebrows. "You got drunk off your concoction?"

"And it's all thanks to Mr. Beecher!"

Our walk had taken us to higher ground, giving us a better view of the lake. Ahead of us, the dogs chased three crows off the path.

We paused to catch our breath and Todd seemed to be lost in memories, staring vaguely out over the water. I continued throwing sticks for the dogs, making sure to aim into the woods rather than over the cliff edge.

"I'd forgotten all about this stuff," Todd mused. "It's wild to real-ize what an important role Jay played in my life. I mean, our paths crossed at such a time of transition for me. I can't imagine what it would have been like without him. He was like a conduit for all these experiences I was craving." Todd's eyes lit up. "He got us to see Van Halen in concert."

"Oh, really?"

"Yeah, and I'd always wanted to go to a rock concert, but at the time it seemed kinda outrageous. I told Jay, 'I don't think my mom would want me to go to that concert.' And he just said, 'Well, then we're not going to tell her.' He would just lay it all out, make it happen. 'You're just gonna be at my house, and we're gonna go to the concert.' And then if a problem arose, he had a solution. Like, 'But we don't have a ride, and we don't want to take the bus.' And Jay was like, 'Can your sister drive us?' And she said yes, so . . .'" Todd shrugged his shoulders, as if to say, "That was that."

Apparently, Jay also had the solution to how they were going to get tickets: "We went to that place downtown that used to sell records and pot paraphernalia," Todd said. "What's it called?"

"Pipefitters?" I asked.

"Right. And we get there and Jay says to me, 'You have to be eigh-teen to go in there, so don't act weird.' And he just walked right up to the counter and said, 'We'd like some Van Halen tickets.' He could just be very matter-of-fact. And, you know, they didn't really care, as long as we weren't buying pot pipes. They just wanted to make the sale—Madison was a different place in those days."

I smiled, remembering all the reckless adventures Jay and I had, too, the things he made possible for us.

"So, yeah, Jay got me into my first rock concert. It was me and Kurt and Jimmy. We all got in the car, and then Jimmy, that dumbass, pulled out a Stridex—you know the pimple medication? The Stridex pads?"

"I guess so?"

"Well Jimmy had a Stridex jar," Todd giggled, "full of joints! And he says to me, 'Here, you hold these when we go in.' And my sister saw, and she goes, 'What is going on?'" Todd mimicked her nagging tone of voice. "I was like, 'Nothing!' And she says, 'Ugh, the more I know about this, the less I like it.'"

"Oh, my God!" I felt like a teenager again, laughing with Todd.

"Isn't that hilarious?" As our laughter faded, Todd looked up at the tall oak we'd stopped beneath, its leaves just starting to turn. "It's amazing to think about how Jay shifted the direction of my life. He got me into adult things that I wanted to do but probably shouldn't have been doing." He smiled conspiratorially. "But, whatever, it was an experience!"

I nodded. I had no judgments about the antics of these young boys. "This is all so cool to hear about, I'm so grateful to you for being open and sharing with me."

"Of course! *Thank you.* Until you reached out the other day, I didn't realize that I had packed a lot of this stuff away. It's funny, I was grocery shopping when I got your message. I was in the dairy section, and had just grabbed a gallon of milk, when I felt my phone buzz. The minute I saw your name on the screen, I just lost it. I had to get out of there. So I left my cart where it was and ran out to my car—"

"Oh, you stopped your shopping?" I stopped walking and Todd paused beside me.

"Yeah! I just felt so sad about everything that happened and also really grateful for the opportunity to talk to you again. And I just sat in my car and cried about everything."

My heart swelled for Todd and I grabbed his arm, picturing this sweet grown man weeping in a parking lot.

"I was pounding the steering wheel, just feeling like, I wish that didn't fucking happen and regrets and missing him and the guilt from the funeral."

"What do you mean?"

"Do you remember?" Todd asked. "You helped me out."

"I hardly remember anything."

"Oh, really? Okay, well, the funeral was really intense. I had only had experience with old people dying. When Jay died, it didn't seem real."

I nodded, aware that every cell in my body was turned toward Todd.

"At the service, for some reason I didn't want my parents to come in with me, and they waited for me outside. So I go inside—"

Sheeta startled me out of my trance by barking sharply, asking me to throw her stick. I did so automatically, still focused on Todd.

He continued. "And we were all standing in that line up to the casket—we're all kids and we're chatting away, giggling while we wait. But then, on the other side of the casket, there was no giggling, there was no talking, there was no anything. Just a lot of crying and a lot of shock."

I began to see the funeral home, the carpeted floor and fluorescent lights.

Todd started off down the path again and I followed. "I was almost up to the casket and I thought, *Okay, I'm just gonna do this. It's unpleasant, but whatever.* But then I looked at his body, in that red and yellow hockey uniform. His face artificially smooth—Oh, God, remember that makeup job they did on him? I mean that was just . . ."

"I don't really remember what he looked like at the funeral, only when I saw him in the hospital." The image of Jay's corpse in a white hospital room swam into view and I had to stop walking. "He was a mess."

We had almost reached the parking lot but stopped at another small beach. The dogs splashed into the lake, lapping at the cold water.

"Yeah, they had to do a lot of work on him. I forget who it was, but somebody warned us that they had put a lot of makeup on him, that when we saw him at the funeral home it might not look like Jay." As he talked, Todd worked his way down the rocks toward the beach, one cautious step at a time.

I inched down behind him, careful not to slip on the mossy stones.

"Oh! And I remember some girl touched his cheek and it moved a section of the filler!"

"Ahh!" I shivered. I noticed a gold-bodied damselfly floating atop the water, seemingly drowning, another of its species flying in circles above it. I reached into the water with Sheeta's stick, stretching carefully to keep from falling into the lake myself, and lifted the soaked creature up and out of the water. Todd and I stood together for a few moments while it dried off, its companion hovering close by.

"So yeah. He was really different. I only looked for a second and then I just turned away. My body started to stiffen. It was really weird, I'd never had that experience. I think I was kind of in shock, seeing something like that. It was just like, boom! It did something to the chemicals in my body and sent me into a kinda panic state."

I felt the edge of panic rising in my own chest. I tried to focus on his words, hoping they would replace the memory of Jay's broken leg, blown-up head, tire-stained chest.

"All of a sudden I was having a really hard time just moving. It was like I was outside of myself. It was just weird. Next thing I know I'm out in the lobby. I was just sitting there in that chair, and I couldn't get up. My arms felt all crampy and weird—I guess I was having a panic attack. You must've noticed me, and you came over and grabbed my hand and held it really tight." Todd turned to face me. "And you just looked at me and said, 'Todd, pull yourself together. Focus, just breathe. In your nose, out your mouth.'" Todd was staring into my eyes as if *he* were teenage Kris and *I* were teenage Todd; the roles had reversed.

I followed the directions and took a deep breath.

Todd smiled. "I did that, and eventually I started to loosen up."

I felt myself loosen, noticing that the wind had picked up and the waves were beginning to spray us as they splashed against the rocks. I gestured toward the shelter of the trees and Todd nodded.

"Anyway," he said as we picked our way back up the steep, rocky steps to the main path. "I've always carried the shame of how I acted. You were going through a horrible time—your whole family was. You'd had enough at that point, I could tell you were strung out. But you were still so kind to me. I mean, you didn't know me that well and . . . I just can't imagine what you and your mom were going through."

The path was wide enough now for me to walk beside him, so I grabbed his arm and held on to it. "There's no need to be ashamed. That was a very healthy response to death."

"Yeah, but your mom looked so, so sad. All these years I've felt so bad for creating this huge fuckin' drama. I made a bad situation much worse. If I was going through *my* brother's death at a funeral, and people started freaking out, I would just be like, 'Okay, this isn't about you. Stop it.' You know?" Todd sighed. "I thought I'd be all cool, and everything would be okay. And it just yanked me."

"I want to honor your response. You loved Jay." We walked arm in arm, the waves crashing harder against the shore. A blue jay squawked overhead.

"Yeah, I did. Thank you." He squeezed my arm. "And thank you for being there. The whole thing was such a blur, but I'll always remember you looking right in my face, calming me down. I would have been lost without you."

We stopped and stood in silence for a moment, looking over the lake. We were almost back to the cars, but I didn't want this walk to end. I felt a current of ancient pain leave my body and move out across the water. In each sparkle of wave, I saw billions of suns opening. I imagined that Jay and all the dead were here for the sharing of this story. Then my golden retriever Toby walked up to us, huffing and snorting in his desperate search for attention, and I knelt to rub his ears. "You need some love, Toby?" I asked.

"Such a classic golden." Todd laughed, throwing Sheeta's stick up the hill.

I stood and turned to face Todd, remembering the topic I had most wanted to address. "So . . . do you know the backstory of—I mean, did you ever hear Jay talk about death or dying or . . . ?"

"No . . ."

"Starting when he was maybe eleven or twelve, Jay would tell us that he was going to die young."

Todd raised his eyebrows, eyes wide.

"And he told us all these details. Like he knew he would be riding his bike and it would have something to do with a green car."

"What! How did he know that?"

"Well, that's one of the mysteries!" My raised voice echoed off the water.

"Huh." Todd seemed lost in thought. "Wow. You know, now that you're telling me this, it makes a lot of sense." He started walking slowly, and I followed. "That's what I was trying to say about Jay's personality. Like with the locker and the concert tickets and stuff—he was kind of like an adult, like he didn't have kid baggage or . . . or drama, or whatever. He could just see a problem and handle it. So if he had some kind of premonition . . . I mean, that just sounds like maybe there's a previous life involved . . ." Todd's pace slowed almost to a standstill.

I turned to watch him, taking the opportunity to throw my arms out wide and stretch my back.

"Maybe Jay knew he was going into another existence after this one. Because if he was saying things like that so young . . ." Sheeta dropped a log in front of Todd. "Should I throw this or is it too big?" he asked.

"You can throw it."

Todd lifted the heavy branch and heaved it into the water. It crashed with a loud splash and Sheeta followed it. "This is fascinating. It's making me think differently about Jay. I suddenly understand why he was so different. I couldn't quite put my finger on it. He never treated me like I was a new friend. He treated me like he knew me."

"And he was so happy, wasn't he?" I asked.

"Yeah!" Todd agreed.

"How do you be fucking happy when you know you are going to die?"

"He was at peace with it." Todd shrugged. "He knew his stint as Jay Amelong was limited, so he just enjoyed it. For as long as he could. He didn't really worry about a whole lot. The real question is, how did he know?"

"Right? That's something else I wanted to ask you about." I began walking again, calling for the dogs to follow, leading our pack through a particularly narrow section of the path. "Jay always told me and my mom that it came to him in his dreams."

"Uh-huh."

"But then, four or five years ago, I spoke with Stevie Anderson and he told me a story in which Jay told Stevie that he learned he would die young while doing LSD, that he had seen it in his acid trip!"

"Yeah." Todd's face remained neutral.

"But do you think it's possible that Jay would have been doing LSD?"

"Oh, yeah," Todd said. "We did it together."

I swung around to face him. "Really?"

"Oh yeah," Todd said again. "Me and Jay and Kurt and—"

"When I talked to Kurt, he denied ever doing acid till high school. And my mom said it was impossible, too, so I started to doubt Stevie's story—he's not the most reliable person."

"No, no, this is another first—"

"But you guys were—what, twelve?" I interrupted. "Thirteen?"

Todd nodded.

"How did you even get your hands on LSD?"

"Speedy Reuter."

"Who?"

"Speedy Reuter."

I felt a tickle of recognition in my brain, then a face came into focus. "Oh, you mean Maurice! I dated him for a bit."

"Yeah, Maurice. So we got LSD from him—"

"You sought it out?" I interrupted again. "Or was he like, 'You guys should try LSD'?"

"I think Kurt was the one who bought it. And then we went over to Speedy's house—or maybe it was Stevie Anderson's house, I can't remember."

"Oh, so Stevie was there?"

"I can't remember. But they got out the stuff and I'm like, 'What's that?' And Jay's like, 'It's acid. We're gonna do LSD.' And I'm like, 'What? What does it do?' 'Well, you know, it'll make you feel really different. You'll be able to see and think a lot differently.' 'Okay . . . Is it safe?' 'Oh, yeah, we'll be fine, we don't have to go anywhere.'"

"So Jay had obviously done acid before then?" I said.

"Oh yeah." Todd said. "So we were in the basement and it had all these colored light fixtures—remember those things in the '70s with the color wheel and all that stuff?"

I nodded.

"And we're listening to *Led Zeppelin III*, and I was just like—" Todd stared blankly into the distance, his neck and hands limp.

"Were you interacting?"

"Yeah, we were laughing about shit, I don't remember what we talked about. But I remember Kurt, he said to me, 'You know, Shantzy, there's just something different about you. You just came to school and we thought, *What a dork!* And now you're tripping on acid with us!'" Todd's last few words turned into giggles. "I was like, 'I know!

When I was in Catholic school, I didn't know any of this existed.' And he's like, 'Well, do you like it?' And I go, 'I think I do, but how long does it last?'"

Our loud laughter startled the dogs, who hurried over to check on me.

"So, was that trip when he had his vision?"

"Not that I was aware of, no. I don't remember him talking about that at all. But what you're saying makes sense because—have you ever done LSD?"

"Not a full trip but a microdose, so I've seen the visuals."

"So you understand that your brain does operate differently, you're able to think outside of yourself."

"Yes."

"You start to think about how things really are. So Jay might have had some sort of epiphany at that time, like to know that he was gonna die. And just like, 'Okay. I accept that that's what will happen.' And most people would be scared or worried about it all the time, or—"

"Or try to make it different!" I cut in.

"Right. But he just went with the flow, all the time." Todd looked softly up at the gray sky, as if he had a view of Jay in heaven. "He was really a nice guy. He helped me out a lot and I miss him." Then he looked at his feet and cleared his throat. "I think about him a lot."

Just then another blue jay—or perhaps the same one—flew overhead, crying loudly. "A jay!" I exclaimed. "Blue jays always make me think of Jay, and they never come this close to me!"

"Wow! I haven't seen one in a while, either." Todd grinned. "That's Jay! That's significant."

"Fucking significant, Todd!" I linked my arm with his again as we headed back to the cars.

—33—

I can hear the sizzle of newborn stars, and know anything of
meaning, of the fierce magic emerging here. I am witness to
flexible eternity, the evolving past, and I know we will live
forever, as dust or breath in the face of stars, in the shifting
pattern of winds.

—Joy Harjo, *Secrets from the Center of the World (Volume 17)*

Almost a year after my walk with Todd, I attended the International Forum on Consciousness. Fall had begun again in Madison, and the maple trees shone red like a million suns as I approached the ultra-modern, glass-fronted building that housed the headquarters of Promega, a biotech corporation.

Walking into the grand, airy lobby, I noticed two tall glass structures that acted as stream beds for vertically flowing water. I stood in front of one of the fountains, stretched my arm around to the other side, and took a few selfies. Life through water, my meditation. I looked at the photos, focusing my attention on how my image seemed to dissolve into waves. I noticed it was past the start time of the event, though many people were still milling around the lobby. I tucked my phone away and decided to investigate the beverage table. As I headed toward the table, a slightly stooped man with short, gray hair stepped into my path.

"I'm Bill," he said, smiling.

"Oh, hi!" I pointed to my name tag. "Kristina."

"Amazing event, yeah? A conference on consciousness. What could be better?"

I nodded.

He turned and pointed to the vertical waters. "What were you doing at the fountain? It seemed like you were about to walk through that one!"

I grinned. "I use photography to study the deeper nature of reality."

"Fascinating. Are you a presenter?"

"No, just interested in consciousness. I find that taking photos helps me stop time."

"Wow, finding the universe in water. That's cool."

"Thank you!" I beamed at him.

"Thank *you*. I'm glad I was brave enough to ask. All of that is much more aligned with my interests than all this alien stuff." He lifted his wineglass to his lips, taking a sip. "What's your interest in psychedelic medicine?"

"Last week I did an assisted psychedelic journey in California."

"A good journey?"

"Yeah, it was really powerful. It expanded my heart, really helped me drop into a space where I could grieve my mom's death."

"That sounds amazing. I haven't used psychedelics since I was a kid."

It was like a bolt of lightning hit the lake of my heart. I grabbed the thick sleeve of his jean jacket to steady myself. Just as quickly, I wanted to pull away—this man was a stranger, after all. But I felt him relax so I didn't let go. He, too, could feel the quickening of our bond.

"Where did you grow up?" I asked.

"Madison."

"And you did psychedelics? How old were you?"

"Fourteen."

"What kind?"

"LSD."

I stared into his glistening brown eyes. "Oh! It's so hard for me to believe that a twelve-year-old would be doing acid."

"Fourteen," he repeated, looking confused.

"I'm sorry. Let me explain. I'm writing a book about my brother who died young. He had a vision of his death, and told us he was okay with his fate. He told the story many times. He said he dreamt it, but recently one of his friends told me that Jay had seen his death while doing LSD. I found it hard to believe, since I wasn't doing acid. I thought I knew everything about Jay. We were best friends."

"I'm so sorry about your brother. Sounds heartbreaking."

"Yes." I wiped away my tears. He set down his empty wineglass and pulled a tissue out of his coat pocket, handing it to me.

"Thank you." I blew my nose and he looked away as he began talking again.

"Yeah, I started taking acid when I was fourteen. Most of my friends did too."

"Really?"

"It was the seventies! You know, that wasn't long after the Beatles released *Sgt. Pepper*—Pink Floyd, Aerosmith, Led Zeppelin . . . It was all part of the culture. Antiwar protests, the riots—remember the bombing at the university?"

"Totally. I remember learning about it when I was only six years old. I learned about war and that some people were trying to stop the killing. That guy, Karl Armstrong, he was my hero."

Bill nodded.

"So you were fourteen, in Madison, doing acid. Does it sound likely to you that younger kids could have gotten their hands on it?"

"Oh, for sure. We'd go to school, do our homework and chores, and spend the rest of our time downtown, watching the college students and dropping acid. Our parents weren't paying attention."

I felt as if I needed to sit down. "I'm realizing that, until this moment, I've really not taken this LSD possibility seriously. I do know Jay was into all the music. I do know how the protests influenced my neighborhood. Stevie and Todd must have been right—Jay must have learned he would die while doing acid."

"I mean, it makes a lot of sense. Acid often gives deep insight, and it affects time perception. Remember in the last talk they were explaining the block universe? Space-time is not a separate space and a separate time, but rather an interconnected process. All time exists all the time."

"Right? I'm excited to go talk to Jeffrey Kripal about it—he's a philosophy professor. I'm seated at his table for the dinner conversations."

"Oh, me too!" Bill checked his watch and looked up at table 4. "Looks like he's already seated there, should we go sit?"

I nodded and followed him to our table.

Bill generously pulled out the open seat next to Jeffrey for me and took the one on the other side.

"Mr. Kripal? Hi, my name is Kristina Amelong."

We shook hands and the rest of the seats filled up at our table, as waitstaff began placing plates of food in front of us. The conversation flowed across the table and I munched my Alaskan halibut and waited for the right moment to share Jay's story. When I did so, unlike most people I've encountered, Jeffrey Kripal seemed unsurprised. "Oh, yes. That sort of thing happens all the time."

"Really? You've heard stories like this before."

"Yes, it's more common than you would think."

I couldn't tell whether I felt affirmed by this. For so long, the mystery surrounding Jay's death had felt so unfathomable. "So you think it's possible he could have discovered his future through LSD?"

"Oh, certainly."

The conversation quickly moved on, and I listened passively, half of my brain still churning on the opening up of this reality. Since my conversation with Todd, I'd begun to consider the likelihood that Jay had seen his future through hallucinogens. That's one of the reasons I had recently decided to do this guided journey. I had experienced firsthand the power of these medicines, when utilized in a safe, supported way.

For so long we had thought Jay had known about his death from his dreams. But now I recalled a conversation I'd had a few years back with a professor from a school of divinity in California who studied dreams. He had written a book on children's dreams for which he had gathered a database of over ten thousand dreams. He said that in all his research, he had never heard a story like Jay's.

"Never?" I asked him.

"Never."

Perhaps it wasn't a dream Jay had had, not in the traditional sense. Perhaps his acid trips had given him access to the deeper nature of the universe.

—34—

*Death ends a life, not a relationship. All the love you created
is still there. All the memories are still there.*
—Morrie Schwartz

I still think about Kurt sometimes, when I pass Goodland Drive on my way to the dog park, when I run into a classmate of mine or Jay's around town. I wish Kurt could have the healing I've had. I'm so grateful to him for even the small amount of time he shared with me and for connecting me with key contacts like Todd. Kurt also put me in touch with John Anderson, a friend and classmate whom I immediately added on Facebook. I found out that John lived in Florida, and I took advantage of a recent trip to Miami for the annual board meeting of the Center for World Philosophy and Religion to meet up with John in person.

We met for dinner near his home in Treasure Island. As we ate at the restaurant in a resort, he told me about the career he'd made of flipping houses. I shared how my journey with chronic illness had led to the launching of my business. Then we sat in his truck in a parking lot and shared a joint. When he reached one of his long, tanned arms over my lap and opened his glove box to grab his stash box, I noticed a handgun nestled atop the owner's manual.

I flinched slightly. "Why do you need a gun?"

"There's some crazy people out here. I take it everywhere I go. Here's a good example." He told the story of a recent day when he had pulled through an intersection and slightly cut someone off. The man he had cut off pulled up to him at the next intersection, furiously flipping him off. "All three of my kids were in the car. And my son said, 'Dad, you have your gun, right?' And I realized it was the first time I didn't have my gun with me." His eyes were wide, serious. "I had all three kids in the car, you know?"

I didn't know what to say.

"Anyway, I swore that was the last time I'd ever leave the house without it. You wanna smoke, by the way?" He extracted a joint from the box and held it up, seeming not to notice my discomfort. "You know, you were the first person I ever smoked weed with."

"Really? Where?"

"It was in your basement. I don't know, I must'a been eleven or twelve?" He flicked the lighter and held it to the twisted end of the hand-rolled joint.

"I can't really remember but I believe you." I strained to picture it: John, Jay, and me falling over each other with laughter, halfway up the basement steps. Smoke spiraling up the narrow stairwell, Shadow purring at my feet.

John asks, *What's that?*

I smirk. *Just suck!*

Do it, Jay insists.

John's voice pulled me from my thoughts. "I don't remember much either. I have a really bad memory—too much of this stuff." He laughed, holding up the joint. "I always kept it under control, though. I'm not like a pothead. Same with other drugs. I mean, sometimes on New Year's my wife and I do a little . . ." He eyed me sheepishly.

I smiled. "Mushrooms? Acid?"

"No, not anymore. I got into it in high school, but those psychedelics are too heavy."

"I've found that microdosing can really help open up emotional space—psilocybin, MDMA."

"Yeah." He exhaled smoke and handed me the burning joint. "Microdosing. But I don't want to think that much. When I want to let loose, I just want to escape. I don't want to go deeper into my thoughts. You know what I mean?"

"I understand." I sucked on the damp tip. "But what else is there?"

"I know. And then sometimes I don't. I don't want to get too deep. It's totally a defense mechanism, because of all the crap I've been through, you know? I just don't want to feel." He took off his black ball cap and rubbed his hand over close-cropped white hair.

"I understand. I spent years after Jay died trying not to feel. Became an alcoholic and drug addict. Eventually I got clean and sober, and over the years I've learned the healing power of going deep, of facing the pain. But I know how hard it is. I appreciate you for having this conversation."

"Well, I want to! There's so many details!" John drummed his fingers on the steering wheel in agitation. "No one wanted to talk about it."

"Right. No one."

"Billy won't go into it. He won't. He never went into it," he said, cracking his window, flicking ash. "Will you keep telling me the story?"

"Absolutely. But first can you tell me what you remember from the funeral?" I offered him the joint back, feeling the THC work its magic.

"Okay. Well, I remember the song, 'Stairway to Heaven.' Used to play it in a band I was in, and it would always make me think of Jay."

"Oh, really? You sang it?"

"And played guitar."

"Let's sing it now!"

"No, no."

I began singing.

"No, come on, I don't even know any of the words."

I sang the next line.

"Seriously, stop. You're gonna make me lose it. I can't listen to that song anymore without crying."

I stopped. "It's okay to cry," I said solemnly.

"No, I don't like to go back to that place, I don't really cry anymore." He shook his head and took a puff of the joint. "I got all my crying out that day, you know, with your mom."

"My mom?"

"At the funeral. I brought Jay's hockey stick. Everyone at school had signed it, and it was my job to deliver it to Jay—you know, we were on the hockey team together." He offered me the joint.

"I'm good, thanks."

"So, anyway, I walked up to the casket and tried not to look, 'cause I had heard he looked kinda weird."

Instead, John said, he thought back to a fond memory of Jay passing him the puck for the winning goal of the state hockey tournament. As he set the stick beside the casket, he experienced something he'd never felt before, a sensation of setting his own body down along with the stick.

"That was when I really looked at the body, and saw someone I didn't recognize. I started shaking. I thought about what Billy had told me when he got back to school on the day it happened: 'It didn't look like Jay. Too long. It wasn't Jay—Jay is small.' He just kept saying that over and over, his face white as a sheet. And I must have looked about the same after seeing inside the casket."

Apparently, my mom had noticed John enter the room with the hockey stick. John had been one of Jay's best friends, and my mom knew him well. She was touched that he had brought Jay's stick and wanted to make sure to tell him, so she hobbled over and waited as he paid his respects. "When I turned away from the casket, your mom was standing there. She startled me, and I was in shock from Jay's body, so I kind of fell into her arms!"

"Whoa!"

"Yeah, and you remember she was on crutches. My knees were giving out and I was trying not to knock her over." We both laughed.

Miraculously, Billy had watched the scene unfold and ran over in the nick of time to catch his friend, saving my mom from a fall.

"We just held each other in the middle of the funeral hall. I was bawling my eyes out, just saying, 'He can't be dead,' over and over."

We sat in silence. I slapped a mosquito on my cheek, wiped the bloody body on my pants.

Then John spoke. "Can you go back to the actual thing again? I want to understand what happened. So they were coming down the hill? Bill's ahead of them, or whatever, Jay and Kurt took off? They ditched him? And then Jay was on the corner or something and that's how he got hit?"

I nodded and prepared to dig back into the story.

"That was something me and Bill never understood. How did Jay die but not *Kurt*?"

Something on John's face made me pause, a sneer. It reminded me of Kurt's words: *Not everyone is nice . . . I'm a private person. I moved away from Wisconsin to be far removed from people . . .*

People like John? I remembered getting the sense from others that Kurt had been seen as a black sheep after Jay's death. There had been some story circulating at the time that cast Kurt as the dark force that had pulled Jay toward smoking and skipping school. I hoped John didn't hold to such beliefs. Before I had a chance to ask him about it, he was talking again.

"I thought it was a girl that hit him. I thought Bill told me that it was a lady. And they were screaming at the lady or something."

"No, it was a man who hit Jay, his name was Robert. He drove a green T-Bird. Did you know that Jay predicted his death?"

"What?"

"Yeah, he told us he would be hit by a green car while riding his bike. And that's exactly what happened."

"What are you saying?"

"Jay started talking to us about his death months before it happened. And he was okay with dying. That's what he told us over and over. He picked the song 'Stairway to Heaven.'"

"You must be shitting me, Kris."

"Jay knew."

"Jay knew. God . . ." John dragged his hand across his face. "I've been waiting for this for forty years, Kris. Thank you. I needed to know what happened. I had heard through the grapevine that Jay had picked the song. But I didn't understand that. I could only blame Kurt. It's so great to know the bigger story. I'm just trying to picture it in my head, what happened exactly."

I described it to the best of my ability: the car hitting Jay, pushing his bike into the curb, pulling him under the car, zigzagging, dragging Jay, slamming into the maple tree.

"Shit. And Kurt's watching the whole thing?"

"And freaking the fuck out, watching a car crush his best friend, watching the blood fill the road."

"Wow." John stared, speechless for several minutes. I stayed silent as well, focusing on my breath, ready to listen to whatever might come next.

"I feel bad," he said. "All these years . . . I've been holding this hatred toward Kurt in my heart—and I know I wasn't the only one. We were just so mad and didn't know who to blame. Kurt was trouble, we said, and it seemed like Kurt was the one who got him into all this stuff. And then Jay died and Kurt lived. It didn't seem right. But now that you're telling me Jay knew it was going to happen—like it was fated or something . . . I mean . . . there's no way Kurt could have caused that. He was just a kid. I mean, that was . . . God . . . or a higher power or whatever." John exhaled another stream of smoke. "Destiny."

Epilogue

For, enlightenment or no enlightenment, consciousness or no
consciousness, nature prepares itself for death.
There is no birth of consciousness without pain.
—Carl Jung

September 3, 2021, was a beautiful, late summer day. It would have been Jay's fifty-fourth birthday. I drove with my three daughters and Rayna's boyfriend, Andrew, out to Richland Center to visit Jay's grave. We all piled into my Subaru, the girls squeezing into the back to give six-foot-tall Andrew the passenger seat, their arms crossing over each other's knees, heads leaning on each other's shoulders. We followed the Wisconsin River past red barns and cornfields, the smells of manure, forest and water reminding me of my whole life.

We weren't going only for Jay. We had chosen this day to scatter my mom's ashes, as per her request. It had been a year and a half since her death—nineteen months of a global pandemic—and we had finally found a time when everyone was in town and had space for this ceremony.

I pulled up the gravel drive of my cousin Marty's house to pick up Mom's ashes. He met us on the same porch he and Jay had swung on when Jay told him he would die. Marty had less hair and more wrinkles, but he had the same charismatic grin he'd had as a boy. He'd had a recent COVID exposure, so we kept some distance, catching up a bit—it was the first time I'd seen him since my mom's funeral, and regret tugged at my heart for the space that always somehow existed between me and my extended family. A dragonfly buzzed overhead as I said, "I'd love to visit you guys more often." Tears welled up in my eyes.

"You know you're always welcome, Kris," Marty said.

I threw my arms around him. "Thanks, Marty, that means a lot." I dried my eyes and got back in the car, hoping I hadn't just contracted COVID. Marty waved as we turned out of the driveway to follow Willow Creek toward the cemetery.

We passed Elephant Trunk Rock, named for the shape it had been carved into by glaciers This was my favorite landmark on this route. As we hit the gravel up the steep hill to the tiny burial ground, I flashed back to a much colder day, Easter 2014.

I drop my car into four-wheel drive, bouncing up the vertical bluff to Neptune Cemetery.

"Kris!" My mom cries from the passenger seat. "Slow down!"

"Sorry." I park along the edge of the adjacent cornfield and turn the ignition off. "Ready, Mom?"

She raises her red umbrella, stepping out of the car. Rain quickly soaks my jacket. I don't mind. I want inside the thickness of this moment, weather and all. The cooing of pigeons echoes from the cement silo across the highway.

We stand together for a moment, surveying the graveyard. I take a deep breath through my nose, savoring the wet, green smell. "It's beautiful here."

My mom nods. "I gave directions in my will to cremate me, but maybe you could bring some of my ashes here."

I look at her, taken aback by her direct commentary about death, but she gazes resolutely into the distance. Then, without another word, she sets off across the cemetery, in the opposite direction of Jay's grave.

I watch her stroll across the uneven ground, unable to imagine that a day will come when my mother will die. One day she will be gone, just like Jay is gone. Then I remember Jay is here; I've come to visit him. I head toward his grave, grass squelching under my boots.

It's been thirty-one years since Jay asked to be buried here, on Easter 1981, thirty-eight days before his death.

Pine trees dance in the wind. Most of the tombstones are two hundred years old. No one else from our family is buried here. The Butte family stones rise tall next to Jay's flat stone. Butte, next to Jay—makes me laugh inside.

I watch the rain bounce off the engraving on his tombstone:

Jay P. Amelong, September 3, 1967–May 27, 1981

I follow the flight of a soaked robin to locate my mother across the cemetery. She is deeply focused, pausing at each member of the Schafer family, rain falling around her umbrella. She looks up for a moment, smiles, and returns her gaze to the next tombstone.

The wind gusts, the rain falls harder, I lie on the soaked grass over Jay's body. I need to feel him. I need to talk to him. The words rush out of my mouth, traveling into the ground, into his bones.

"Jay, do you hear the wind? Can you feel the rain? I miss you so much. I think about you every day. I'm writing a book about you, Jay. And you know what? I have you to thank for so many blessings in my life. I started a business because of you—because I followed your signs. Most of all, I am coming to understand how you could see your future, how consciousness is primary."

I long to share everything about my life, evolutionary journey, family, memoir. I look up to find our mom, still roaming the far side of the cemetery.

"I named my daughter Rayna Jay after you." I wonder what he

would think—I see my thirteen-year-old brother laughing to find out I have a daughter.

My mom appears over me, wearing a bemused expression. "You must be soaked!"

"Yes."

She rolls her eyes. "I'm going back to the car, it's cold."

"I'll be there in a minute, and then change my clothes."

I listen to her footsteps slosh away. I breathe in the wet smell of the earth. Then I get back to my feet and speak again: "We stay connected, Jay. Ours is a love story."

Back in the present, the sky was a sapphire blue and a warm breeze wafted gently through green-leaved oak trees. Our small party wandered toward Jay's plot, solemn yet at ease, taking in the glory of the day. Andrew and Rayna held hands. Johannah linked her arm through mine. When we reached Jay, we all looked at each other.

"Should we each say something about Gran?" I asked.

They nodded.

"You go first," Taran said, nudging her glasses with the back of her hand. "And scatter some ashes."

I unscrewed the urn's lid and reached into the plastic bag nestled inside, stuffing my fist with the fine, white particles. "I miss you, Mom. I wonder where the journey of your consciousness takes you now. I wonder if parts of you are the dappled sunshine in the clouds above us." I looked up at the puffy clouds moving across the sky and felt time expand.

As I bent over and sprinkled the being who brought me through her body into the grass on top of Jay's grave, memory took me away again.

* * *

The sun sets behind me as I slide open the glass door, pushing the heavy curtains aside, walking into my mom's dark living room. The squishy carpet under my foot startles me. So does my mom. Her eyes are closed, mouth open. I don't see breathing.

The oxygen machine puffs air like a whale. I feel frozen, standing so close to death, watching, watching, watching until I see her chest rise and fall in shallow breaths. I relax, bend down, and pet Budi.

"Oh, you're back," she says. "Can you take down the garbage for me?"

I catch her eyes. She looks away. I want to hug her; instead I turn, grab the garbage bags, and head downstairs. The stairwell air feels thick. I pull open the door and walk across to the far end of the garage, concentrating on the echo of each footstep.

Me. Here. Alive. In intimacy with how it took every moment of all-of-life to bring my mom and me to this moment. A life cycle. I could even feel our repair in eternity.

I turn the handle to open the garbage room, squint in the darkness, and set the garbage on the left side and the recycling on the right. I hold my breath so I won't pass out—the room smells like a mix of rotten food and an oil spill.

I shut the door and begin to breathe again, lifting my hand to feel my heart pound, allowing a shiver of utter delight to surge through my body. I love my mom. I want to hold her and not let her go.

Back in the apartment, I fill a glass of water from the filter in the fridge and bring it to my mom in the living room.

She takes it from me wordlessly and takes a sip. As I head back to the kitchen she asks, "Want to play cards?"

"Sure." I help her to the table with her glass. Sitting across from her, I am struck at how swollen and shiny her lips are.

I shuffle the cards, but as I start to deal she grabs my wrists with both of her hands, gasping for breath. "Where is my next morphine? I . . . feel like I'm . . . drowning."

My heart hurts for my mother, sinking in the sea of lung death.

As if reading my mind, she says, "I am not dying." In fact, she will die sixty hours later.

I squeeze her hand. I help her swallow her pill. I deal the cards.

It's a tight game, but at the end of the last round she throws in her final cards, a satisfied grimace on her face. "It was a close one, but hearts was the best I had," she rasps.

"Good one, Mom."

She nods, coughing again. I see the alarm has returned to her eyes.

I hold out her water and rub her back. "It's okay, Mom. I'm here. I won't leave."

"Mommy?" Rayna touched my shoulder, her soil-brown eyes asking me if I was done.

I shook my head, looking down at the urn and noticing how the ash that had clung to my hand had imprinted the lines of my finger on the silver vessel. Some of what remained of my mom had formed a shape of my body. "Mom, I wonder if your suffering around death is over. I want to imagine you are now enmeshed in the full infinity of our entangled and participatory universe." I met the eyes of each of the people standing with me—Johannah's round face beaming encouragement; Taran's expression serious and loving; Rayna's eyes rimmed in red; Andrew looking down shyly. "Most of all, Mom, I love you. I love you forever. One lifetime isn't long enough for the beauty of our relationship."

Taran went next, the ash coating the silver rings on her right hand. "It's hard to believe you've been gone a year and a half."

We all nodded.

"Thank you for being such a wonderful grandmother. I feel so lucky to have had you." She let the ash fall gently around the flowers that grew on Jay's grave, then went to lean up against her big sister.

Johannah put her arm around her, looking to Rayna to see if she was ready.

Rayna nodded, reaching for the urn. "I'm so glad you're in a better place now, but I miss you so much." She wiped a tear from her cheek with her forearm and leaned over the grave to trickle the white dust. She held the urn tightly to her abdomen, as if clinging to her grandmother. I pictured Rayna as a three-year-old, wrapped around Gran's still sturdy body, going everywhere she went. When Rayna finished speaking, Johannah asked Andrew if he wanted to say anything.

"Well." Andrew squeezed his large hand into the small urn opening. "All I can say is, I know Gran was a very special person, and I wish I could have met her." He dropped the fistful of dust in a small pile in the grass, then went back to Rayna's side where she buried her wet face in his chest.

Johannah stepped forward. "I've had this song in my head all day, when I picked these flowers and as we drove out here, and I want to teach it to you all. It's called 'Wildflowers' by Tom Petty." She began the chorus, voice full of emotion yet clear. After she repeated each line a couple times, we all joined in as I filmed.

We joined hands as the song ended and shared a moment of silence, staring at my mom's urn, which rested on the gravestone. A shaft of light fell perfectly across the flowers and the urn, so I knelt to capture it with my camera. Soon I was snapping away, lost in the beauty of nature and thoughts of my mother. When I stood, I noticed Johannah had sat on a flat stone nearby, and Rayna had come to perch on her knee. They motioned Taran to join them, and she wrapped a tanned arm around each of their shoulders so the three girls could lean their heads together.

When everyone seemed ready, we headed back to the car. As we walked through the grass and away from the grave, I said, "I, too, will be leaving the planet sometime, and I will miss it, and all of you."

On our drive home along the river, we played euchre in the car. The game is so second-nature to me at this point, almost like breathing, so I can easily drive and play with the help of my self-driving

Subaru. It requires each person to announce which card they are playing, since it can be hard to see.

"Queen of clubs," Rayna declared.

"King of clubs," I crowed, having bumped, or "euchred" Rayna and Andrew's team.

"Euchre's the name of the game," Rayna said, a frequent saying of my mom's.

As Johannah dealt the next hand, I looked down at the urn, nestled between Andrew's feet on the floor of the front seat. I could hear my mom's laugh, and I saw Jay's face. I was transported back to our kitchen table, the three of us playing cards.

I thought about how all time exists all the time. What other unique forms do Jay and Mom and I take throughout eternity?

I picked up my new hand of cards. "Jack of hearts," I called, smiling at the mystery.

Acknowledgments

I am profoundly grateful to all those who have inspired me and whose shoulders I stand on, too many artists and thought leaders to name, including those I have quoted. This fifteen-year project would not have been possible without the loving support and labor of so many.

My early writing was cradled by the beautiful container of Miriam Hall's writing group, and I appreciate you all for making space for my writer's voice to develop. Richard Ely was my first editor and saw the potential in my writing before I did, reading early chapters and following the process through to the end. Thank you for your keen eye and big heart—and for the genius title idea!

I'm grateful to Ron Kuka, who taught as he edited and gave me new confidence in my story and my ability to tell it. You were such a pleasure to work with! I thank Brooke Warner for early inspiration in writing a memoir and for creating such a powerful and cutting-edge hybrid publisher! And my deepest appreciation to everyone at She Writes Press for doing what you do and making so many dreams realities. I am forever indebted to those who read drafts of the manuscript and provided invaluable feedback, support, and blurbs: Samantha Krause, Becca Gardener, Jeffrey Kripal, Kristina Kincaid, Judy Reeves, Bridget Birdsall, John Nichols, and Carol Herndon.

I gratefully acknowledge Johannah CordonHill, my cherished stepdaughter, whose unwavering support, meticulous project management, and insightful editing breathed life into these pages. Your love, dedication, and attention to detail have not only shaped this memoir but have also illuminated Jay's story. I adore you.

I am privileged to have studied with brilliant and loving mentors who are willing to look directly at the existential risks that humanity currently faces. Thank you to Kathleen Wescott, whose Indigenous perspective on God and nature has shaped me and can be felt in every chapter of my memoir and my life. I owe an eternal debt of gratitude to my teacher Marc Gafni for the love, rigor, depth, and devotion that serves as a guiding light for me and so many. Thank you also to my beloveds in the Center for World Philosophy and Religion community and to all my pickleball buddies!

Big love and hugs and never-ending appreciation for my family of origin and the one that I helped shape. Our relationships have sustained me, and your love and connection makes so much possible in my life. To those of you who made it into the pages of this book, whether or not you ever read it, I'm grateful. Special thanks to Taran, Rayna, Mike, Genio, and Nina—you all mean the world to me; to Jay, for opening my mind to all that is and for journeying with me forever; and to my mom and dad, Carol and Steve, for giving me the gift of this life.

To those whose voices and stories fill these pages, no amount of thanks is sufficient. You are the lifeblood of this book. Without the conversations we had and messages you sent, I would still be stumbling in the dark. Thank you for opening your hearts to me and sharing your stories, painful as they may be. You all have a place in my heart, forever.

Thank you to Marty, for being such a great cousin and a safe place to start; to Stevie and Sheri for your tears; to Billy, Michael, and Jimmy for reliving that tragic day for me; to Char for loving and remembering my mom; to John for your forgiveness.

Thank you to Aunt Alice, Aunt Ruth, Uncle Mike, and Mark for your valuable perspectives.

Thank you to Robert, for staying on the phone; to Marcy, Shannon, and Phillip for the profound conversations we shared; to Todd, for a beautiful walk in the woods, for so much crucial insight, and for your loving feedback on the final draft—it's been a gift to reconnect with you.

Thank you to Denise, for guiding and following me through life, love, and death.

Finally, my deepest gratitude and appreciation for Kurt, and I'm so sorry for all that happened. Thank you for loving Jay.

About the Author

photo credit: Maureen Cassidy

Kristina Amelong lives on the east side of Madison, Wisconsin, just a few miles from where she grew up. From a working-class childhood filled with abuse, addiction, and loss, she has overcome addiction and chronic illness, raised four children, and founded a successful holistic health business, Optimal Health Network. She's developed natural protocols that have helped thousands heal from a wide range of digestive and other chronic issues. She is the writer of the self-published book, *Ten Days to Optimal Health: A Guide to Nutritional Therapy and Colon Cleansing*.

Kristina is a senior board member for the Center for World Philosophy and Religion, a nonprofit organization dedicated to a reweaving of the human story that will guide humanity through the current evolutionary crisis. She has a passion for photography, gardening, backyard chicken raising, and pickleball. She has two dogs and three grand-dogs that she walks on frozen lakes every winter.

Looking for your next great read?

We can help!

Visit www.shewritespress.com/next-read
or scan the QR code below for a list
of our recommended titles.

She Writes Press is an award-winning
independent publishing company founded to
serve women writers everywhere.